Children's Exposure to Domestic Violence

This book bridges together research, theory, and practice to offer future directions for new treatment policy and context-based intervention with children exposed to domestic violence.

Centering the voices of children, this book aims to reveal and fill in the gaps of knowledge concerning deep levels of exposure to the domestic violence phenomenon. The book begins with a critical review of the whole field, covering theory, research, intervention, and policy. The author then puts forward a new data-based conceptualization for understanding this field of abuse and its application in practice. Drawing on her rich academic and clinical experience, Carmel includes treatment recommendations, planning, and intervention strategies as well as suggestions for how to deal with the phenomenon at policy level in the legal, social, community, and education fields.

Calling for the involvement of legal, educational, and community systems, this book is essential reading for researchers in psychology, law, social work, education, gender studies, and sociology, as well as therapeutic practitioners, such as clinicians, educational consultants, art therapists, and policymakers.

Yifat Carmel, PhD, is an expert in trauma and trauma recovery. Her main field of research and practice is children exposed to domestic violence.

Children's Exposure to Domestic Violence

Theory, Practice, and Implications for Policy

Yifat Carmel

NEW YORK AND LONDON

Cover Image by Keren Weinstein

First published 2024
by Routledge
605 Third Avenue, New York, NY 10158

and by Routledge
4 Park Square, Milton Park, Abingdon, Oxon, OX14 4RN

Routledge is an imprint of the Taylor & Francis Group, an informa business

© 2024 Yifat Carmel

The right of Yifat Carmel to be identified as author of this work has been asserted in accordance with sections 77 and 78 of the Copyright, Designs and Patents Act 1988.

All rights reserved. No part of this book may be reprinted or reproduced or utilised in any form or by any electronic, mechanical, or other means, now known or hereafter invented, including photocopying and recording, or in any information storage or retrieval system, without permission in writing from the publishers.

Trademark notice: Product or corporate names may be trademarks or registered trademarks, and are used only for identification and explanation without intent to infringe.

Library of Congress Cataloging-in-Publication Data
Names: Carmel, Yifat, author.
Title: Children's exposure to domestic violence: theory, practice, and implications for policy / Yifat Carmel.
Description: New York, NY: Routledge, 2024. | Includes bibliographical references and index.
Identifiers: LCCN 2023029217 (print) | LCCN 2023029218 (ebook) | ISBN 9781032427737 (hardback) | ISBN 9781032427720 (paperback) | ISBN 9781003364221 (ebook)
Subjects: LCSH: Family violence–Prevention. | Abused children–Services for. | Children and violence.
Classification: LCC HV6626 .C374 2024 (print) | LCC HV6626 (ebook) | DDC 362.82/92--dc23/eng/20230815
LC record available at https://lccn.loc.gov/2023029217
LC ebook record available at https://lccn.loc.gov/2023029218

ISBN: 978-1-032-42773-7 (hbk)
ISBN: 978-1-032-42772-0 (pbk)
ISBN: 978-1-003-36422-1 (ebk)

DOI: 10.4324/9781003364221

Typeset in Times New Roman
by Deanta Global Publishing Services, Chennai, India

This book is lovingly dedicated to the memory of my maternal grandmother who had the unique gift of being able to see the internal essence of a person. She devoted her life to healing, nurturing, and rehabilitating children from a variety of sectors in society, regardless of religion, race, or gender.

And with love and deep respect for the hundreds of children whom I have encountered throughout the years of my professional and academic activity in the field of domestic violence. I promised them that their voices will be heard.

Contents

About the author xii
Preface xiii
Acknowledgments xv

Introduction 1

1 Scientific background 11

   1.1 Children exposed to interparental violence: Definition 11
   1.2 The influence of interparental violence on children:
       Theoretical approaches 12
   1.3 The impact of interparental violence on children: Research
       review and renewed theoretical evaluation 12
       1.3.1 Negative impacts of interparental violence on
            children's development 12
       1.3.2 Broadening the theoretical formulation in light of the
            research results 16
       1.3.3 Factors that mediate the impact of interparental
            violence on the children's development 16
       1.3.4 Resiliency among children exposed to interparental
            violence 19
       1.3.5 Theoretical reevaluation in light of the research
            results 19
       1.3.6 Exposure to interparental violence: Direct abuse 20
       1.3.7 Limitations of the research 21
       1.3.8 Critical learning of the limitations of the research
            described thus far 22
       1.3.9 Summary of children's exposure to interparental
            violence 23

1.4 Children's experience of interparental violence 23
    1.4.1 Recollection: Negotiation of what happened 24
    1.4.2 Causality: Negotiation of what happened 24
    1.4.3 Moralization: Negotiation of what it means 24
    1.4.4 Living with the Secret 25
    1.4.5 Living with Conflicts of Loyalty 25
    1.4.6 Living in Terror and Fear 25
    1.4.7 Adopting the Violent Model 25
1.5 Limitations of the aforementioned research and the critical lessons learned from them 27
1.6 Escalation of violence in intimate relationships 30
    1.6.1 Critical learning in the field of violence against an intimate partner 34

2 Intervention with children exposed to interparental violence   51

2.1 The theoretical and empirical basis for shaping interventions for children exposed to interparental violence 51
    2.1.1 Social learning theory 51
    2.1.2 Cognitive-contextual theory 52
    2.1.3 The theory of emotional security 52
    2.1.4 Family system theory 53
    2.1.5 Trauma theory 53
    2.1.6 Dynamic perspectives and attachment theory 54
2.2 Interventions for children exposed to interparental violence 54
    2.2.1 Interventions with children exposed to interparental violence and with their mothers: First wave of evaluation (mid-1980s to the beginning of the 2000s) 55
    2.2.2 Interventions with children exposed to interparental violence and their mothers: Second wave of evaluation (from the beginning of the 2000s to the present) 60
    2.2.3 Critical learning of knowledge building in the field of intervention for children exposed to violence 67
2.3 Adolescents' experiences of interparental violence and its implications for intervention 69
2.4 Evidence-based intervention for treating children who have experienced maltreatment 71
    2.4.1 The ecological-transaction model of development 71

2.4.2 *Trauma-focused cognitive-behavioral therapy* 72
  2.4.3 *The question of tailoring the evidence-based intervention programs to the context of children exposed to violence: A critical analysis* 74
 2.5 *Summary and conclusions* 75

3 **Treatment policy for the phenomenon of exposure to interparental violence**   86

 3.1 *Historical review* 86
 3.2 *Critical learning of the history of treatment policy for the phenomenon of exposure to interparental violence* 92
 3.3 *Interventions with violent men and with women victims of domestic violence reflected in the treatment policy for the phenomenon of exposure to interparental violence* 103
  3.3.1 *Intervention with violent men as fathers* 103
  3.3.2 *Intervention with mothers who are victims of domestic violence* 104

4 **The phenomenology of the experience of exposure to interparental violence**   114

 4.1 *Study 1. The perception of daily reality among children exposed to their father's violence against their mother: An intense bipolar experience* 116
  4.1.1 *Introduction* 116
  4.1.2 *Literature review* 116
  4.1.3 *The research questions* 118
  4.1.4 *Study method* 118
  4.1.5 *Sample and participants* 118
  4.1.6 *Research instrument* 121
  4.1.7 *Data collection* 122
  4.1.8 *Data analysis* 123
  4.1.9 *Findings* 123
  4.1.10 *Discussion* 133
 4.2 *Study 2. The perception of escalation of interparental conflicts among children exposed to their father's violence against their mother: Characteristics of the exposure to violence and its connection to child sexual abuse* 137
  4.2.1 *Introduction* 137
  4.2.2 *Literature review* 137

   4.2.3 *Study method 138*
   4.2.4 *Findings 139*
   4.2.5 *Discussion 150*

5 **Intervention with children exposed to interparental violence: Change in trends and the implications of this**   159

 5.1 *The experience of children exposed to interparental violence—new dimensions for understanding 159*
 5.2 *What is the connection between art and living in a domestic violent reality? 161*
 5.3 *Art therapy—use of nonverbal language to gain insights, reconstruction of self, and change 162*
  5.3.1 *The process of creating art as therapy 163*
  5.3.2 *Images of art as helping to evoke verbal communication surrounding personal issues, emotions, and conflicts (art psychotherapy) 164*
 5.4 *Art education—the arts as important tools for developing complex and refined forms of thinking 164*
 5.5 *Art therapy groups 165*
  5.5.1 *Art psychotherapy groups 165*
  5.5.2 *Open studio groups or art studio groups 166*
 5.6 *Intervention with children exposed to interparental violence—principles 166*
  5.6.1 *Integrating the principles of art education in a process of creating art 168*
  5.6.2 *Integrating art psychotherapy through a process of creating art 169*
  5.6.3 *Therapy in small groups 170*
 5.7 *Context-focused intervention: Children exposed to interparental violence 171*
 5.8 *Deepening the therapy in the field of children exposed to interpersonal violence 175*
  5.8.1 *Stage 2 of the intervention: Assessing the type of experience that characterizes the child's reality and drafting the appropriate intervention 176*
 5.9 *Exposure to interparental violence: Implications of the nature of the abuse for working in the school context 186*
 5.10 *Children exposed to interparental violence—conclusions in relation to the drafting of new policy in the field 188*

6	Treatment modality: Treatment recommendations, planning, and intervention strategies	192
	6.1 First dimension 193 *6.2 Second dimension 195* *6.3 Third dimension 196* *6.4 Fourth dimension 198*	
7	Summary and implications for policy	206
	Index	*221*

About the author

Yifat Carmel, PhD, is a teaching fellow at the School of Creative Arts Therapies, Faculty of Welfare and Health Sciences, and a researcher at the Emily Sagol CATs Research Center at the University of Haifa, Israel. Dr Carmel is also a senior lecturer in the Faculty for Counseling, Therapy, and Educational Support, Beit Berl College, Kfar Saba, Israel. Her academic and professional expertise is in trauma and trauma recovery and in child abuse, specifically abuse in the field of children exposed to domestic violence. She has published several articles in these fields, and her research includes, inter alia, the development of context-based intervention programs. As part of Dr Carmel's clinical consulting work, for two decades, she was head of therapy for children exposed to domestic violence in one of the large shelters in Israel for battered women and their children. At the same time, she was head of therapy at a large center for the treatment and prevention of family violence. During her ongoing work, she developed a unique body of knowledge and intervention in the field, which she disseminates among social workers, therapists, educators, legal professionals, law enforcement authorities, medical and public health practitioners, and researchers from various disciplines. Today, Dr Carmel is working on creating an interdisciplinary therapeutic, legal, and sociological language to facilitate work based on predetermined uniform criteria. She believes that this will be helpful in providing a more precise response for children who experience abuse in the context of domestic violence that is characterized by terrorization and pathological control. In this context, she participates in professional panels dealing with psychology and law and collaborates with a legal clinic in the Faculty of Law at Bar Ilan University.

Preface

The field of children exposed to domestic violence is being increasingly recognized in the scientific literature as having a damaging effect on children, at least to the same extent as other fields of child abuse—sexual, physical, and psychological abuse, and neglect. Nonetheless, specifically in this field, recognition expressed in the research has not penetrated the practice field. The gaps are manifest also in practitioners' lack of understanding of the essential nature of the abuse and its special, multifaceted, and complex character, as well as in the law courts' inconsistency regarding visitation arrangements and custody issues, in cases where domestic violence is present, frequently involving men's violence against women. This book attempts to examine the source of these perceptible gaps between the research and practice levels via a rough critical review of the entire knowledge field. In addition, the book proposes a new conceptualization for understanding this field of abuse and its application in practice. Drawing on a weighting up of the insights, the book presents new social conceptualizations in the field as well as novel directions for working with these children, calling on the involvement of legal, educational, and community systems.

This is the first book of its kind in the field that gives voice exclusively to the children. Thus, it constitutes a change in perspective by exposing the act of blurring the intensity of abuse that the children undergo, examining what may lie behind this blurring, and bringing the children's voices to the fore by publishing my widescale phenomenological study. This study exposes the children's experience, including their perceptions and behavior throughout all the different escalation stages of the interparental conflict.

Another aspect of the book's innovation is in offering a perspective that integrates academic research and practical activity. Thus, the book is pioneering not only because it deals with a new conceptualization based on grounded theory on the experiences of children living with domestic violence but also because it translates the conceptualization into practice. Through my longstanding experience of consulting and clinical work with the child population under discussion,

I was able to shape a new intervention model built on complex clinical themes based on the children's experiences as they emerged from the study. Moreover, since the themes themselves dictated the (art-based) direction for intervention, the chosen intervention approach was based, for the first time, on the clinical nature of the problem exposed.

Another, final aspect, that sets this book apart from others in the field is an exposure to the existence of gendered and legal issues, which influenced the development of the research and policy undertaken with this child population. These issues are related to the broader sphere of the phenomenon of exposure to violence—a domestic violence reality that is part of a wider context of men's violence against women. Therefore, attention is drawn, for the first time, to the relevance of this field of abuse to other disciplines, mainly law, gender, education, society in its wide political sense, and art therapy. The conclusions of the critical-theoretical research have important implications for the field of law-society-parenthood and for the shaping of policy.

Acknowledgments

Endless thanks to my husband, Liran, for his constant presence, support, and deep understanding and for being with me on every step of the journey of writing this book.

And to my daughters, Leehee and Ori, for giving up so many of their hours with me so that I could bring the children's voices to the fore.

Introduction

Children's exposure to their father's violence against their mother is a phenomenon that has negative short-term and long-term personal, health, and social implications (Arai et al., 2021; Cameranesi & Piotrowski, 2020; Lawson, 2019; McTavish et al., 2016; Øverlien, 2010). Moreover, this area of child abuse is becoming increasingly recognized as having a damaging impact on children just like other areas of child abuse (Black et al., 2020; Geffner, 2016; MacMillan et al., 2013; Parsons et al., 2020; World Health Organization, 2013, 2016). Over the years, this phenomenon has expanded to epidemic proportions globally, including in Israel. During the 1990s, it was estimated that, in the United States, 10 million children were suffering from the problem (Straus, 1991). In the year 2000 in Israel, according to a survey of family violence and children at-risk (Eisikovits et al., 2000), it was estimated that the problem was affecting approximately 260,000 children. A national survey in the United States in 2009 (Finkelhor et al., 2009) revealed that 16.3 million children between 2 and 17 years had witnessed their father's violence against their mother at some point during their lives. Data in the United States in 2011 reported that approximately 17.9 million children aged 17 and under were exposed to domestic violence at some stage (Hamby et al., 2011). The estimates in Israel and the United States indicate a very widespread phenomenon. Researchers currently assume that the numbers are even greater because less severe violence in families remains unreported[1] and because between 40% and 60% of children who are victims of physical and/or sexual abuse are exposed, in addition, to interparental violence (Carmel, 2016; Graham-Bermann & Howell, 2010; Lyn et al., 2015). Regarding the frequency of exposure, researchers believe that the experience recurs throughout the entire period of a child's development (McCloskey, 2011; Smokowski & Evans, 2019). The growing prevalence of the phenomenon as well as its negative implications are a kind of time bomb on the threshold of society. Therefore, it is imperative to recognize the phenomenon as a cross-border social problem and to place it high on the agenda in the global public discourse.

DOI: 10.4324/9781003364221-1

The body of knowledge in the field to date has dealt widely with the results of children's exposure to interparental violence, thus advancing the perception that they are a population at-risk, in need of assistance and support. Nevertheless, this body of knowledge has scarcely examined the way in which these risks are played out. Hence, limited information exists regarding the complexity of the problem and the way in which to cope with the phenomenon. In other words, the body of knowledge emphasizes the need for social intervention but provides limited tools for its implementation. This lacuna might be derived from the way in which the phenomenon develops into a general social problem. First, the problematic nature of the phenomenon must be stressed and only later, once it has received the status of a social problem, can coping strategies be developed. However, in light of the knowledge that has accumulated in the field, the outcomes of children's exposure to their father's violence against their mother and the establishment of this knowledge in recent years, it is quite astonishing that research continues to focus on that direction rather than investigating the essence of the phenomenon. This choice may be due to the fear of placing the children at fault or implying that they shoulder some of the responsibility, as persons involved in the process. Today, however, since a clear picture has formed of the negative influences of the exposure itself and since the issue of responsibility is understood (responsibility for the violence falls on the man as the perpetrator against the woman), the time is ripe to deal with the process. Therefore, another explanation for the aforementioned lack might be the complexity involved in the context in which exposure to violence occurs—the phenomenon of men's violence against women. This context might involve sensitive political and ethical issues that might be evoked more strongly following a deepening of the knowledge in the field of complexity of child abuse, which might in turn have an influence on the research directions in this area.

In light of the above, the aim of the book is to expose the complexity of the phenomenon known as "children exposed to violence," in its background context—men's violence against women—and of its unique internal background characteristics—direct and indirect abuse of children. I will examine the characteristics of the harm to children with reference to the dimensions mentioned above. In addition, I will examine the emphases and existing lacunae in the knowledge field under discussion to learn about the issues that might be involved in knowledge development, their potential influence on selected directions for study, and the nature of treatment for this population. Based on all of this (the establishment of the existing knowledge and its critical examination), I will suggest new directions for intervention and policy for treating the population of children exposed to violence on a number of levels: clinical, educational, legal, and parental. I will also emphasize the critical need to distinguish between the field of violence toward women and the field of severe conflicts in couple relationships that have run aground. This is to avoid chaos in the interpersonal relationships field by confusing dysfunctional arguments that escalate to violence in a normative context with arguments leading to all-out violence in the context of violence against women. Such blurring of fields may lead to erroneous decisions regarding the whole issue of custody and visiting rights between children and parents, may provide an opening for taunting, and may exacerbate the tension between women and men in society in general.

The following paragraphs provide an organizational framework for the reader:

1. The order of the chapters is inherent to the book's rationale. By way of explanation, the aim of the book is to expose the unique abuse that constitutes witnessing violence that, for years, has not been researched. Therefore, as a **first stage** of this inquiry, I attempt to examine why a subject in need of research, for so long, has not yet been studied. The **scientific review and critical examination relate to three knowledge fields**: theory and research dealing with children's exposure to violence (Chapter 1), interventions in the field of exposure to violence (Chapter 2), and policy in the context of this phenomenon through the years (Chapter 3).

Following identification of the gap in research that was created and its causes, I attempt to fill this gap in the scientific literature by presenting the findings of a broad, data-based, phenomenological study (in Chapter 4). **The children's experience of exposure to violence is learned for this study regarding all stages of the escalating interparental conflict.** Besides the fundamental questions posed by this study, for the first time in the existing body of knowledge, its uniqueness lies in its methodological strength (size and characteristics) that enable cautious generalization to additional cultural contexts. Much has been written in the scientific literature about the absence of first-hand knowledge of children's perspectives and understanding. This study intends to introduce the children's voices in a way that provides a stage on which to present their many thick descriptions. The findings of the study and the understandings that emerge from them are based strictly on this rich information.

Based on the conclusion regarding the motives for creating the lacuna in the scientific literature, **as well as on** my empirical findings, which enabled me to develop a new theoretical conceptualization, I suggest a **context-based intervention** program (in Chapters 5 and 6). Specifically, this program focuses on themes learned as problematic and responsible for creating difficulty among this child population. The nature of the treatment, including its planning and use of strategies, is also included. Nonetheless, it is important to note that this book is not a manual but provides an outline for a new concept and a design for ways in which to work.

The final chapter, Chapter 7, **serves as a connecting thread.** It explains how the motives for creating the gap in the scientific literature and the research findings regarding the children's complex experience are intended to influence **future directions of work in this field.**

2. The conceptualization of children exposed to domestic violence as a phenomenon in the context of men's violence toward women needs attention and clarification: Over the years, the terminology of the phenomenon known as family violence—first researched in the 1970s—changed. The different terms expressed different understandings, ideologies, and a certain construct of reality. Thus, victims of family violence began to be referred to as battered women, then as abused women. The phenomenon then became known as domestic violence, simultaneously as intimate partner violence, and, in the 2000s, as violence against women (Breiding et al., 2015; Garcia-Moreno et al., 2005).

While all those terms in the first 30 years of violence research centered on men's aggressive, violent, controlling, and coercive behaviors toward women, in the last 20 years, these terms were extended to describe other phenomena (Breiding et al., 2015; Council of Europe, 2011; European Union Agency for Fundamental Rights, 2014; Garcia-Moreno et al., 2005; Haselschwerdt, 2019; Johnson, 2008; Katz, 2022). Although these other phenomena center on behaviors including elements of power (e.g., one-time violence; incitement and use of children during divorce disputes; and psychological abuse or use of physical aggression not based on couple relations involving obsessive control), they are not characterized specifically by creating a system of captivity and pathological control. The wider use of these terms has blurred and confused phenomena that contain essentially similar, and yet different, elements. Even worse, however, it has led to a broadening of the concepts of perpetrator and victim, leading to problems in defining and measuring phenomena.

Today, researchers point to the fact that the way in which violence is defined and measured will have a direct impact on findings regarding the prevalence and scope of the phenomenon as well as on the understanding of its essence (Black et al., 2020; Buntin, 2015). In fact, the significance is that the domestic violence phenomenon, termed as such to emphasize the relationship characterized by men's pathological control of women, which is legitimized by a patriarchal sociocultural construct (the home as an imitation of a social structure), has come to "accommodate" additional phenomena that do not represent domestic violence. Despite the statistical finding that, in other phenomena as well, most abuse is perpetrated by men against women (e.g., WHO, 2013, 2016; Black et al., 2020), women's violence against men also exists as a phenomenon and is sufficiently prevalent to deserve examination. Until now, those areas have received in-depth study in the context of women's gender studies (Parsons et al., 2020). In contrast, in domestic violence involving control that creates a state of captivity, the central characteristic, as found empirically, is abuse of women (e.g., Buntin, 2015; Garcia-Moreno et al., 2005; Johnson, 2001, 2008; Monckton Smith, 2020). The term "violence against women," applied to the phenomenon in the 2000s, expresses this understanding.

In this last context, two important points must be emphasized:

a. Most of the studies, to date, on children exposed to domestic violence were conducted in battered women's shelters. Therefore, the characteristics of the phenomenon were learned in a gender context of violence against women (Arai et al., 2021; Carmel, 2010; Graham-Bermann & Levendosky, 2011).
b. As explained above, in the domestic violence context, the perpetrator–victim dynamics needs to be learned mainly regarding cases under the overall title of man-perpetrator and woman-victim. It was found, however, that the escalation dynamics between couples contains "alternating" perpetrator–victim relationships that are a product of the captivity dynamics itself: the man's perception of the woman's behavior as threatening the "proper" couple setup; the man's escalation based on this; and the woman, as captive, not being able to read the situation in the aforementioned context and thus reacts in her own defense—a situation that the man interprets as a deliberate attempt to harm him (Eisikovits et al., 2002; Winstok, 2007; Winstok et al., 2002). An outsider, who does not take the captivity dynamics into consideration, might mistakenly interpret the situation as mutual violence.

The children's perspective, as learned in my comprehensive study and presented in Chapter 4, reinforces this understanding. That is to say, there is a gap between the children's **description** of what happens at home (a description supporting the reality of the man in control, deliberately escalating the conflict and behaving violently toward the woman) and their **perception** of what is happening. The children understand the escalating conflicts as normative arguments and perceive both sides as responsible for arousing and developing the conflicts. This gap between the overt and covert dimensions results from the act of blurring the violence at home (as part of the captivity dynamics) until the internal home dynamics are constructed as normative for the children. The gaps, their meaning, and the way they are constructed in the violent domestic reality are detailed, as mentioned, in Chapter 4.

3. The literature review and its adaptation to a global context—points for emphasis:

a. The domestic violence phenomenon was initially researched in the United States and the United Kingdom. It eventually began to gain momentum as a research field in other countries that identify as individualistic and Western (e.g., Canada, Israel, Australia, and in the last decade, Western European countries; Arai, 2021; Howell et al., 2016; Lawson, 2019, Liel et al., 2020; Richardson-Foster et al., 2012). Culturally sensitive learning has taken place in those Western cultures themselves as part of the attempt to develop a culturally sensitive discourse surrounding different minorities (e.g., Eisikovits et al., 2008; Mazher Idriss & Abbas, 2010). This discourse is based mainly on finding a solution to the woman's safety that will take cultural factors into account. The assumption was that the phenomenon learned in a Western cultural context would exist, but to a greater extent, in traditional cultures characterized by patriarchal ideologies (Geffner, 2016; Parsons et al., 2020). Only in recent years has the subject been broached in relation to more traditional and conservative cultures which, because of their closed and cohesive nature, scarcely allow entry of outsiders; therefore, empirical knowledge about them is limited (based mainly on content analysis of World Health Organization surveys; WHO, 2013, 2016).

Multicultural learning demands the creation of unified definitions, agreed-upon standards which, because of norm differences, become very complex. Therefore, statistical analyses have not yet been used to obtain validated findings on a global scale. Until these guidelines are consolidated (based on a meaningful database taking culturally sensitive influences and interpretations into account), there is a consensus among researchers in the field regarding the generalizability of the data to a global context based on the body of research knowledge accumulated in Western countries while exercising the necessary caution (e.g., Geffner, 2016; Parsons et al., 2020). The implications of what has been written above regarding research of the phenomenon on children exposed to domestic violence, in the global context, are clear—that this body of knowledge is missing. Therefore, in the context under discussion as well, the learned phenomenon is based on empirical findings collected in a context of cultures centered around Western ideology (Parsons et al., 2020).

From this perspective, the scientific review in Chapters 1–3 (on which the critical analysis is based) gives expression also to **the historical development** of understanding the phenomenon known as domestic violence and to aspects of **global processes** that influence the development of research in the field. In other words, the reviews include older bibliographical sources that are milestones for understanding the field as well as more recent sources relating to culturally sensitive perspectives.

b. The comprehensive phenomenological study presented in Chapter 4, which is the basis for the new theoretical conceptualization in the knowledge field of children exposed to violence, was conducted in Israel. As mentioned in section a) above, Israel makes an important contribution to the accumulating database in the context of Western countries. Specifically, to building the body of knowledge on the experience of children exposed to violence (e.g., Arai et al., 2020), to the field of intervention with this child population (e.g., Graham-Bermann & Levendosky, 2011), and to developing research in culturally sensitive contexts (e.g., Eisikovits et al., 2008). The possibility of generalization to additional global cultural contexts (i.e., to cultures based on traditional values) is derived, as mentioned, from the theoretical assumption that patriarchal cultures include elements of control that may create more powerful states of captivity than in cultures not based around this ideology.

Note

1 An estimate that appears to be true based on data published in relation to COVID-19. Reports from various countries indicate a marked increase in the number of complaints of domestic violence since the outbreak of the pandemic (Avgar, 2020; WHO, 2020).

References

Arai, L., Shaw, A., Feder, G., Howarth, E., MacMillan, H., Moore, T. H. M., Stanley, N., & Gregory, A. (2021). Hope, agency, and the lived experience of violence: A qualitative systematic review of children's perspectives on domestic Violence and abuse. *Trauma, Violence, and Abuse*, *22*(3), 427–438. https://doi.org/10.1177/1524838019849582

Avgar, I. (2020). *Collected data for the international day for the elimination of violence against women.* https://m.knesset.gov.il/EN/activity/mmm/ViolenceAgainstWomen--Data.pdf

Black, T., Fallon, B., Nikolova, K., Tarshis, S., Baird, S., & Carradine, J. (2020). Exploring subtypes of children's exposure to intimate partner violence. *Children and Youth Services Review*, *118*, Article 105375. https://doi.org/10.1016/j.childyouth.2020.105375

Breiding, M. J., Basile, K. C., Smith, S. G., Black, M. C., & Mahendra, R. R. (2015). *Intimate partner violence surveillance: Uniform definitions and recommended data elements version 2.0.* National Center for Injury Prevention and Control. https://www.cdc.gov/violenceprevention/pdf/ipv/intimatepartnerviolence.pdf

Buntin, J. (2015). Intimate partner violence. *International Encyclopedia of the Social and Behavioral Sciences*, *2*(12), 685–688. https://doi.org/10.1016/B978-0-08-097086-8.35026-7

Cameranesi, M., & Piotrowski, C. C. (2020). Critical review of theoretical frameworks elucidating the mechanisms accounting for the adverse developmental outcomes observed in children following exposure to intimate partner violence. *Aggression and Violent Behavior*, *55*, Article 101455. https://doi.org/10.1016/j.avb.2020.101455

Carmel, Y. (2010). *Escalation of interparental conflicts from the children's perspective* (Unpublished doctoral dissertation). University of Haifa, Israel (Hebrew).

Carmel, Y. (2016). Children exposed to their father's violence against their mother: The link between the children's perception of escalation and their experience of complex psychological physical and sexual abuse. *Academic Journal of Creative Art Therapies*, *6*(1), 355–377. http://ajcat.haifa.ac.il/images/June_2016/Yifat_Carmel_article_english_formatted.pdf

Council of Europe. (2011, April 12). *Council of Europe convention of preventing and combating violence against women and domestic violence.* Council of Europe.

Eisikovits, Z., Buchbinder, E., & Bshara, A. (2008). Between the person and the culture: Arab couples' perceptions of police intervention in intimate partner violence. *Journal of Ethnic and Cultural Diversity in Social Work*, *17*(2). https://doi.org/10.1080/15313200801941531

Eisikovits, Z., Fishman, G., Mesh, G., & Gusinsky, R. (2000). *A review of family violence and children at risk*. The Minerva Center for Youth Studies (Hebrew).

Eisikovits, Z., Winstok, Z., & Gelles, R. (2002). Structure and dynamics of escalation from the victim's perspective. *Families in Society*, *83*(2), 142–152. https://doi.org/10.1606/1044-3894.29

European Union Agency for Fundamental Rights. (2014). *Violence against women: An EU-wide survey*. European Union Agency for Fundamental Rights. https://fra.europa.eu/en/publication/2014/violence-against-women-eu-wide-survey-main-results-report

Finkelhor, D., Turner, H., Ormrod, R., & Hamby, S. L. (2009). Violence, abuse and crime exposure in a national sample of children and youth. *Pediatrics*, *124*(5), 1411–1423. https://doi.org/10.1542/peds.2009-0467

Garcia-Moreno, C., Jansen, H. A. F., Ellsberg, M., Helse, L., & Watts, C. (2005). *WHO multi-country study on women's health and domestic violence against women: Initial results on prevalence, health outcomes and women's responses*. World Health Organization.

Geffner, R. (2016). Children exposed to intimate partner violence and abuse: Current research on the effects and adjustment. *Journal of Child and Adolescents Trauma*, *9*(2), 95–96. https://doi.org/10.1007/s40653-016-0097-9

Graham-Bermann, S. A., & Howell, K. H. (2010). Child abuse in the context of intimate partner violence. In J. E. B. Myers (Ed.), *APSAC handbook on child maltreatment* (3rd ed., pp. 167–180). Sage.

Graham-Bermann, S. A., & Levendosky, A. A. (Eds.). (2011). *How intimate partner violence affects children*. American Psychological Association.

Hamby, S. L., Finkelhor, D., Turner, H. A., & Ormrod, R. (2011). *Children's exposure to intimate partner violence and other family violence* (Juvenile justice bulletin, pp. 1–12). U.S. Government Printing Office.

Haselschwerdt, M. L., Hlavaty, K., Carlson, C., Schneider, M., Maddox, L., & Skipper, M. (2019). Heterogeneity within domestic violence exposure: Young adults' retrospective experiences. *Journal of Interpersonal Violence*, *34*(7), 1512–1538. https://doi.org/10.1177/0886260516651625

Howell, K. H., Barnes, S. E., Miller, L. E., & Graham-Bermann, S. A. (2016). Developmental variations in the impact of intimate partner violence exposure during childhood. *Journal of Injury and Violence Research*, *8*(1), 43–57. https://doi.org/10.5249/jivr.v8i1.663

Johnson, M. (2001). Conflict and control: Symmetry and asymmetry in domestic violence. In A. Booth, C. Crouter, & C. Clements (Eds.), *Couples in conflict* (pp. 95–104). Lawrence Erlbaum.

Johnson, M. (2008). *A typology of domestic violence: Intimate terrorism, violent resistance, and situational couple violence*. Northeastern University Press.

Katz, E. (2022). *Coercive control in children's and mothers' lives*. Oxford University Press.

Lawson, J. (2019). Domestic violence as child maltreatment: Differential risks and outcomes among cases referred to child welfare agencies for domestic violence exposure. *Children and Youth Services Review, 98*, 32–41. https://doi.org/10.1016/j.childyouth.2018.12.017 https://doi.org/10.1111/j.2044-8287.2012.02072.x

Liel, C., Ulrich, S. M., Lorenz, S., Eickhorst, A., Fluke, J., & Walper, S. (2020). Risk factors for child abuse, neglect and exposure to intimate partner violence in early childhood: Findings in a representative cross-sectional sample in Germany. *Child Abuse and Neglect, 106*, Article 104487. https://doi.org/10.1016/j.chiabu.2020.104487

Lyn, M. A., Franchek-Roa, K., & Giardino, A. P. (2015). The connection between intimate partner violence and child maltreatment. In A. P. Giardino, L. Shaw, P. Speck, & E. R. Giardino (Eds.), *Recognition of child abuse for the mandated reporter* (4th ed., pp. 145–160). STM Learning.

MacMillan, H. L., Wathen, C. N., & Varcoe, C. M. (2013). Intimate partner violence in the family: Considerations for children's safety. *Child Abuse and Neglect, 37*(12), 1186–1191. https://doi.org/10.1016/j.chiabu.2013.05.005

Mazher-Idriss, M., & Abbas, T. (Eds.). (2010). *Honor, violence, women, and Islam*. Routledge-Cavendish. https://doi.org/10.4324/9780203846988

McCloskey, L. A. (2011). The impact of intimate partner violence on Adolescents. In S. A. Graham-Berman & A. A. Levendosky (Eds.), *How intimate partner violence affects children* (pp. 225–246). American Psychological Association.

McTavish, J. R., MacGregor, C. D., Wathen, C. N., & MacMillan, H. L. (2016). Children's exposure to intimate violence: An overview. *International. Review of Psychiatry, 28*(5), 505–518. https://doi.org/10.1080/ 09540261.2016. 1205001.

Monckton-Smith, J. (2020). *In control: Dangerous relationships and how they end in murder*. Bloomsbury.

Øverlien, C. (2010). Children exposed to domestic violence: Conclusions from the literature and challenges ahead. *Journal of Social Work, 10*(1), 80–97. https://doi.org/10.1177/1468017309350663

Parsons, A. M., Heyman, R. E., Mitnick, D. M., & Smith Slep, A. M. (2020). Intimate partner violence and child maltreatment: Definitions, prevalence, research, and theory through a cross-cultural lens. In H. W. Kim & V. D. V. Fons (Eds.), *Cross-cultural family research and practice* (pp. 249–285). Elsevier.

Richardson-Foster, H., Stanley, N., Miller, P., & Thomson, G. (2012). Police intervention in domestic violence incidents where children are present: Police and children's perspectives. *Policing and Society, 22*(2), 220–234.

Smokowski, P. R., & Evans, C. B. R. (2019). Bullying in intimate partner relationships: Teen dating violence and adult intimate partner violence as forms of bullying. In P. R. Smokowski & C. B. R. Evans (Eds.), *Bullying and victimization across the lifespan: Playground politics and power* (pp. 167–182). Springer.

Straus, M. A. (1991). Children as witnesses to marital violence: A risk factor for lifelong problems among a nationally representative sample of American men and women. In D. F. Schwartz (Ed.), *Children and violence: Report of the 23rd Ross Roundtable on critical approaches to common pediatric problems* (pp. 98–104). Ross.

Winstok, Z. (2007). Toward an interactional Perspective on intimate partner violence. *Aggression and Violent Behavior, 12*(3), 348–363. https://doi.org/10.1016/j.avb.2006.12.001

Winstok, Z., Eisikovits, Z., & Gelles, R. (2002). Structure and dynamics of escalation from the batterer's perspective. *Families in Society, 83*(2), 129–141. https://doi.org/10.1606/1044-3894.37

World Health Organization. (2013). *Global and regional estimates of violence against women: Prevalence and health effects of intimate partner violence and non-partner sexual violence.* https://apps.who.int/iris/bitstream/10665/85239/1/9789241564625_eng.pdf

World Health Organization. (2016). *Global plan of action to strengthen the role of the health system within a national multisectoral response to address interpersonal violence, in particular against women and girls, and against children.* https://www.who.int/reproductivehealth/publications/violence/global-plan-of-action/en/

Chapter 1

Scientific background

The aim of this chapter is to review the existing body of knowledge in the field of children exposed to interparental violence by examining the mode of development and the establishment of the field.

1.1 Children exposed to interparental violence: Definition

Three stages can be identified in the description of children living in a reality in which the father behaves violently toward the mother. Initially, these children were referred to as "the silent victims," "the forgotten victims," and "the unintended victims." These terms reflected a passive orientation on the children's part and related to them as being randomly harmed by the violence. Later, because of the understanding that the children were both present at the scene of the confrontation and affected by it, the terminology changed, referring to them as "witnesses of violence." Nevertheless, this concept does not emphasize the serious harm to the children as a result of what they experience. Since the 2000s, the terms "exposed to violence" or "experiencing violence" have come into use, concepts that emphasize the children's active orientation and their being central victims of the violence.

In the scientific literature, exposure to violence is defined as a variety of ways in which children experience a violent event between their parents, even if they are neither present at the scene of the occurrence nor directly watching the event (Feder & MacMillan, 2015; Holden, 2003). Modes of exposure include direct observation of the violence, hearsay evidence, involvement in the conflict, the abuser's use of the children to harm the mother (e.g., by threatening the children that if they take their mother's side, they will be physically harmed or taken hostage in order to force the mother to return to him), observing the outcomes of the conflict and not the conflict itself (this experience may include seeing that the mother is injured, a father who moves between physical violence and helping, police intervention to keep the father at a distance, and evacuation of the mother to a battered women's shelter; Gilbert et al., 2009; Hollin, 2016; MacMillan

DOI: 10.4324/9781003364221-2

& Wathen, 2014; Mariscal, 2020), and the child being a target for direct harm (Callaghan et al., 2018; Carlson, 2000; Graham-Bermann & Howell, 2010; Katz, 2022). Introducing the term "interparental violence" defined the violence against women in the sense that takes into consideration the children's presence in the confrontational environment (Carmel, 2010).

1.2 The influence of interparental violence on children: Theoretical approaches

Several theories offered explanations for the development of the psychopathology of children exposed to their father's violence against their mother. The leading theories among these are social learning theory, intergenerational transmission theory, and family system theory (Geffner et al., 2003). According to social learning theory, children who are exposed to interparental violence learn ineffective ways to resolve conflicts and observe their parents' aggressive behavior. This serves as a model for them when coping with interpersonal confrontations both inside and outside the family (Lee et al., 2022; O'Brien et al., 1991). Intergenerational transmission theory suggests that children who live in such a family environment undergo long-term socialization, according to which they learn gender and parenting roles. Therefore, these children are at risk of becoming either violent men or women victims of violence (Kimber et al., 2018; Widom, 1989). Family system theory holds that the great impact of a state of tension on children is mediated by the education that they receive from their parents. If the tension hinders parental education, the children are at greater risk of developing adjustment problems. Disturbances to parental education tend to occur in the context of interparental violence when the parents adopt ineffective patterns of communication and problem-solving, which do not make a separation between the couple subsystem and the parent–child system (Anderson & Cramer-Benjamin, 1999; Fusco, 2017).

1.3 The impact of interparental violence on children: Research review and renewed theoretical evaluation

1.3.1 Negative impacts of interparental violence on children's development

Research on children exposed to interparental violence has dramatically increased since 1980 and testifies to the behavioral, emotional, social, and cognitive problems, both short term and long term, among this population, compared to children from normative families (e.g., Artz et al., 2014; Bedi & Goddard, 2007; Black et al., 2020; Evans et al., 2008; Graham-Bermann & Levendosky, 2011; Hollin, 2016; Kimber et al., 2018; Wolfe et al., 2003). Even though the accumulated knowledge in the field is based on different investigative methods and measurement tools, all the studies show, unequivocally, that exposure to violence has a damaging effect on children's development (Edleson et al., 2007; Holt et al., 2008; MacMillan et al., 2013; McTavish et al., 2016; Onyskiw, 2003; Parsons et al., 2020). The synthesis of this body of knowledge was based on three central meta-analyses in the field (Chan & Yeung, 2009; Kitzmann et al., 2003; Vu et al., 2016). It is noteworthy that the following review will include new emphases in research: The influence of exposure to interparental violence on children's physical health (Hollin, 2016) and on language development (Conway et al., 2021). These two areas have implications for children's psychological, social, and cognitive development. Another area on which research focuses today is teen dating violence (Smokowski & Evans, 2019).

In the behavioral field, studies found that children exposed to interparental violence complain of physical problems and manifest aggressive and antisocial behaviors ("externalized" behavioral problems) as well as fear and avoidance behaviors ("internalized" behavioral problems; e.g., Chan & Yeung, 2009; Graham-Bermann & Levendosky, 2011; Kitzmann et al., 2003; Smagur et al., 2017; Vu et al., 2016).

It was also found that adolescents are dysfunctional and manifest aggressive behaviors within the peer group, toward romantic partners and toward their parents. At the same time, many behaviors related to victimhood were found as well (e.g., Artz et al., 2014; Cao et al., 2016; Ellis et al., 2009; Foshee et al., 2001; Foshee et al., 2005; Hlavaty & Haselschwerdt, 2019; McClosky, 2011). Moreover, it was found that adolescents tend to use drugs and alcohol and try to attain "emotional relief" through either early marriage or pregnancy (e.g., Faulkner et al., 2014; Foy et al., 2011; Smagur et al., 2017).

Contemporary research focuses on effects of exposure to violence on teen dating relationships (e.g., Hollin, 2016). These effects have come to light through analyzing romantic relationship characteristics among adolescents who reported violence in their dating relationships and through learning the risk factors for developing violent romantic relationships in adolescence and adulthood (e.g., Smokowski & Evans, 2019; Richardson et al., 2021). The findings show that risk factors for romantic relationships in adolescence that are characterized by an abusive behavioral pattern of (physical, psychological/emotional, and sexual) control exist on individual, family, and social levels. Witnessing violence and child abuse is included specifically on the family level (Smokowski & Evans, 2019). Teen dating violence is a predictor for violence in romantic relationships later in life. At the same time, similar risk factors were found for intimate partner violence in adults (Richardson et al., 2021). Early parenthood was also found to be a risk factor for violent intimate relationships (Smokowski & Evans, 2019). From the development of research in this area, it can be concluded that exposure to interparental violence characterized by a coercive control pattern predicts such involvement in that type of intimate relationship in adolescence and adulthood.

In the emotional field, it was found that children and adolescents suffer from severe feelings of loss, anger, sadness, confusion, guilt, shock, fear, lack of confidence and low self-esteem, as well as of constant tension as a result of the threat of being harmed themselves. In addition, these children and adolescents tend to experience a lack of confidence and uncertainty regarding what to do and how to behave. They sometimes feel responsible for the violence itself (e.g., D'Andrea & Graham-Bermann, 2017; Hester et al., 2007; Huang et al., 2015; Jenney & Alaggia, 2012; McClosky, 2011; Rogers & Berger, 2022; Shen, 2009; Vu et al., 2016). Other studies in the emotional field found that this child and adolescent population showed more anxiety, depression, mood swings, posttraumatic reactions, and suicidal thoughts (DeBoard-Lucas & Grych, 2011; Graham-Bermann et al., 2008; Horn et al., 2017; Margolin & Vickerman, 2007; Nowakowski et al., 2016; Sonego et al., 2018). Specifically, it was found that among internalizing disorders, exposure to violence has the greatest influence on the development of PTSD (Kitzmann et al., 2003; Evans et al., 2008; Noonan & Pilkington, 2020).

Exposure to interparental violence was found to have an influence also on children's and adolescents' social development. In this context, studies revealed problems in several areas of social interaction (Evans et al., 2008; Foy et al., 2011; Lyn et al., 2015; Kitzmann et al., 2003; Bender et al., 2022). Specifically, it was found that these children were more socially isolated than their peers and showed little interest in activities appropriate to their age group (e.g., Artz et al., 2014; Grych et al., 2000; Howell et al., 2016; Rhoades, 2008; Gao et al., 2021). Children who were frequently exposed to severe violence had difficulty understanding social situations and the thoughts and emotions of people involved in such situations, and as a result, they had a tendency toward aggressive reactions (Graham-Bermann & Levendosky, 2011; Grych et al., 2000; Kiesel et al., 2016; McDonald et al., 2007; Fong et al., 2017). These children were also found to lack problem-solving and conflict-resolving skills and tended to use ineffective strategies, such as verbal, physical, and passive aggression (Bedi & Goddard, 2007; Chan & Yeung, 2009; Foy et al., 2011; Smagur et al., 2017; Vu et al., 2016).

Another group of studies examined the effect of exposure to violence on the children's cognitive competence. The findings in this area showed that these children were at risk of cognitive delay and had low academic abilities (Cage et al., 2021; Edleson et al., 2007; Kiesel et al., 2016; Samuelson, 2012). In addition, the children had a tendency to absenteeism from school and suffered from attention and concentration difficulties (Supol et al., 2021; Jayasinghe et al., 2009). Another category of problems related to the cognitive field is the approach that children develop toward the use of violence and conflict resolution. In this context, it was found that children exposed to interparental violence may develop approaches that justify the use of violence, for example, that violence is an appropriate way to solve problems in intimate relationships; that abusive behavior and threats are effective ways of exerting power and control over others; that violence is an essential strategy for the release of tension; and that the victims brought the violence upon themselves through their behavior. It emerged that a large number of children expressed these approaches when "warring" with the peer group (Graham-Bermann & Levendosky, 2011; Garrigan et al., 2018; Katz, 2022; Miller, 2015).

Research on the influence of interparental violence on children's physical health began at a later stage. Findings of studies in this field show that women who were exposed to domestic violence during pregnancy had a much higher rate of complications than other women, including miscarriages and stillbirths. The infants had a tendency toward low birthweight and preterm birth, requiring intensive specialist care (Mondal & Paul, 2020; Silverman et al., 2006; Silverman et al., 2007). In addition, long-term effects of exposure were documented, which continued to predict childhood health problems. Evidence of immunodeficiency was found, increasing the children's vulnerability to illness (Burke et al., 2008; Petroccelli, 2019). School-age children were found to suffer from more eating and sleeping problems, and pain complaints, and in adolescence, they had a higher tendency toward self-harm than their peers who had not been exposed to interparental violence (Lyn et al., 2015; Lamers-Winkelman et al., 2012; Holmes et al., 2022). Studies also report that these children often continue to cope with a diversity of health issues into adulthood, such as cardiovascular diseases, obesity, liver diseases, cancer, and chronic pulmonary disease (Callaghan et al., 2018; Lazenbatt, 2010).

Another area of recent research is the impact of exposure to interparental violence on children's language development. Only a few studies have examined the relationship between exposure to violence and language development (e.g., Cobos-Cali et al., 2018; Gilbert et al., 2013; Peterson et al., 2019). Research is lacking in spite of the two following pieces of empirical evidence: 1) that stress and distress in childhood may be a risk to the development of the nervous system, including language development (Shonkoff & Garner, 2012) and 2) proof that a healthy home environment and the mother's psychological well-being are crucial to children's intact language development (Ahun & Cote, 2019; Gilkerson et al., 2018). Most studies conducted to date provide evidence that exposure to interparental violence may have a negative influence on children's language development. Specifically, it was found that exposure to violence in the first four years of life is associated with poor language skills in middle childhood (e.g., Conway et al., 2021). This can lead to negative consequences later on, such as low academic achievement, limited social abilities, and mental health implications.

Other parallel research areas that address the health and language implications of exposure for children (inter alia based on the understanding that these are overlapping, relevant fields) are immunological and neurological problems that develop as a result of exposure to violence (Bair-Merrit et al., 2012; Mueller & Tronick, 2019; Teicher & Samson, 2016), as well as immunological reactions that affect blood cells and are related, inter alia, to the development of allergy-related diseases (Bair-Merrit et al., 2015).

Several studies examined the long-term developmental impacts of exposure to interparental violence on children. These studies drew on retrospective reports by adults and archival documentation or on longitudinal studies. Research in this field found a link between depression, traumatic symptoms, aggressiveness, low social adjustment, and low self-esteem in adulthood and exposure to violence during childhood, compared to populations who were not exposed to violence (e.g., Cater et al., 2015; Felitti & Anda, 2010; Kimber et al., 2018; McTavish et al., 2016; Sternberg et al., 2006b). Several researchers reported a strong connection between exposure to interparental violence in childhood and either violent or victim behavior in adulthood (Ehrensaft et al., 2003; Richardson et al., 2021; Widom & Jay, 2017).

1.3.2 Broadening the theoretical formulation in light of the research results

The theory of social learning, the theory of intergenerational transmission, and family system theory can explain how exposure to violent models can lead to both externalized and internalized behavioral problems (Ehrensaft et al., 2003; Fusco, 2017; Voisin & Hong, 2012). Nevertheless, these models cannot explain the myriad problems experienced by children who are exposed to violence, such as posttraumatic symptoms, low self-image, depression, and interpersonal problems. Therefore, when research documented the association between exposure to violence and a variety of emotional, cognitive, and social problems, additional theoretical frameworks were used to explain the children's severe distress (Carlson, 2000; Geffner et al., 2009). The perspective of stress and of coping with stress (Lazarus & Folkman, 1984) were drawn on to explain how children react to the stress factor of interparental violence, which they may assess as unchangeable or as emotionally threatening to the extent that they cannot cope with it. The trauma perspective (Graham-Bermann et al., 2008; Silvern & Kaersvang, 1989) was enlisted to explain the range of reactions to events perceived as threatening in the context of domestic violence toward the children themselves or toward significant figures in their close environment. These reactions may include flashbacks, hyperarousal, or emotional freezing.

1.3.3 Factors that mediate the impact of interparental violence on the children's development

Even though research has clearly shown that exposure to interparental violence has a direct negative impact on children's development, another wave of studies contradicts the deterministic perception of the phenomenon. These studies pointed to a series of personal and environmental factors that might mediate (strengthen or weaken) the negative developmental impact of the exposure. These factors include variables such as age, gender, socioeconomic status, frequency and type of violence, direct abuse and exposure to violence, mother–child relationships, and the children's coping skills (e.g., Allen et al., 2003; Davies & Sturge-Apple, 2006; Geffner, 2016; Hlavaty & Haselschwerdt, 2019; MacMillan & Wathen, 2014; Martinez-Torteya et al., 2009; Vu et al., 2016; Arai et al., 2021).

1.3.3.1 Age

Several studies compared differences in the reactions of children of different ages. In general, these studies found that **preschool-age children** suffered from physical symptoms of anxiety (such as stomach cramps, bedwetting, and sleep disturbance) whereas **elementary-school-age children** expressed their fears openly, both behaviorally and emotionally. **High-school-age children** may attempt to attain emotional "relief" by drug use, early marriage, or pregnancy. It can be said that the age variable has an impact in the sense in which children are capable of understanding or giving meaning to their experiences and the range of possibilities at their disposal of expressing distress or anxiety (Cater et al., 2015; Graham-Bermann & Perkins, 2010; Kimber et al., 2018; Sternberg et al., 2006a).

1.3.3.2 Gender

Studies found that boys, on the whole, demonstrated "externalized" behavioral problems (such as hostility and aggression), whereas girls demonstrated mainly "internalized" behavioral problems (such as depression and somatic problems). Nevertheless, some findings contradicted this observation, showing no differences between the genders regarding the type of problems manifested. Therefore, gender can be defined as a variable that affects the impact of exposure to violence, even though aggressive reactions among boys and anxious-depressive reactions among girls cannot be unequivocally determined (Bogat et al., 2005; Cater et al., 2015; Smaur et al., 2017).

1.3.3.3 Socioeconomic status

This variable has an impact on the way in which the authorities treat families in addition to the woman's ability to cope and find solutions to the violence that she experiences. This is an area worthy of examination since most research to date has studied samples of low-income families (Graham-Bermann et al., 2009; Martinez-Torteya et al., 2009). Recently, an attempt was made to examine the link between low socioeconomic status and children's adoption of coping strategies (e.g., Ahmad et al., 2017; Wang & Maguire-Jack, 2018; Hiilamo et al., 2021). In this context, a positive relationship was found between adopting coping strategies/resiliency and socioeconomic status/education.

1.3.3.4 Frequency and types of violence

In this area, findings show that repeated exposure to violence and victimization increases children's sensitivity and distress. Similarly, it was found that the greater the children's exposure to more forms of violence (e.g., verbal, physical, and sexual abuse), the more they expressed behavioral, emotional, and other types of problems (Callaghan & Alexander, 2015; Charak et al., 2019; Davies & Sturge-Apple, 2006; Finkelhor et al., 2009; Katz, 2016, 2022).

1.3.3.5 Direct abuse and exposure to violence

Studies in which direct child abuse was the control variable found that children who were exposed to interparental violence as well as experiencing abuse themselves expressed the greatest distress. Researchers referred to this experience as "double abuse" (Callaghan et al., 2018; Carlson, 2000; Edleson et al., 2007; Farrell & Zimmerman, 2019; Graham-Bermann & Howell, 2010; MacMillan & Wathen, 2014; McDonald et al., 2016). Recently, it has been suggested that since children have similar experiences to women, as part of their exposure to the domestic violence dynamics, they should be seen as direct victims of the same male coercive control (Alexander et al., 2016; Fellin et al., 2018; Katz, 2022).

1.3.3.6 Mother–child relationships

Several studies found that when the mother–child attachment is damaged and mothers are unable to support their children because of their state of tension, the negative impact of exposure to violence is increased. The negative impacts were found to be stronger in early childhood (Graham-Bermann et al., 2009; Gustafsson et al., 2017; Johnson & Lieberman, 2007; McIntosh et al., 2021; Noonan & Pilkington, 2020; Visser et al., 2016). A recent study found that posttraumatic symptoms in the mother often appear in the children, a phenomenon termed "relational posttraumatic stress" (Galano et al., 2020).

1.3.3.7 Children's coping strategies

Studies in this field have suggested that children are not passive toward their environment, and many of them choose to react in what they perceive to be the best way of improving their situation and of coping with tension and negative experiences (Allen et al., 2003; Arai et al., 2021; Anderson, 2012, 2017; Bender, 2022; Callaghan et al., 2018; Eriksson et al., 2005; Fellin et al., 2018; Fellin et al., 2019; Graham-Bermann et al., 2009; Katz, 2015, 2016; Øverlien, 2016; Zolkoski & Bullock, 2012). These reactions were found to depend on the children's extent of emotional and behavioral development (Eisikovits & Winstok, 2001; Øverlien, 2016), on their personal coping style, and on the nature of their experience of harm, which affects psychological stress (Anderson, 2012; El-Sheikh et al., 2008; Noble-Carr et al., 2019). Strategies that were recorded included reactions such as keeping their distance from or entering into the violent event; physical intervention against the perpetrator; passing on information and attempting to receive external assistance from formal and informal authorities; and behaviors to protect the mother, such as taking responsibility at home, or alternatively, staying close to the father to guard against further outbursts (Alexander et al., 2016; Mullender et al., 2002; Øverlien, 2014; Øverlien & Hyden, 2009; Ravi & Casolaro, 2018; Katz, 2022).

1.3.4 Resiliency among children exposed to interparental violence

In the literature dealing with the impact of interparental violence on children's development, a small stream of burgeoning research has examined the resiliency developed by these children (Cameranesi et al., 2022; Carmel et al., 2014; Fogarty et al., 2019; Gewirtz & Edleson, 2007; Howell, 2011; Kitzmann et al., 2003). Resiliency is a universal capability, enabling a person, group, or community to develop normatively despite a difficult life reality (Luthar et al., 2000). This capability is determined by means of complex interactions between the individual and the environment (Cicchetti, 2013). Among factors found to be protective against the traumatic influence of children's exposure to violence were positive self-esteem, the way in which the children interpreted the event, their ability to cope with stress, availability of the mother or of other people who served as the children's primary caregivers, good relationships with a supportive and concerned adult outside of the family, engagement and connectedness among siblings, psychological hardiness that facilitates resistance to or rejection of negative factors at home, effective social skills, sense of hope for the future, respect for and empathy with others, and the development of a sense of control in life (American Psychological Association Presidential Task Force on Violence and the Family, 1996; Benavides, 2015; Bender, 2022; Cameranesi et al., 2022; Dankoski, et al., 2006; Fogarty et al., 2019; Hellman & Gwinn, 2017; Hambrick, 2019; Howell , 2011; Margolin et al., 2009; Mariscal, 2020; O'Dougherty Wright et al., 2013; Riesen & Porath, 2004).

1.3.5 Theoretical reevaluation in light of the research results

Based on the results of studies that revealed that some children developed severe problems whereas others did not, researchers proposed several theoretical formulations that took a more integrative approach (Carlson, 2000). The developmental psychopathological perspective (Cicchetti & Cohen, 2006; Hecht & Hansen, 2001) and the resiliency perspective (Gewirtz & Edleson, 2007; Luthar et al., 2000) attempted to explain the differential influence of children's exposure to violence as a result of the child's current developmental stage and the presence of risk factors and of protective variables. In addition, these approaches explain differently why some children will develop one type of adjustment problem (e.g., behavioral problems) whereas others will develop a different type of problem (either cognitive or emotional problems; Howell,2011; Howell et al., 2016). Some other theoretical formulations that proposed a more integrative approach for understanding the differential influence of exposure to violence while still working within a narrow framework (social learning theory and trauma theory) included Grych and Fincham's model (Grych & Fincham, 1990; Grych et al., 2000), composed of variables of interparental conflict, context, primary, and secondary level cognitive processes, coping behavior, and behavior that has an effect on how the conflict progresses. Cummings (1998) proposed a model for children's adjustment to interparental conflict in terms of emotional security attained by emotion regulation, internal representation of family relationships, and regulation of exposure to family influence. Attachment theory (Bowlby, 1982) was proposed as a useful framework for understanding the mechanisms involved in the generational transmission of maladaptive patterns (Levendosky et al., 2012). In this context, several attachment-focused interventions were developed to strengthen positive parenting and to promote secure attachment between mothers and children surrounding exposure to interparental violence (e.g., Howell et al., 2015).

1.3.6 Exposure to interparental violence: Direct abuse

Research in the field of exposure to violence provides cross-sectional evidence of a direct link between living in a violent reality and direct physical and sexual abuse of children (Graham-Bermann & Howell, 2010; Jenney & Alaggia, 2012; McDonald et al., 2016). This is notwithstanding the use of various samples throughout these studies and of methodologies that make it difficult to perform a systematic comparison (Holt et al., 2008; Kitzmann et al., 2003; Vu et al., 2016). Specifically, many studies that examined the relationship between exposure to violence and physical abuse of children reported an overlap rate of 32% to 53% (Edleson, 1995; Osofsky, 2003; Downes, 2019). Other studies that examined the relationship between exposure to violence and sexual abuse found a correlation of 40% to 70% (Saunders, 2003; Bancroft et al., 2012; Sitney & Kaufman, 2021).

Despite the high percentages revealed in the context of sexual abuse when examined both from the angle of exposure to violence as well as regarding clinical samples of abused children, no theoretical or empirical attempt was made to explain the high overlap between exposure to violence and child sexual abuse. The relationship between exposure to violence and physical abuse was explained against the background of an aggressive individual's inherent abuse potential toward his environment (McCloskey, 2001) and the tension-inducing circumstances (e.g., Slep & O'Leary, 2001).

1.3.7 Limitations of the research

The cumulative body of knowledge built in the field of children's exposure to interparental violence enabled the development of understanding regarding the outcomes of the exposure for these children. Nevertheless, the various researchers pointed out the fact that these studies, as a group, have significant limitations, even though their methodological planning has improved since the 1980s, when this field of research was begun (e.g., Carlson, 2000; Holt et al., 2008).

The foci of the problems, as identified by researchers who summarized three decades of studies in the field (Carlson, 2000; Holt et al., 2008) were as follows: 1) Most studies were based on samples of children living in battered women's shelters. It is a known fact that shelters receive the most severe cases of violence, giving rise to the problem of generalizing the findings to larger populations of children who are exposed to interparental violence but who have never either been in a shelter or received any kind of social services. 2) Shelter-based studies may be biased because of the stress effect of living in a shelter. 3) Most of the samples were small, raising the problem of the number of variables that can be considered when attempting to understand the impact of witnessing violence. This is a serious limitation in view of the complexity of the problem. 4) Most studies examined the impact of physical violence, and only a small number took into account the psychological or verbal violence against the mother. 5) Even though the majority of the studies used standardized methods, in most of them, the information about the children was obtained via the mother. Direct interviews with the children were conducted in only a small number of studies.

Recently, researchers raised an additional problem related to learning about the violence phenomenon in global contexts (Geffner, 2016; Parsons et al., 2020). Learning on such a multicultural scale demands complicated statistical analyses, which have not yet been implemented to produce valid, culturally sensitive findings. Specifically, as part of the need to bring the findings of severe child abuse that is the result of exposure to interparental violence to a global level, researchers from different disciplines have increased their focus on this phenomenon (Cameranesi & Piotrowski, 2020; Hollin, 2016; Parsons et al., 2020). However, 1) children, specifically, have not been researched, only the context. In other words, the prevalence of the domestic violence phenomenon has been studied, but children's exposure to that violence has not (Parsons et al., 2020). 2) Even in the context under discussion (domestic violence), data were analyzed based on surveys in various countries. This analysis requires creation of empirically based criteria for family violence (e.g., Heyman & Slep, 2019) as well as learning about cultural nuances that can influence interpretation of experiences and implications which must then be considered (e.g., Mann & Takyi, 2009). 3) Data from low-income countries are scarce, making it difficult to identify and understand diversity and to develop interventions (Parsons et al., 2020). 4) Existing data on child abuse are not specific to children who were exposed to violence in situations centered on relationships of psychological control. Rather, these data focus on physical and sexual abuse and neglect as part of the general field of child abuse. Even though research has proven congruence in high rates of exposure to violence and direct child abuse, witnessing violence serves as the basis of this type of abuse (Black et al., 2020). In any case, even the general field of child abuse in the global context lacks empirically based criteria (Parsons et al., 2020).

Notwithstanding the aforementioned deficits, there is a foundation of data based on which it can be assumed that exposure to violence is a widescale global phenomenon with a common denominator. Researchers claim the need for caution when generalizing the phenomenon, alongside ongoing intensive study worldwide that is particularly sensitive to cultural nuances (i.e., learning about the culture and its significance in intervention contexts; Parsons et al., 2020).

Another problematic area is that studies in the last decade have revealed a more complex picture than initially acknowledged regarding the factors influencing the outcomes of exposure to violence. This is yet another obstacle in the problem of sampling and in splitting up the role of the different variables in producing the different negative symptoms (Cameranesi & Piotrowski, 2020; Geffner, 2016). In this context, researchers in the field of exposure to violence (D'Andrea & Graham-Bermann, 2017) have recently raised the need to reexamine the theoretical frameworks that are suitable for use as a basis for studies in the field.

1.3.8 Critical learning of the limitations of the research described thus far

An analysis of the limitations of the research reveals inadequate sampling in many of the studies described above (samples based mainly on shelters and far less on other service populations, limiting their generalization potential). They also lack information sources (effects of exposure to violence are learned from the mothers and scarcely from the children themselves). Alongside these deficits, however, the researchers noted an improvement in methodological planning of the studies over the years.

The gap between identifying the problematic points of the research and the nature of the change that researchers have tried to introduce in order to improve the situation is astonishing. If the problem lies in the nature of the samples, then why not approach much larger samples for better generalization of the research findings? For example, the service user population of violence prevention centers is relatively large and, not living in a total institution, is not stricken with the stress effect of leaving the house or of transferal to a closed institution. In addition, this population might be exposed to more moderate forms of violence (since the shelter is reserved for extreme cases), allowing better generalization of the service population sample. Similarly, childcare experts could have been recruited to interview these children directly about their feelings, coping, and modes of thinking. Information provided by the victims themselves would have been more trustworthy. Why were these obvious research directions not adopted instead of the effort that was made to improve the use of samples from shelters for research purposes?

1.3.9 Summary of children's exposure to interparental violence

The literature review on exposure to violence, which covers four decades of research, shows a clear relationship between men's violence toward their wives or partners and abuse of children. (Research in the field reveals that between 30% and 40% of children exposed to violence are at risk of developing psychopathology.) On the most basic level, exposure to violence against the mother is equivalent to emotional abuse, with implications for mental health and interpersonal relationships in the future. Furthermore, many researchers agree that children may be exposed to violence in various ways that do not involve direct observation, such as hearsay evidence, involvement in conflict, and observing the results of the violence. Nevertheless, researchers are divided regarding the influence of such evidence, taking into consideration the studied variables and protective factors.

Interparental violence is also an important predictor of the risk of direct physical and sexual child abuse. In cases of direct abuse, in addition to witnessing violence, the impact of the abuse on the children was found to be especially severe. Therefore, the impact of exposure to violence in this context was named "double abuse."

1.4 Children's experience of interparental violence

A later wave of studies, at the beginning of the 1990s, mainly qualitative and clinical, offered knowledge based on the child's internal perspective. This knowledge helps us understand, to a certain depth, the complex experience of the child exposed to violence (Ericksen & Henderson, 1992; Humphreys, 1991; Peled, 1993).

Peled (1998), as a summarization, suggested four characteristic types of experience: **Living with the Secret**, meaning that the child denies the existence of the violence and acts as if it does not exist; **Living with Conflicts of Loyalty**, in which the child is aware of the violence but cannot choose sides; **Living in Terror and Fear**, in which the child is completely aware of the violence and identifies with the victim; and **Adopting the Violent Model**, in which the child is aware of the violence, but identifies with the aggressor.

Eisikovits et al. (1998) elaborated on these processes that lead to the appearance of the defined structures or subjects and deepened understanding of their influence on the child's system of constructing meaning. The aim of their work was to conceptualize the experience of children exposed to interparental violence using an interpretive-constructivist perspective. In the context under discussion, the researchers identified the child's experience as shaped through a three-stage process via violent events assimilated in the child's understanding of the family context. The three stages that were exposed as components of the assimilation process are: 1) "**Recollection**," negotiation of what happened; 2) "**Causality**," negotiation of why it happened, and 3) "**Moralization**," negotiation of what it means.

1.4.1 Recollection: Negotiation of what happened

This stage begins after the violence occurs. Family members try to negotiate within the boundaries of the event in order to determine what happened, who did what to whom, etc. The aim of this negotiation is to reach a consensus regarding a script for the violent event. At this stage, the couple can exaggerate, dramatize, minimize, or discover disagreements about the incident.

The children who experienced the violence itself as well as the negotiation process learn how collective memory is constructed and how to live with the gap between what they witnessed and what is to be remembered.

1.4.2 Causality: Negotiation of what happened

At this stage, the negotiation leaves the descriptive boundaries of the event. The causes attributed to the incident can move from the aggressor's emotional and psychological state (e.g., "Dad came home from work feeling depressed") to mystical beliefs (e.g., "He's a Taurus so has a tendency to outbursts"). During this stage, the children learn how to attribute causality and to adapt events and causes to each other. For this purpose, they might be assisted by categories of "folk psychology," which help to introduce logic to the events. Moreover, the children learn to lay responsibility for certain causes on specific objects. One possibility is that the child turns into the one who is responsible for the event; another possibility is that one or other of the parents becomes responsible; and yet another possibility is that no one is perceived as responsible.

1.4.3 Moralization: Negotiation of what it means

In the third stage, the child "draws a picture" of the moral outcomes of what happened. For example, the child may judge the violent event as either deserved or undeserved and may perceive violence as either a legitimate or an illegitimate means of achieving a particular goal. This moral judgment leads children to understanding that is beyond the boundaries of the event and toward developing a general approach to family culture and overall reality.

In light of the processes detailed here, the four types presented in the literature (Peled, 1998) have been expanded as summarizing the experience of children exposed to violence (Eisikovits et al., 1998).

1.4.4 Living with the Secret

In the recollection stage, the violence is diminished, given a lower profile, and frequently denied. It turns into a secret with the self and others. This situation contains both physical and emotional risks for the children. They might not be completely aware of the extent of the severity of the violence and of the potential physical risk involved. They do not proceed to the causality stage because, in the eyes of all the participants, nothing has happened. The children develop a belief that it is seemingly dangerous to cope with the reality of admitting to violence and prefer to be deaf and blind than to undermine the foundations of the family and to carry a feeling of guilt. The collective moral lesson learned in these families is that some subjects are taboo. Denial tactics are generalized beyond the violent situations and become a regular strategy for coping with stressful situations. The children assimilate a perception of a secret reality, which becomes part of their existential worldview.

1.4.5 Living with Conflicts of Loyalty

The presence of partner violence in the family is recognized and processed through the recollection and causality stages in a way that places the children in a position of emotional conflict. They might feel empathy toward the victimized parent's pain and suffering as well as anger toward the aggressor because of his wicked and brutal behavior. At the same time, they might be disgusted or feel contempt for the weak parent while admiring the aggressor's displays of power. Moreover, the children might simultaneously experience contradictory feelings for that parent, such as love and hate, emotional closeness and alienation, and physical closeness and repulsion. Gradually, the children internalize a perception that becomes a general moral lesson that the world is a place that is determined and managed by conflicts.

1.4.6 Living in Terror and Fear

In the processes of recollection and causality regarding the violent event, the children are guided to take the victim's stance. As a result, they have a tendency to worry and are afraid, both for themselves and for their mother. This fear is justified by the belief that violence against the mother tends to lead to violence against themselves. The actual and potential violence create an environment in which expectations of violence and terror become a daily reality. The world is interpreted as a dangerous place in which people must be frightened. Such a moral lesson usually leads to feelings of helplessness, depression, introversion, and an absence of trust.

1.4.7 Adopting the Violent Model

In the processes of recollection and causality to the violent events, children are guided to take the stance of the aggressor, which, for them, means connecting to a life pattern characterized by aggression and dominance. As a result, emotions of anger turn into a central theme in the child's emotional world, and manipulative and violent behaviors are adopted. When control is successfully attained through violence, its accompanying behaviors become stronger and will be chosen in the future, inter alia in peer group relationships. The moral lesson learned from this approach is that the world is a jungle, either eat or be eaten. This perception is included in the use of aggression and violence as rules for survival in the family context and in the broad existential context.

The interpretation suggested for parent–child relationships was expanded into a conceptual formulation that includes an external social context (Eisikovits & Winstok, 2001). The broad formulation includes "significant others" (people/institutions) that serve as mediators between the parents' expectations and the children's construction of their experiences. As such, they might either strengthen or contradict the parental expectations.

Specifically, when the child has a normative construction of reality notwithstanding the parents' expectations, the external impact factor will be great, whereas when the child's construction of reality is in line with the parents' expectations, external influences will be marginal. The significance of this theoretical formulation is that despite the negative influences that can lead to nonnormative cognitive constructions, this child population shows resiliency.

Since the beginning of the 2000s, studies in the field of interpreting the experiences of children and adolescents (Alexander et al., 2016; Allen et al., 2003; Anderson, 2012, 2017; Arai et al., 2021; Beetham, 2019; Callaghan & Alexander, 2015; Davies & Sturge-Apple, 2006; Fellin et al., 2018, 2019; Goldblatt & Eisikovits, 2005; Katz, 2015, 2016; Mullender et al., 2002; Noble-Carr et al., 2019; Øverlien, 2014, 2016; Rogers & Berger, 2022) have strengthened the findings of previous studies, showing that the children's efforts to give meaning to their experiences were dynamic while they navigated around the complexity and terror of domestic violence. Inter alia, a variety of coping strategies used by children were observed, ranging from integration to distancing. Through an integration strategy, children can normalize the violence, minimize its impact, or even incorporate violence into their own behavior (Hines, 2015; Noble-Carr et al., 2019; Ravi & Casolaro, 2018; Miranda et al., 2022).

Following on from this, the children's perception and understanding in the abusive context changed from passive to active (Arai, 2021; Callaghan et al., 2018; Holt et al., 2008; Øverlien, 2016), and the serious harm to the children was recognized not only by the fact of their presence at the scene of the confrontation but also as a result of what they experienced themselves (Callaghan et al., 2016; Carmel, 2010; Katz, 2022; Øverlien & Hyden, 2009; Rogers & Berger, 2022). It is noteworthy that over the last 15 years, the limited stream of research dealing with the children's experience has grown. However, these studies focused mainly on the children's coping strategies rather than on the phenomenology of how they experienced all the stages and complexities of the domestic violence dynamics.

1.5 Limitations of the aforementioned research and the critical lessons learned from them

In the second wave of studies that constructs the body of knowledge in the field of children exposed to violence, the research performed is limited and knowledge is provided mainly in the context of adolescents (Arai et al., 2021). In addition, a considerable amount of knowledge was constructed on theoretical developments, which, after conceptualization, were not examined empirically. If we compare this picture to the one received from the first wave of studies that examined the relationships between exposure to violence and its outcomes, we may identify **common elements** in their research limitations.

The first wave of studies focused mainly on shelter samples that, by nature, lacked generalizability. The **second wave of studies** was based on qualitative research, which, to build a body of knowledge, requires a broad examination of various microsocial units. Thus, in both cases, the body of knowledge had limited generalizability. In the context of the first wave of studies, therefore, why did the researchers not approach a wider sample of the service population to allow greater generalizability? (Samples from the last decade, although larger, are still limited.) In the context of the second wave of studies, why was further research not performed as a foundation for the knowledge and why the leap toward theoretical conceptualizations instead of deeper study of the experience and its complexity? The last question is even more piercing in view of the systematic review in the field of children's experience of violence (Arai et al., 2021), which emphasizes the following research limitations: 1) The particularly small amount of research (only about 33 qualitative studies over the years); 2) very small samples (half of them with between 4 and 6 participants and the other half with between 10 and 14 participants); and 3) studies based mainly on populations living in shelters (convenience samples that do not allow a "pure" examination of the experience of violence).

Moreover, even though, in the **second wave of studies**, most of the knowledge is acquired through the eyes of the children (as opposed to through the eyes of the mothers and the children's therapists in the first wave of studies), it relies mainly on descriptions by older children and adolescents and on theoretical knowledge developed externally by the researchers. Therefore, in both cases, in the context of the first and second waves of studies, the knowledge pertaining to the serious consequences of exposure to violence is not founded sufficiently on the children's perspective.

An examination of the body of knowledge to date in the field of children exposed to interparental violence may reveal the existence of a gap between the way the body of knowledge develops and the way it is established. Regarding its development, advancement can be seen, and this is consistent with a phenomenon that requires social attention. In other words, the first wave of studies dealt with the attempt to prove the problematic nature of the phenomenon, and as soon as it was proven worthy of attention as a social problem, the second wave of studies attempted to examine the problem's complexity.

The picture is different regarding the establishment of the body of knowledge. Indeed, establishing the phenomenon of exposure to violence as a social problem draws on studies that lack generalizability and information on which they are founded. Therefore, the phenomenon's problematic status is left subject to additional proof. In a similar way, but with a difference, the multilayered and complicated nature of the problem that arises from the studies was not learned in-depth. Since the number of studies was small and the knowledge was obtained mainly from the adult age group, they provided limited knowledge regarding the complexity of the problem and how to cope with it.

A deeper search is needed to reveal the sources of the gap between the development and the establishment of the body of knowledge (a point not yet learned to date). Clearly, researchers have faced some objective difficulty that has stopped them taking the necessary action to establish the phenomenon's status as a social problem, which would facilitate its learning in depth. A hint that may help us to explore the source of the problem is the absence of reference to samples based on the service population outside of battered women's shelters, despite repeated criticism voiced on the subject. This gap in the samples over so many years may be evidence of an intentional choice because of the problems involved in conducting surveys and research among this population. We must, then, ask what differentiates the child population in the shelter from the population, for example, in the centers for treatment and prevention of family violence.

The answer might be that in battered women's shelters, the children are only with their mothers, who have custody and are able to protect them on account of their being in the shelter. Moreover, the women's special state of risk gives them a special legal status, in which the children are entitled to immediate treatment without the father's consent. This is not the case in violence prevention centers, where children's treatment is subject to the consent of both parents, even if they are not separated, leading to cases of potentially serious conflict in which the consent of both sides is essential. This situation, which makes it difficult to treat the children within the framework of violence prevention centers because of the need for the father's consent, is also what may create difficulties in recruiting children for the study. I encountered this problem during my research project (Carmel, 2010) while attempting to recruit 27 children for an in-depth qualitative study, for which I needed the consent of both fathers and mothers. In the pilot study, the mothers gave their immediate consent, whereas the fathers completely refused, even when I enlisted the help of male therapists. To obtain the fathers' consent, I developed a special method. It required an in-depth study of the violent men's experience and the development of unique skills as to how to approach them and exactly what to say to them so that they would not see me as representing systems that they perceived as threatening (welfare and academia). In light of the above, we can understand why the number of qualitative studies attempting to learn about the complexity of the experience of exposure to violence is limited. It is also clear why researchers turned to a theoretical conceptualization of the children's understanding of the violent family context before attempting to gain a deeper empirical understanding of the meaning attributed by the children to the complex domestic reality.

Another topic for study is the exposure of information through asking and interviewing the children rather than through sources who speak on their behalf. This topic appears to be especially problematic in the context of the first wave of studies, which, even when focusing on shelter samples, scarcely questioned the children themselves but turned to their mothers and therapists for information about them. The issue is slightly less problematic in the second wave of studies. However, even though researchers interviewed the children themselves, they far more frequently spoke to older children or adolescents and hardly ever to younger children of 7 to 12 years old. (Data in this context can be learned from a recent critical review of children's perspectives of domestic violence; Arai et al., 2021). These two factors, a) the scarcity of interviews with the children themselves and b) even when children were interviewed, the focus being mainly on the adolescent group, might indicate another problem regarding establishment of the data in the body of knowledge of children exposed to violence. This is fear and/or lack of knowledge of "how to talk to children," especially young children.

In this context also, I will bring an example from my research project (Carmel, 2010), referring to reactions that I encountered when meeting with caregivers of children in the framework of violence prevention centers as part of my research. In this context, it is important to me to make two things clear: 1) I am full of admiration for the staff whom I met and who helped me, eventually, to reach the children. 2) My words are not, in any way, intended as criticism but merely reflect the honest, genuine desire to clarify the extent to which the cultural world of adults lacks knowledge of the children's world.

Therapists who had treated men and women (who helped me to recruit parents whose children fitted my research criteria) reacted very positively and identified with the important need for knowledge obtained from the children themselves. Child therapists, however, were preoccupied with fears about how the interviews would affect the children and what potential damage they might cause. It seemed to me, for a moment, that they had forgotten that I, too, had spent many years working with children and had acquired skills as a clinical-consultant child therapist. The focus of their energies was this point, rather than the new knowledge to be gathered from the children's perspective, enriching the understanding of everyone involved in dealing with the children's world. In this context, it is important for me to emphasize that, during my many years of working with children who were exposed to their fathers' violence against their mothers in a battered women's shelter and in a violence prevention center, I have learned that children's culture and adults' culture are completely different and that children's physical smallness and inexperience do not detract from their mental strength and capabilities. They understand the world differently and interpret it through their own special tools and perspectives, but we are talking about difference and not about weakness. Children have powers and strengths, and it is sometimes enough just to listen to them from the purest possible place in order to understand the extent of their creativity, strengths that we have lost because, when we were children, no one showed us their importance or beauty.

Furthermore, speaking on behalf of the children and their thinking may lead to far more serious errors and far worse damage than speaking to them directly. (The price might be irrelevant treatment at best and harmful treatment, at worst.) Thus, making them think about what occurred and asking questions will not weaken them but will enable them to rethink about what happened to them, redefine the reality of their lives, and arouse their vitality and creativity to find solutions and seek help. And we, as therapists and researchers, who are skilled in treating children, will be there for them in cases when thinking is too difficult or too painful, the type that requires help to gather strength.

1.6 Escalation of violence in intimate relationships

An examination of the continued development of a body of knowledge in the field of exposure to violence reveals that in-depth learning of the complexity of the children's experience of the violent reality has reached a standstill. This is despite the necessity for this deeper learning in view of the revelation that the children play an active role in the escalating interparental dynamics. Instead, it is as if the body of knowledge has taken a few steps backward and is dealing, once again, with proving the relationship between living in a violent reality and the development of negative and psychopathological symptoms (see studies from the 2000s onward, Sections 1.3.1, 1.3.3, and 1.3.4). Notwithstanding the logic of this in light of the problematic generalization in studies on the subject, a halt in the development of this body of knowledge might hinder the ability to build context-based interventions. That is to say, the limited information regarding the complexity of the problem might interfere with the understanding of the ways that one can and should deal with the issue. Moreover, continued establishment of the existing knowledge might have been accomplished parallel to exploring the new knowledge.

We may be able to shed light on what is behind this standstill by taking a look at the development of the body of knowledge on violence against women, since this is the context in which to learn about the experience of children who are exposed to the violence. The children's experience is constructed in relation to the escalating interparental dynamics.

The literature review in the field of violence against women (Winstok, 2008) raises the point that, for many years, researchers dealt with the definition of the phenomenon.[1] In this context, the various prevalent approaches to understanding intercouple violence were emphasized. The feminist approach (Dekeseredy & MacLeod, 1997) defined violence against women by means of the term "domestic violence," with reference to the home as a patriarchal social construct that strengthens inequality and legitimizes men's use of power over women. The family system approach (Straus, 1979, 1990) defined the phenomenon as "intimate partner violence" in relation to the development of the conflict itself, involving violent behavior by both sides. The separation between the context of violence against women and violent behavior enabled placing mutual responsibility on the sides involved in the escalation regarding their "contribution" to the development of the quarrel (Winstok, 2008). The different theoretical assumptions of the central approaches to understanding intimate partner violence were the basis for the start of a key polemic in the field, named "gender symmetry or asymmetry" (Johnson, 2011). This polemic, which began in the mid-1990s, was deepened with the publication of the meta-analysis by Archer (2000) and the global research by Straus (2008) on dating violence, who presented a gender symmetry approach. Although they provide support for the existence of bidirectional violence, various researchers note the problems involved in relating to bidirectionality as symmetry and emphasize the importance of relating to the duration, frequency, severity, and type of abuse (Langhinrichsen-Rohling et al., 2012; Tjaden & Thoennes, 2000; Hamby, 2009).

There is a broad consensus in the literature that escalation is an emotional process involving intense feelings such as anxiety, anger, helplessness, humiliation, shame, guilt, jealousy, hostility, low self-esteem, and sense of failure (e.g., Gergen, 1994). The presence of such emotions leads to an imbalance, which in turn leads to an experience of a lack of control and the loss of the ability to predict, plan, and navigate through life. Under these conditions, the violence turns into a tool perceived as having the capacity to attain power and control (e.g., Scheff & Retzinger, 1991).

Most theories dealing with escalation examined its components rather than the dynamics of the process involved. For example, Brockner and Rubin (1985) claimed that escalation describes a decision-making process in which each side is entrenched in his/her stance. Goffman (1967) suggested that the need to maintain one's self-image and the perception of changing one's mind as a weakness is what lies behind this process. Even though the various theories can be distinguished by the emphasis placed on the variables that contribute to the escalation, there is widespread agreement in the literature regarding the centrality of the threat and of counterthreat reactions (e.g., Patterson, 1982).

Retzinger's conflict and escalation model (Retzinger, 1991a, 1991b) addresses a process within the context of intimate violence. The researcher distinguishes between dyads with a safe relationship that lead to conflict-free interpersonal relations and dyads in which the relationship is threatened, the parties become estranged, and feel attacked by the other side. While Retzinger's model is an important step in the ability to help the distinction between functional and dysfunctional conflicts in intimate relationships; it focuses on emotions and does not deal with additional details—constructive components of escalation and the interactional dynamics between them.

Later studies that dealt with escalation in the intimate violence context (Eisikovits et al., 2002; Winstok et al., 2002; Winstok, 2007) attempted to develop a theoretical model that exposes the structure and dynamics of violence in intimate relationships from the perspective of the perpetrator, the victim, and the couple.

In this context, it was found that men perceive their activity during confrontations as a reaction to the behavior of their female partners. They tend to focus on their partner's actions, which they perceive as undermining the interpersonal balance and threatening their existential reality. Accordingly, they perceive their activities as directly channeled toward the need to recreate the balance (Winstok et al., 2002). Specifically, the findings show that men perceive themselves as entitled and obliged to protect their existential dyadic system while acknowledging the costs and the advantages involved in using violence to accomplish this goal. They create rules, pass judgment when their rules are violated, and take steps to enforce them. These men's evaluation of their control through these activities and the consideration of the advantages and disadvantages regarding them have a tremendous influence on their attempts to restore the lost balance in their couple life.

The men's process of constructing the action as a reaction to their partner's behavior is composed of two distinct, yet interlinked, stages: **The first** relates to identifying the partner's behavior and constructing it as an action worthy of a reaction, and **the second** is the construction of an appropriate reaction (Winstok et al., 2002).

In contrast, the women see the transition from a nonviolent to a violent reality as a process. They appraise the change as marked by distinct intersections, each with the potential either for escalation or for an escape route. Control of the situation is a key variable in managing the process, which may or may not lead to violence, which explains why they stay together despite the violence (Eisikovits et al., 2002).

The attempt to unify both viewpoints while weighing the points of difference and similarity between the genders led to an overall view. According to this view, both the man and the woman have the potential, from their internal perspective, to see themselves as both perpetrators and victims. Nevertheless, when the focus of the conflict moves from a specific issue to a more general problem that threatens the couple's relationship, then both of them might perceive violence as an action worth taking. At this point, a new problem might be created that will send the conflict out of control (Winstok, 2013).

Learning about the process of interparental conflict escalation to all-out violence within the framework of intimate violence from the perspective of the perpetrator and the victim was a breakthrough regarding the construction of the body of knowledge in the field of violence against women. Indeed, it served to authorize critical examination of the prevalent approaches to understanding the violence and the creation of a structural and integrative model in the field.

In the context under discussion, Winstok (2008) relates to the lacunae in both the family system approach and the feminist approach. Regarding the family system approach, he pointed to the fact that the researchers were not concerned with identifying a motive for the process (Straus, 1979, 1990; Straus et al., 1996, in Winstok, 2008). He also remarked that they provided evidence only of an escalation schema on a time continuum (Feld & Straus, 1989, in Winstok, 2008) and not of a gradual schema of de-escalation. In his opinion, these gaps, which disregard the intentional component of the escalation, as emerges clearly from the study of the dynamics of the escalation from the men's perspective, are a weakpoint in the construction of the theoretical and definitive framework of understanding the violence. In fact, the revelation of the intentional component of the escalation provides clear-cut evidence of the absolute necessity of learning about the violent intercouple dynamics within the context of violence against women. In contrast, examining the dynamics of the escalation from the women's perspective strengthens the need to learn about the escalation process from the viewpoint of all participants involved and not only from an external perspective. This is because, from the internal perspective of the sides involved in the conflict, the violence is perceived as a problem-solving tactic. That is to say, the weak point in the theoretical and definitional framework of the feminist approach contradicts the family system approach, disregarding the internal perspective of those involved in the escalation dynamics (Winstok, 2008).

The integrative view, which is the result of this critical learning, is that the escalation dynamics of the intercouple relationships must be learned in the context of the definition of the man as the aggressor and the woman as the victim. In other words, placing the situational responsibility on the man, as initiator of the escalation, will eliminate the fear of learning about the escalation dynamics, whose internal characteristic is the changing relationships between perpetrator and victim (Winstok, 2008). Johnson (2011) suggested that the data that emerged from the various studies on intimate violence should be interpreted broadly, namely as the existence of different violence perpetrator patterns. He claims that what appears to be gender symmetry in research reviews is actually a greater reflection of intercouple situational violence than of the alarming violence that has gender-related patterns of intimate terror.

This integrative view has very important implications for developing the knowledge field of children exposed to interparental violence. This is because the situational responsibility placed on the man as the initiator of the violence, which enables us to learn about the escalation dynamics from the internal perspective of its participants, is also what removes the fear of casting a stain or of placing any kind of responsibility on the children themselves as a result of researching the nature of their involvement and how they understand what is happening between their parents (Carmel, 2010). From this point of view, the body of knowledge in the field of violence against women was completely synchronized with the development of the body of knowledge in the field of children exposed to violence and even prepared the ground for continued exploration and learning of the field. Nevertheless, it must be noted that despite the fact that this integrative theoretical understanding was formed only in 2008, the study findings that made this possible already existed in 2002. Furthermore, the first study in the field of children exposed to violence, which was a direct outcome of the integration of this theory, was conducted in 2010 by the author of this book (Carmel, 2010). Since then, despite the complex and difficult findings that warranted continued research in the proposed direction, I have found no such studies to date. The difficulty arises also from another direction; the writing of interventions for the child population exposed to violence. In this context, the researchers repeatedly emphasized the paucity in this field as well as demonstrating only partial, and not sufficiently validated, success of these interventions. These findings are directed toward the need to continue to learn about the complexity in the field of exposure to violence (Carlson, 2000; Graham-Bermann & Levendosky, 2011; McTavish et al., 2016; Miranda et al., 2022; Muir et al., 2022; Romano et al., 2021). The body of knowledge dealing with interventions for children exposed to violence will be addressed in the second chapter of this book.

Based on the above, the lack of continuation of research in the knowledge field of children exposed to violence is even less comprehensible, raising the possibility that there is a certain interest at stake.

1.6.1 Critical learning in the field of violence against an intimate partner

An in-depth examination of the prevalent approaches to explaining violence against women may, in my view, be a direction worth developing to understand the vacuum that has been created. As mentioned, the feminist approach to intercouple violence explains men's violence against women in a gender-related context, namely as a social construct that legitimizes the use of power against women. This theoretical conceptualization infers that escalation has a motivational component designed to achieve optimal balance in the family (according to patriarchal society criteria of gender-based role division between women and men). This theoretical conceptualization has an empirical basis on studying the escalation dynamics from the violent men's perspective (Winstok et al., 2002). Therefore, understanding these dynamics from the children's perspective as well as examining their involvement in the escalation process could have provided additional empirical proof for the presence of a motivational component in the escalating intercouple confrontation, thus establishing the rationale behind the approach. Similarly, but in a different way, the family system approach, by investigating the children's point of view, might have earned at least partial empirical support for the thesis that advocates the presence of gender symmetry (maybe not in the context of initiating the escalation, for example, but in other conflictual contexts). If that is the case, and if studying the children's understanding of the interparental escalation process could have shed new light, not only on the experience of the children themselves but also on the general phenomenon of violence against women, the question to be asked is: What prevented the researchers from doing this? More precisely, why did they not immediately move in this research direction? It would appear to be in the interest of both schools of researchers to establish the thesis of each approach. Alternatively, to achieve an integrated theoretical construct in the field that will be able to advance it on the sociopolitical level and to build context-tailored intervention programs for all those involved in the experience of the violence.

The answer to this question may lie in the attempt to understand the possible accompanying outcomes of learning about the phenomenology of the children's experience, in all its dimensions, beyond developing in-depth understanding in the field. The outcomes of such learning should have exposed the nature and intensity of the harm to the children more deeply and precisely, which would have immediately placed the responsibility on the man as the perpetrator, not only against the women but also against the children (to a greater extent than was thought in the past). At the same time, such learning may also have exposed the woman's difficulty as a captive who, over time, is unable to release herself. Since she perceives the reality from the position of her captivity, her complex situation does not always enable her to protect the children emotionally, psychologically, and physically. **On the practical level**, the results of such learning may lead not only to official recognition that violent men are also abusive fathers, with all the implications of that, but also that children who are exposed to violence need to be treated separately from their mothers. This is a morally challenging situation of secondary victimization from the women's perspective, who might feel as though they have been turned into victims of the society as well.

The critical analysis offered here may show that there are stakes involved in the reasons for the stagnated learning about the experience of exposure to violence. The stagnation might be interpreted as an expression of researchers' social responsibility to prevent a situation in which protecting the women and protecting the children turns into a conflict of interests. This might lead to a situation in which women are afraid to cooperate on issues related to the children. In addition, it can be hypothesized that placing additional responsibility on the abusive men might be problematic in the political-gender context, since it is relevant to quite a large group of men within the general population (despite research evidence that studying the field in this context is, in fact, expedient). This politically and socially problematic state regarding the men, which is morally problematic regarding the women, is what seems to determine the construction of the body of knowledge in the field.

The analysis put forward here leads to complex conclusions. In the next chapter, therefore, I will review current interventions with children exposed to violence to see if they shed additional light, possibly from a different angle, on the construction of the body of knowledge in the field of children exposed to violence.

Note

1 The study of the phenomenon of violence against women began in the 1970s.

References

Ahmad, S., Ishtiaq, S. M., & Mustafa, M. (2017). The role of socio-economic status in adaption of coping strategies among adolescents against domestic violence. *Journal of Interpersonal Violence*, *32*(18), 2862–2881. https://doi.org/10.1177/0886260516635321

Ahun, M. N., & Cote, S. M. (2019). Maternal depressive symptoms & early childhood cognitive development: A review of putative environmental mediators. *Archives of Women's Mental Health*, *22*(1), 15–24. https//doi.org/10.1007/s00737-018-0870-x

Alexander, J. H., Callaghan, J. E. M., Sixsmith, J., & Fellin, L. (2016). Children's corporeal agency and use of space in situations of domestic violence. In B. Evans, J. Horton, & T. Skelton (Eds.), *Play, recreation, health and wellbeing: Geographies of children and young people* (vol. 9, pp. 523–543). Springer. https://doi.org/10.1007/978-981-4585-96-523-1

Allen, N. E., Wolf, A. M., Bybee, D. I., & Sullivan, C. M. (2003). Diversity of children's immediate coping responses to witnessing domestic violence. In R. Geffner, R. S. Igleman, & J. Zellner (Eds.), *The effects of intimate partner violence on children* (pp. 123–147). Haworth American.

American Psychological Association Presidential Task Force on Violence and the Family. (1996). *Violence and the family: Report of the APA presidential task force*. American Psychological Association.

Anderson, K. (2017). Children's protective strategies in the context of exposure to domestic violence. *Journal of Human Behavior in the Social Environment*, *27*(8), 835–846. https://doi.org/10.1080/10911359.2017.1339654

Anderson, K. M. (2012). Fostering resilience in daughters of battered women. In D. Becvar (Ed.), *Handbook of family resilience* (pp. 495–514). Springer.

Anderson, S. A., & Cramer-Benjamin, D. B. (1999). The impact of couple parenting and children: An overview and clinical implications. *The American Journal of Family Therapy*, *27*(1), 1–19. https://doi.org/10.1080/019261899262069

Arai, L., Shaw, A., Feder, G., Howarth, E., MacMillan, H., Moore, T. H. M., Stanley, N., & Gregory, A. (2021). Hope, agency, and the lived experience of violence: A qualitative systematic review of children's perspectives on domestic Violence and abuse. *Trauma, Violence, and Abuse*, *22*(3), 427–438. https://doi.org/10.1177/1524838019849582

Archer, J. (2000). Sex differences in aggression between heterosexual partners: A meta-analytic review. *Psychological Bulletin, 126*(5), 651–680. https://doi.org/10.1037/0033-2909.126.5.651

Artz, S., Jackson, M. A., Rossiter, K. R., Nijdam-Jones, A., Geczy, I., & Porteous, S. (2014). A comprehensive review of literature on the impact of exposure to intimate partner violence for children and youth. *International Journal of Child, Youth and Family Studies, 5*(4), 493–587. https://doi.org/10.18357/ijcyfs54201413274

Bair-Merritt, M. H., Johnson, S. B., Okelo, S., & Page, G. (2012). Intimate partner violence exposure, salivary cortisol, and childhood asthma. *Child Abuse and Neglect, 36*(7–8), 596—601. https://doi.org/10.1016/j.chiabu.2011.12.002

Bair-Merrit, M. H., Voegtline, K., Ghazarian, S. R., Granger, D. A., Blair, C., Johnson, S. B., Vernon Feagans, L., Cox, M., Burchinal, P., Burton, L., Crnic, K., Crouter, A., Garrett-Peters, P., Greenberg, M., Lanza, S., Mills-Koonce, R., Skinner, D., Werner, E., & Willoughby, M. (2015). Maternal intimate partner violence exposure, child cortisol reactivity and child asthma. *Child Abuse and Neglect, 48*, 50–57. https://doi.org/10.1016/j.chiabu.2014.11.003

Bancroft, L., Silverman, J. G., & Ritchie, D. (2012). *The batterer as parent: Addressing the impacts of domestic violence on family dynamics* (2nd ed.). Sage.

Bedi, G., & Goddard, C. (2007). Intimate partner violence: What are the impacts on children? *Australian Psychologist, 42*(1), 66–77. https://doi.org/10.1080/00050060600726296

Beetham, T., Gabriel, L., & James, H. (2019). Young children's narrations of relational recovery: A school-based group for children who have experienced domestic violence. *Journal of Family Violence, 34*(6), 565–575. https://doi.org/10.1007/s10560-014-0339-3

Benavides, L. E. (2015). Protective factors in children and adolescents exposed to intimate partner violence: An empirical research review. *Child and Adolescent Social Work Journal, 32*(2), 93–107. https://doi.org/10.1007/s10560-014-0339-3

Bender, A. E. (2022). *An exploration of sibling relationships in middle childhood among children exposed to intimate partner violence* (Unpublished doctoral dissertation). Case Western Reserve University.

Bender, A. E., McKinney, S. J., Schmidt-Sane, M. M., Cage, J., Holmes, M. R., Berg, K., Salley, J., Bodell, M., Miller, E. K., & Voith, L. A. (2022). Childhood exposure to intimate partner violence and effects on social-emotional competence: A systematic review. *Journal of Family Violence,* 1–19. https://doi.org/10.1007/s10896-021-00315-z

Black, T., Fallon, B., Nikolova, K., Tarshis, S., Baird, S., & Carradine, J. (2020). Exploring subtypes of children's exposure to intimate partner violence. *Children and Youth Services Review, 118*, Article 105375. https://doi.org/10.1016/j.childyouth.2020.105375

Bogat, G. A., Levendosky, A. A., & von Eye, A. (2005). The future of research on intimate partner violence: Person-oriented and variable-oriented perspectives. *American Journal of Community Psychology, 36*(1–2), 49–70. https://doi.org/10.1007/s10464-005-6232-7

Bowlby, J. (1982). Attachment and loss: Retrospect and prospect. *American Journal of Orthopsychiatry, 52*(4), 664–678. https://doi.org/10.1111/j.1939.0025.1982.tb01456.x

Brockner, J., & Rubin, J. Z. (1985). *Entrapment in escalating conflicts.* Springer.

Burke, J. G., Lee, L. C., & O'Campo, P. (2008). An exploration of maternal intimate partner violence experiences and infant general health and temperament. *Maternal and Child Health Journal, 12*(2), 172–179. https://doi.org/10.1007/s10995-007-0218-z

Cage, J., Kobulsky, J. M., McKinney, S. J., Homes, M., Berg, K., Bender, A. E., & Kemmerer, A. (2021). The effect of exposure to intimate partner violence on children's academic functioning: A systematic review of the literature. *Journal of Family Violence, 37*(8), 1337–1352. https://doi.org/10.1007/s10896-021-00314-0

Callaghan, J. E. M., & Alexander, J. H. (2015). *Understanding agency and resistance strategies (UNARS): Children's experiences of domestic violence.* European Commission project JUST/2012/DAP/AG/3461. University of Northampton.

Callaghan, J. E. M., Alexander, J. H., Sixsmith, J., & Fellin, L. C. (2016). Children's experiences of domestic violence and abuse: Siblings' accounts of relational coping. *Clinical Child Psychology and Psychiatry, 21*(4), 649–668. https://doi.org/10.1177/1359104515620250

Callaghan, J. E., Alexander, J. H., Sixsmith, J., & Fellin, L. C. (2018). Beyond "witnessing": Children's experiences of coercive control in domestic violence and abuse. *Journal of Interpersonal Violence, 33*(10), 1551–1581. https://doi.org/10.1177/0886260515618956

Cameranesi, M., & Piotrowski, C. C. (2020). Critical review of theoretical frameworks elucidating the mechanisms accounting for the adverse developmental outcomes observed in children following exposure to intimate partner violence. *Aggression and Violent Behavior, 55*, Article 101455. https://doi.org/10.1016/j.avb.2020.101455

Cameranesi, M., Shooshtari, S., & Piotrowski, C. C. (2022). Investigating adjustment profiles in children exposed to intimate partner violence using a biopsychosocial resilience framework: A Canadian population-based study. *Child Abuse and Neglect, 125*, 105453.

Cao, Y., Li, L., Zhang, Y., Guo, X., Zhang, Y., & Luo, X. (2016). Effects of exposure to domestic physical violence on children's behavior: A Chinese community-based sample. *Journal of Child and Adolescent Trauma, 9*(2), 127–135. https://doi.org/10.1007/s40653-016-0092-1

Carlson, B. E. (2000). Children exposed to intimate partner violence: Research findings and implications for intervention. *Trauma, Violence, and Abuse, 1*(4), 321–342. https://doi.org/10.1177/1524838000001004002

Carmel, Y. (2010). *Escalation of interparental conflicts from the children's perspective* (Unpublished doctoral dissertation). University of Haifa, Israel. (Hebrew).

Carmel, Y., Sigad, L., Lev-Wiesel, R., & Eisikovits, Z. (2014). Pathways to resilience among Israeli child victims of abuse and neglect. *Child Indicators Research, 8*(3), 551–570. https://doi.org/10.1007/s12187-014-9255-5

Cater, Å. K., Miller, L. E., Howell, K. H., & Graham-Bermann, S. A. (2015). Childhood exposure to intimate partner violence and adult mental health problems: Relationships with gender and age of exposure. *Journal of Family Violence, 30*(7), 875–886. https://doi.org/10.1007/s10896-015-9703-0

Chan, Y. C., & Yeung, J. W. K. (2009). Children living with violence within the family and its sequel: A meta-analysis from 1995–2006. *Aggression and Violent Behavior, 14*(5), 313–322. https://doi.org/10.1016/j.avb.2009.04.001

Charak, R., Ford, J. D., Modrowski, D. A., & Kerig, P. K. (2019). Polyvictimization, emotion dysregulation, symptoms of posttraumatic stress disorder, and behavioral health problems among justice-involved youth: A latent class analysis. *Journal of Abnormal Child Psychology, 47*(2), 287–289. https://doi.org/10.1007/s10802-018-0431-9

Cicchetti, D. (2013). Annual research review: Resilient functioning in maltreated children—Past, present and future perspectives. *Journal of Child Psychology and Psychiatry, 54*(4), 402–422. https://doi.org/10.1111/j.1469-7610.2012.02608.x

Cicchetti, D., & Cohen, D. H. (2006). *Developmental psychopathology* (vol. 2). John Wiley & Sons.

Cobos-Cali, M., Ladera, V., Petra, M. V., & Garcia, R. (2018). Language disorders in victims of domestic violence in children's homes. *Child Abuse and Neglect, 86,* 384–392. https://doi.org/10.1016/j.chiabu.2017.02.028

Conway, L. J., Cook, F., Cahir, P., Brown, S., Reilly, S., Gartland, D., Mensah, F., & Giallo, R. (2021). Children's language abilities at age 10 and exposure to intimate partner violence in early childhood: Results of an Australian prospective pregnancy cohort study. *Child Abuse and Neglect, 111,* Article 104794. https://doi.org/10.1016/j.chiabu.2020.104794

Cummings, E. M. (1998). Children exposed to marital conflict and violence: Conceptual and theoretical directions. In G. W. Holden, R. Geffner, & E. N. Jouriles (Eds.), *Children exposed to marital violence* (pp. 55–93). American Psychological Association.

D'Andrea, W., & Graham-Bermann, S. (2017). Social context and violence exposure as predictors of internalizing symptoms in mothers and children exposed to intimate partner violence. *Journal of Family Violence, 32*(2), 145–155. https://doi.org/10.1007/s10896-016-9869-0

Dankoski, M. E., Keiley, M. K., Thomas, V., Choice, P., Lloyd, S. A., & Seery, B. L. (2006). Affect regulation and the cycle of violence against women: New directions for understanding the process. *Journal of Family Violence, 21*(5), 327–339. https://doi.org10.1007/s10896-006-9028-0

Davies, P. T., & Sturge-Apple, M. L. (2006). The impact of domestic violence on children'as development. In T. L. Nicholls & J. Hamel (Eds.), *Family interventions in domestic violence: A handbook of gender inclusive theory and treatment* (pp. 165–189). Springer.

DeBoard-Lucas, R. L., & Grych, J. H. (2011). The effects of intimate partner violence on school-age children. In S. A. Graham-Bermann & A. A. Levendosky (Eds.), *How intimate partner violence affects children* (pp. 155–178). American Psychological Association.

DeKeseredy, W. S., & MacLeod, L. (1997). *Women abuse: A sociological story*. Harcourt Brace.

Downes, J., Kelly, L., & Westmarland, N. (2019) 'It's a work in progress': Men's accounts of gender and change in their use of coercive control. *Journal of Gender-Based Violence, 3*(3). https://doi.org/10.1332/239868019X15627570242850

Edleson, J. I. (1995, March). Mothers and children: Understanding the links between woman battering and child abuse. Paper presented at the Strategic Planning Workshop on Violence against Women, Washington, DC. National Institute of Justice.

Edleson, J. L., Ellerton, A. L., Seagren, E. A., Kirchberg, S. L., Schmidt, S. O., & Ambrose, A. T. (2007). Assessing child exposure to adult domestic violence. *Children and Youth Services Review*, *29*(7), 961–971. https://doi.org/10.1016/j.childyouth.2006.12.009

Ehrensaft, M. K., Cohen, P., Brown, J., Smailes, E., Chen, H., & Johnson, J. G. (2003). Intergenerational transmission of partner violence: A 20-year prospective study. *Journal of Consulting and Clinical Psychology*, *71*(4), 741–753. https://doi.org/10.1037/0022-006X.71.4.741

Eisikovits, Z., & Winstok, Z. (2001). Researching children's experience of interparental violence: Towards a multidimensional conceptualization. In J. L. Edleson & S. A. Graham-Bermann (Eds.), *Domestic violence in the lives of children* (pp. 203–218). American Psychological Association.

Eisikovits, Z., Winstok, Z., & Enosh, G. (1998). Children's experience of interparental violence: A heuristic model. *Children and Youth Services Review*, *20*(6), 547–568. https://doi.org/10.1016/S0190-7409(98)00025-5

Eisikovits, Z., Winstok, Z., & Gelles, R. (2002). Structure and dynamics of escalation from the victim's perspective. *Families in Society*, *83*(2), 142–152. https://doi.org/10.1606/1044-3894.29

Ellis, W. E., Crooks, C. V., & Wolfe, D. A. (2009). Relational aggression in peer and dating relationships: Links to psychological and behavioral adjustment. *Social Development*, *18*(2), 253–269. https://doi.org/10.1111/j.1467-9507.2008.00468

El-Sheikh, M., Cummings, E. M., Kouros, C. D., Elmore-Staon, L., & Buckhalt, J. (2008). Marital, psychological and physical aggression and children's mental and physical health: Direct, mediated, and moderated effects. *Journal of Consulting and Clinical Psychology*, *76*(1), 138–148. https://doi.org/10.1037/0022-006x.76.1.138

Ericksen, J. R., & Henderson, A. D. (1992). Witnessing family violence: The children's experience. *Journal of Advanced Nursing*, *17*(10), 1200–1209. https://doi.org/10.1111/j.1365-2648.1992.tb01836.x

Eriksson, M., Hester, M., Keskinen, S., & Pringle, K. (2005). *Tackling men's violence in families: Nordic issues and dilemmas*. Policy Press.

Evans, S. E., Davies, C., & DiLillo, P. (2008). Exposure to domestic violence: A meta-analysis of child and adolescent outcomes. *Aggression and Violent Behaviour*, *13*(2), 131–140. https://doi.org/10.1016/j.avb.2008.02.005

Farrell, C., & Zimmerman, G. M. (2019). Violent lives: Pathways linking exposure to violence to suidical behavior in a national sample. *Archives of Suicide Tesearch*, *23*(1), 100–121. https://doi.org/10.1080/13811118.2017.1404517

Faulkner, B., Goldstein, A. L., & Wekerle, C. (2014). Pathways from childhood maltreatment to emerging adulthood: Investigating trauma-mediated substance use and dating violence outcomes among child protective services-involved youth. *Child Maltreatment*, *19*(3–4), 219–232. https://doi.org/10/1177/1077559514551944

Feder, G., & MacMillan, H. I. (2015). Intimate partner violence. In L. Goldman & A. I. Schafer (Eds.), *Goldman's Cecil medicine* (25th ed.). Elsevier Saunders.

Feld, S. L., & Straus, M. A. (1989). Escalation and desistance of wife assault in marriage. *Criminology*, *27*(1), 141–161. https://doi.org/10.1111/j.1745-9125.1989.tb00866.x

Felitti, V. J., & Anda, R. F. (2010). The relationship of adverse childhood experiences to adult medical disease, psychiatric disorders, and sexual behavior: Implications for

healthcare. In R. Lanius & E. Vermetten (Eds.), *The hidden epidemic: The impact of early life trauma on health and disease* (pp. 77–87). Cambridge University Press.
Fellin, L. C., Callaghan, J. E. M., Alexander, J. H., Harrison-Breed, C., Mavrou, S., & Papthanassiou, M. (2019). Empowering young people who experienced domestic violence and abuse: The development of a group therapy intervention. *Clinical Child Psychology and Psychiatry*, *24*(1), 170–189. https://doi.org./10.1177/1359104518794783
Fellin, L. C., Callaghan, J. E. M., Alexander, J. H., Mavrou, S., & Harrison-Breed, C. (2018). Child's play? Children and young people's resistances to domestic violence and abuse. *Children and Society*, *33*(2), 126–141. https://doi.org/10.1111/chso.12302
Finkelhor, D., Turner, H., Ormrod, R., & Hamby, S. L. (2009). Violence, abuse and crime exposure in a national sample of children and youth. *Pediatrics*, *124*(5), 1411–1423. https://doi.org/10.1542/peds.2009-0467
Fogarty, A., Giallo, R., Wood, C., Kaufman, J., & Brown, S. (2019). Emotional-behavioral resilience and competence in preschool children exposed and not exposed to intimate partner violence in early life. *International Journal of Behavioral Development*, *44*(2), 97–106. https://doi.org/10.1177/0165025419830241
Fong, V. C., Hawes, D., & Allen, J. A. (2017). A systematic review of risk and protective factors for externalizing problems in children exposed to intimate partner violence. *Trauma, Violence, and Abuse*, 1–19. https://doi.org/10.1177/ 1524838017692383
Foshee, V. A., Ennett, S. T., Bauman, K. E., Benefield, T., & Suchindran, C. (2005). The association between family violence and adolescent dating violence onset. Does it vary by race, socioeconomic status, and family structure? *Journal of Early Adolescence*, *25*(3), 317–344. https://doi.org/10.1177/0272431605277307
Foshee, V. A., Linder, F., MacDougall, J. E., & Bangdiwala, S. (2001). Gender differences in the longitudinal predictors of adolescent dating violence. *Preventive Medicine*, *32*(2), 128–141. https://doi.org/10.1006/pmed.2000.0793
Foy, D. W., Furrow, J., & McManus, S. (2011). Exposure to violence, post-traumatic symptomatology, and criminal behaviours. In V. Ardino (Ed.), *Post-traumatic syndromes in childhood and adolescence: A handbook of research and practice* (pp. 199–210). Wiley-Blackwell.
Fusco, R. A. (2017). Socioemotional problems in children exposed to intimate partner violence: Mediating effects of attachment and family supports. *Journal of Interpersonal Violence*, *32*(16), 2515–2532. https://doi.org/ 10.1177/0886260515593545
Galano, M. M., Grogan-Kaylor, A. C., Stein, S. F., Clark, H. M., & Graham-Bermann, S. A. (2020). Dynamic profiles of posttraumatic stress symptoms in mothers and children experiencing intimate partner violence. *Child Psychiatry and Human Development*, *51*(6), 943–955. https://doi.org/10.1007/s10578-020-00973-y
Gao, S., Assink, M., Liu, T., Chan, K. L., & Ip, P. (2021). Associations between rejection sensitivity, aggression, and victimization: A meta-analytic review. *Trauma, Violence, and Abuse*, *22*(1), 125–135. https://doi.org/10.1177/1524838019833005
Garrigan, B., Adlam, A. L. R., & Langdon, P. E. (2018). Moral decision-making and moral development: Toward an integrative framework. *Developmental Review*, *49*, 80–100. https://doi.org/10.1016/j.dr.2018.06.001
Geffner, R. (2016). Children exposed to intimate partner violence and abuse: Current research on the effects and adjustment. *Journal of Child and Adolescents Trauma*, *9*(2), 95–96. https://doi.org/10.1007/s40653-016-0097-9

Geffner, R., Griffin, D. A., & Lewis, J., III (Eds.). (2009). *Children exposed to violence: Current issues, intervention and research*. Taylor & Francis.

Gergen, K. J. (1994). *Realities and relationships*. Harvard University Press.

Gewirtz, A. H., & Edleson, J. L. (2007). Young children's exposure to intimate partner violence: Towards a developmental risk and resilience framework for research and intervention. *Journal of Family Violence*, *22*(3), 151–163. https://doi.org/10.1007/s10896-007-9065-3

Gilbert, A. L., Bauer, N. S., Carroll, A. E., & Downs, S. M. (2013). Child exposure to parental violence & psychological distress associated with delayed milestones. *Pediatrics*, *142*(4), 11. https://doi.org/10.1542/peds.2013-1020

Gilbert, R., Widom, C. S., Browne, K., Fergusson, D., Webb, E., & Janson, S. (2009). Burden and consequences of child maltreatment in high-income countries. *Lancet*, *373*(9657), 68–81. https://doi.org/10.1016/S0140-6736(08)61706-7

Gilkerson, J., Richards, J. A., Warren, S. F., Oller, D. K., Russo, R., & Vohr, B. (2018). Language experience in the 2nd year of life & language outcomes in late childhood. *Pediatrics*, *142*(4), 11. https://doi.org/10.1542/peds.2017-4276

Goffman, E. (1967). *Interaction ritual*. Anchor.

Goldblatt, H., & Eisikovits, Z. (2005). Role taking of youth in a family context: Adolescents exposed to interparental violence. *American Journal of Orthopsychiatry*, *75*(4), 644–657. https://doi.org/10.1037/ 0002-9432.75.4.644

Goldstein, S., & Brooks, R. B. (2013). Why study resilience? In S. Goldstein & R. B. Brooks (Eds.), *Handbook of resilience in children* (2nd ed.) (pp. 3–14). Springer.

Graham-Bermann, S. A., Gruber, G., Howell, K. H., & Girz, L. (2009). Factors discriminating among profiles of resilience and psychopathology in children exposed to intimate partner violence (IPV). *Child Abuse and Neglect*, *33*(9), 648–660. https://doi.org/10.1016/j.chiabu.2009.01.002

Graham-Bermann, S. A., & Howell, K. H. (2010). Child abuse in the context of intimate partner violence. In J. E. B. Myers (Ed.), *APSAC handbook on child maltreatment* (2nd ed.). Sage.

Graham-Bermann, S. A., Howell, K. H., Habarth, J., Krishnan, S., Loree, A., & Bermann, E. A. (2008). Toward assessing traumatic events and stress symptoms in preschool children from low-income families. *American Journal of Orthopsychiatry*, *78*(2), 220–228. https://doi.org/10.1037/ a0013977

Graham-Bermann, S. A., & Levendosky, A. A. (2011). Introduction. In S. A. Graham-Bermann & A. A. Levendosky (Eds.), *How intimate partner violence affects children* (pp. 3–16). American Psychological Association.

Graham-Bermann, S. A., & Perkins, S. C. (2010). Contributions of age of first exposure and intimate partner violence (IPV) on child adjustment. *Violence and Victims*, *25*(4), 427–439. https://doi.org/10.1891/0886-6708.25.4.427

Grych, J. H., & Fincham, F. D. (1990). Marital conflict and children's adjustment: A cognitive-contextual framework. *Psychological Bulletin*, *108*(2), 267–290. https://doi.org/10.1037/0033-2909.108.2.267

Grych, J. H., Jouriles, E. N., Swank, P. R., McDonald, R., & Norwood, W. D. (2000). Patterns of adjustment among children of battered women. *Journal of Consulting and Clinical Psychology*, *68*(1), 84–94. https://doi.org/10.1037/0022-006X.68.1.84

Gustafsson, H. C., Mills-Koonce, W. R., & Cox, M. J. (2017). Intimate partner violence and children's attachment representations during middle childhood. *Journal of Marriage and Family, 79*, 865–878. doi, https://doi.org/10. 1111/jomf.12388

Hambrick, E. P., Brawner, T. W., Perry, B. D., Brandt, K., Hofmeister, C., & Collins, J. O. (2019). Beyond the ACE score: Examining relationships between timing of developmental adversity, relational health and developmental outcomes in children. *Archives of Psychiatric Nursing, 33*(3), 238–247. https://doi.org/10.1016/j.apnu.2018.11.001

Hamby, S. (2009). The gender debate about intimate partner violence: Solutions and dead ends. *Psychological Trauma: Theory, Research, Practice, and Policy, 1*(1), 24–34. https://doi.org/10.1037/a0015066

Hecht, D. B., & Hansen, D. J. (2001). The environment of child maltreatment: Contextual factors and the development of psychopathology. *Aggression and Violent Behavior, 6*(5), 433–457. https://doi.org/10.1016/S1359-1789(00)00015-X

Hellman, C. M., & Gwinn, C. (2017). Camp hope as an intervention for children exposed to domestic violence: A program evaluation of hope, and strength of character. *Child Adolescents Social Work Journal, 34*(3), 269–276. https://doi.org/10.1007/s10560-016-0460-6

Heyman, R. E., & Slep, A. M. S. (2019). Relational disorders and beyond. In B. H. Fiese, M. Celano, K. Deater-Deckard, E. N. Jouriles, & M. A. Whisman (Eds.), *Family therapy and training, Vol. 3. APA handbook of contemporary family psychology* (pp. 19–34). American Psychological Association. https://doi.org/10.1037/0000101-002

Hiilamo, A., Hiilamo, H., Ristikari, T., & Virtanen, P. (2021). Impact of the great recession on mental health, substance use and violence in families with children: A systematic review of the evidence. *Children and Youth Services Review, 121*, Article 105772. https://doi.org/10.1016/j.childyouth.2020.105772

Hines, L. (2015). Children's coping with family violence: Policy and service recommendations. *Child and Adolescent Social Work Journal, 32*(2), 109–119. https://doi.org/10.1007/s10560-014-0333-9

Hlavaty, K., & Haselschwerdt, M. L. (2019). Domestic violence exposure and peer relationships: Exploring the role of coercive control exposure. *Journal of Family Violence, 34*(8), 757–767. https://doi.org/10.1007/s10896-019-00044-4

Holden, G. W. (2003). Children exposed to domestic violence and child abuse: Terminology and taxonomy. *Clinical Child and Family Psychology Review, 6*(3), 151–160. https://doi.org/10.1023/A:1024906315255

Hollin, C. R. (2016). *The psychology of interpersonal violence* (pp. 77–89). John Wiley & Sons.

Holmes, M. R., Berg, K. A., Bender, A. E., Kobulsky, J. M., Davis, A. P., & King, J. A. (2022). The effect of intimate partner violence on children's medical system engagement and physical health: A systematic review. *Journal of Family Violence, 37*(8), 1221–1244. https://doi.org/10.1007/s10896-021-00291-4

Holt, S., Buckley, H., & Whelan, S. (2008). The impact of exposure to domestic violence on children and young people: A review of the literature. *Child Abuse and Neglect, 32*(8), 797–810. https://doi.org/10.1016/j.chiabu.2008.02.004

Horn, S. R., Miller-Graff, L. E., Galano, M. M., & Graham-Bermann, S. A. (2017). Post-traumatic stress disorder in children exposed to intimate partner violence: The clinical picture of physiological arousal symptoms. *Child Care in Practice, 23*(1), 90–103. https://doi.org/10.1080/13575279.2015.1126229

Howell, K. H. (2011). Resilience and psychopathology in children exposed to family violence. *Aggression and Violent Behavior, 16*(6), 562–569. https://doi.org/10.1016/j.avb.2011.09.001

Howell, K. H., Barnes, S. E., Miller, L. E., & Graham-Bermann, S. A. (2016). Developmental variations in the impact of intimate partner violence exposure during childhood. *Journal of Injury and Violence Research, 8*(1), 43–57. https://doi.org/10.5249/jivr.v8il.663

Huang, C. C., Vikse, J. H., Lu, S., & Yi, S. (2015). Children's exposure to intimate partner violence and early delinquency. *Journal of Family Violence, 30*(8), 953–965. https://doi/10.1007/s10896-015-9727-5.

Humphreys, J. (1991). Children of battered women: Worries about their mothers. *Pediatric Nursing, 17*(4), 342–345.

Jayasinghe, S., Jayawardena, P., & Perera, H. (2009). Influence of intimate partner violence on behaviour, psychological status and school performance of children in Sri Lanka. *Journal of Family Studies, 15*(3), 274–283. https://doi.org/10.5172/jfs.15.3.274

Jenney, A., & Alaggia, R. (2012). Children's exposure to domestic violence: Integrating policy, research, and practice to address children's mental health. In R. Alaggia & C. Vine (Eds.), *Cruel but not unusual: Violence in Canadian families* (pp. 303–336). Wilfrid Laurier University Press.

Johnson, M. P. (2011). Gender and type of partner violence: A response to an anti-feminist literature review. *Aggression and Violent Behavior, 16*(4), 289–296. https://doi.org/10.1016/j.avb.2011.04.006

Johnson, V. K., & Lieberman, A. F. (2007). Variations in behavior problems of preschoolers exposed to domestic violence: The role of mothers' attunement to children's emotional experience. *Journal of Family Violence, 22*(5), 297–308. https://doi.org/10.1007/s10896-007-9083-1

Katz, E. (2015). Domestic violence, children's agency and mother-child relationships: Towards a more advanced model. *Children and Society, 29*(1), 69–79. https://doi.org/10.1111/chso.12023

Katz, E. (2016). Beyond the physical incident model: How children living with domestic violence are harmed by and resist regimes of coercive control. *Child Abuse Review, 25*(1), 46–59. https://doi.org/10.1002/car.2422

Katz, E. (2022). *Coercive control in children's and mothers' lives*. Oxford University Press.

Kiesel, L. R., Piescher, K. N., & Edelson, J. L. (2016). The relationship between child maltreatment, intimate partner violence exposure, and academic performance. *Journal of Public Child Welfare, 10*(4), 434–456. https://doi.org/10.1080/15548732.2016.1209150

Kimber, S., Adham, S., Gill, S., McTavish, J., & MacMillan, H. L. (2018). The association between child exposure to intimate partner violence (IPV) and perpetration of IPV in adulthood—A systematic review. *Child Abuse and Neglect, 76*, 273–286. https://doi.org/10.1016/j.chiabu.2017.11.007

Kitzmann, K. M., Gaylord, N. K., Holt, A. R., & Kenny, E. D. (2003). Child witnesses to domestic violence: A meta-analytic review. *Journal of Consulting and Clinical Psychology, 71*(2), 339–352. https://doi.org/10.1037/0022-006X.71.2.339

Lamers-Winkelman, F., De Schipper, J., & Oosterman, M. (2012). Children's physical health complaints after exposure to intimate partner violence. *British Journal of Health Psychology, 17*(4), 771–784.

Langhinrichsen-Rohling, J., Misra, T. A., Selwyn, C., & Rohling, M. L. (2012). Rates of bidirectional versus unidirectional intimate partner violence across samples, sexual orientations, and race/ethnicities: A comprehensive review. *Partner Abuse, 3*(2), 199–230. https://doi.org/10.1891/1946-6560.3.2.199

Lazarus, R., & Folkman, S. (1984). *Stress, appraisal, and coping*. Springer.

Lazenbatt, A. (2010). *The impact of abuse and neglect on the health and mental health of children and young people*. Research briefing, NSPCC reader in childhood studies. Queen's University Belfast.

Lee, H., Russell, K. N., O'Donnell, K. A., Miller, E. K., Bender, A. E., Scaggs, A. L., Harris III, L. A., Holmes, M. R., & Berg, K. A. (2022). The effect of childhood intimate partner violence (IPV) exposure on bullying: A systematic review. *Journal of Family Violence*, 1–8. https://doi.org/10.1007/s10896-021-00299-w

Levendosky, A. A., Lannert, B., & Yalch, M. (2012). The effects of intimate partner violence on women and child survivors: An attachment perspective. *Psychodynamic Psychiatry, 40*(3), 397–434. https://doi.org/10.1521/pdps.2012.40.3.397

Luthar, S. S., Cicchetti, D., & Becker, B. (2000). The construct of resilience: A critical evaluation and guidelines for future work. *Child Development, 71*(3), 543–562. https://doi.org/10.1111/1467-8624.00164

Lyn, M. A., Franchek-Roa, K., & Giardino, A. P. (2015). The connection between intimate partner violence and child maltreatment. In A. P. Giardino, L. Shaw, P. Speck, & E. R. Giardino (Eds.), *Recognition of child abuse for the mandated reporter* (4th ed.) (pp. 145–160). STM Learning.

MacMillan, H. L., & Wathen, C. N. (2014). Children's exposure to intimate partner violence. *Child and Adolescent Psychiatric Clinics of North America, 23*(2), 295–308. https://doi.org/10.1016/j.chc.2013.12.008

MacMillan, H. L., Wathen, C. N., & Varcoe, C. M. (2013). Intimate partner violence in the family: Considerations for children's safety. *Child Abuse and Neglect, 37*(12), 1186–1191. https://doi.org/10.1016/j.chiabu.2013.05.005

Mann, J. R., & Takyi, B. K. (2009). Autonomy, dependence or culture: Examining the impact of resources and socio-cultural processes on attitude towards intimate partner violence in Ghana, Africa. *Journal of Family Violence, 24*(5), 323–335. https://doi.org/10/1007/s10896-009-9232-9

Margolin, G., & Vickerman, K. A. (2007). Post-traumatic stress in children and adolescents exposed to family violence: I. Overview and issues. *Professional Psychology:, Research and Practice, 38*(6), 613–619. https://doi.org/10.1037/0735-7028.38.6.613

Margolin, G., Vickerman, K. A., Ramos, M. C., Serrano, S. D., Gordis, E. B., Iturralde, E., & Spies, L. A. (2009). Youth exposed to violence: Stability, co-occurrence, and context. *Clinical Child and Family Psychology Review, 12*(1), 39–54. https://doi.org/10.1007/s10567-009-0040-9

Mariscal, E. S. (2020). Resilience following exposure to intimate partner violence and other violence: A comparison of Latino and non-Latino youth. *Children and Youth Services Review, 113*, Article 104975. https://doi.org/10.1016/j.childyouth.2020.104975

Martinez-Torteya, C., Bogat, G. A., von Eye, A., & Levendosky, A. A. (2009). Resilience among children exposed to domestic violence: The role of risk and protective factors. *Child Development, 80*(2), 562–577. https://doi.org/10.1111/j.1467-8624.2009.01279.x

McCloskey, L. A. (2001). The "Medea Complex" among men: The instrumental abuse of children to hurt wives. *Violence and Victims, 16*(1), 19–37. https://doi.org/10.1891/0886-6708.16.1.19

McCloskey, L. A. (2011). The impact of intimate partner violence on Adolescents. In S. A. Graham-Bermann & A. A. Levendosky (Eds.), *How intimate partner violence affects children* (pp. 225–246). American Psychological Association.

McDonald, R., Jouriles, E. N., Briggs-Gowan, M. J., Rosenfield, D., & Carter, A. S. (2007). Violence toward a family member, angry adult conflict, and child adjustment difficulties: Relations in families with 1- to 3-years-old children. *Journal of Family Psychology, 21*(2), 176–184. https://doi.org/10.1037/0893-3200.21.2.176

McDonald, S. E., Graham-Bermann, S., Maternick, A., Ascione, F. R., & Williams, J. H. (2016). Patterns of adjustment among children exposed to intimate partner violence: A person-centered approach. *Journal of Child and Adolescents Trauma, 9*(2), 137–152. https://doi.org/10.1007/s40653-016-0079-y

McIntosh, J. E., Tan, E. S., Levendosky, A. A., & Holtzworth-Munroe, A. (2021). Mothers' experience of intimate partner violence and subsequent offspring attachment security ages 1–5 years: A meta-analysis. *Trauma, Violence, and Abuse, 22*(4), 885–899. https://doi.org/10.1177/1524838019888560

McTavish, J. R., MacGregor, C. D., Wathen, C. N., & MacMillan, H. L. (2016). Children's exposure to intimate violence: An overview. *International. Review of Psychiatry, 28*(5), 505–518. https://doi.org/10.1080/09540261.2016.1205001

Miller, L. E. (2015). Perceived threat in childhood: A review of research and implications for children living in violent households. *Trauma, Violence, and Abuse, 16*(2), 153–168. https://doi.org/10.1177/1524838013517563

Miranda, J. K., Olivares, N., & Crockett, M. A. (2022). Growing up with intimate partner violence at home: Adolescents' narratives on their coping strategies. *Journal of Family Violence*. https://doi.org/10.1007/s10896-021-00345-7

Mondal, D., & Paul, P. (2020). Association between intimate partner violence and child nutrition in India: Findings from recent National Family Health Survey. *Children and Youth Services Review, 119*, Article 105493. https://doi.org/10.1016/j.childyouth.2020.105493

Mueller, L., & Tronick, E. (2019). Early life exposure to violence: Development consequences on brain and behavior. *Frontiers in Behavioral Neuroscience, 13*, Article 156. https://doi.org/10.3389/fnbeh.2019.00156

Muir, C., Adams, E. A., Evans, V., Geijer-Simpson, E., Kaner, E., Phillips, S. M., Salonen, D., Smart, D., Winstone, L., & McGovern, R. (2022). A systematic review of qualitative studies exploring lived experiences, perceived impact, and coping strategies of children and young people whose parents use substances. *Trauma, Violence, and Abuse* https://doi.org/10.1177/15248380221134297

Mullender, A., Hague, G., Iman, U., Kelly, L., Malos, E., & Regan, L. (2002). *Children's perspectives on domestic violence*. Sage.

Noble-Carr, D., Moore, T. H., & McArthur, M. (2019). Children's experiences and needs in relation to domestic and family violence: Findings from a meta-synthesis. *Child and Family Social Work, 25*(1), 182–191. https://doi.org/10.1111/cfs.12645

Noonan, C. B., & Pilkington, P. D. (2020). Intimate partner violence and child attachment: A systematic review & meta-analysis. *Child Abuse and Neglect, 109*, Article 104765. https://doi.org/10.1016/j.chiabu.2020.104765

Nowakowski, S., Choi, H., Meers, J., & Temple, J. (2016). Inadequate sleep as a mediating variable between exposure to interparental violence and depression severity in adolescents. *Journal of Child and Adolescents Trauma, 9*(2), 109–114. https://doi.org/10.1007/s40653-016-0091-2

O'Brien, M., Margolin, G., John, R. S., & Krueger, L. (1991). Mothers' and sons' cognitive and emotional reactions to simulated marital and family conflict. *Journal of Consulting and Clinical Psychology, 59*(5), 692–703. https://doi.org/10.1037/0022-006X.59.5.692

O'Dougherty Wright, M., Masten, A. S., & Narayan, A. J. (2013). Resilience processes in development: Four waves of research on positive adaption in the context of adversity. In S. Goldstein & R. B. Brooks (Eds.), *Handbook of resilience in children* (2nd ed., pp. 15–38). Springer.

Onyskiw, J. E. (2003). Domestic violence and children's adjustment: A review of research. In R. Geffner, R. S. Igelman, & J. Zellner (Eds.), *The effects of intimate partner violence on children* (pp. 11–45). Haworth.

Osofsky, J. D. (2003). Prevalence of children's exposure to domestic violence and child maltreatment: Implications for prevention and intervention. *Clinical Child and Family Psychology Review, 6*(3), 161–170. https://doi.org/10.1023/A:1024958332093

Øverlien, C. (2014). "He didn't mean to hit mom, I think:" Positioning, agency and point in adolescents' narratives about domestic violence. *Child and Family Social Work, 19*(2), 156–164. https://doi.org/10.1111/j.1365-2206.2012.00886.x

Øverlien, C. (2016). "Do you want to do some arm wrestling?" Children's strategies when experiencing domestic violence and the meaning of age. *Child and Family Social Work, 22*(2), 680–688. https://doi.org/10.1111/cfs.12283

Øverlien, C., & Hyden, M. (2009). Children's actions when experiencing domestic violence. *Childhood, 16*(4), 479–496. https://doi.org/10.1177/0907568209343757

Parsons, A. M., Heyman, R. E., Mitnick, D. M., & Smith Slep, A. M. (2020). Intimate partner violence and child maltreatment: Definitions, prevalence, research, and theory through a cross-cultural lens. In H. W. Kim & V. D. V. Fons (Eds.), *Cross-cultural family research and practice* (pp. 249–285). Elsevier.

Patterson, G. (1982). *Coercive family process*. Castalia.

Peled, E. (1993). *The experience of living with violence for preadolescent witnesses of women abuse* (Unpublished doctoral dissertation). University of Minnesota.

Peled, E. (1998). The experience of living with violence for preadolescent children of battered women. *Youth and Society, 29*(4), 395–430. https://doi.org/10.1177/0044118X98029004001

Peterson, C. C., Riggs, J., Guyon-Harris, K., Harrison, L., & Huth-Boeks, A. (2019). Effects of intimate partner violence and home environment on child language development in the first 3 years of life. *Journal of Developmental and Behavioral Pediatrics, 40*(2), 112–121. https://doi.org/10.1097/DBP.0000000000000638

Petrocelli, K., Davis, J., & Berman, T. (2019). Adverse childhood experiences and associated health outcomes: A systematic review and meta-analysis. *Child Abuse and Neglect, 97*, Article 104127. https://doi.org/10.1016/j.chiabu.2019.104127

Ravi, K. E., & Casolaro, T. E. (2018). Children's exposure to intimate partner violence: A qualitative interpretive meta-synthesis. *Child and Adolescent Social Work Journal, 35*(3), 283–295. https://doi.org/10.1007/s10560-017-0525-1

Retzinger, S. M. (1991a). Shame, anger and conflict: Case study of emotional violence. *Journal of Family Violence, 6*(1), 37–59. https://doi.org/10.1007/BF00978525

Retzinger, S. M. (1991b). *Violent emotions: Shame and rage in marital quarrels*. Sage.

Rhoades, K. A. (2008). Children's responses to interparental conflict: A meta-analysis of their associations with child adjustment. *Child Development, 79*(6), 1942–1956. https://doi.org/10.1111/j.1467-8624.2008.01235.x

Richardson, H., Kloess, J. A., Patel, A., & Farr, J. (2021). How do young people who have experienced parental intimate partner abuse make sense of romantic relationship? A qualitative analysis. *Child Abuse and Neglect, 113*, Article 104942. https://doi.org/10.1016/j.chiabu.2021.104942

Riesen, Y., & Porath, M. (2004). Self-worth and social support of children exposed to marital violence. *Canadian Journal of School Psychology, 19*(1–2), 75–97. https://doi.org/10.1177/082957350401900104

Rogers, K., & Berger, E. (2022). A systematic review of children's perspectives of fathers who perpetrate intimate partner violence. *Trauma, Violence, and Abuse*, 1–20. https://doi.org/10.1177/15248380221124268

Romano, E., Weegar, K., Gallitto, E., Zak, S., & Saini, M. (2021). Meta-analysis on interventions for children exposed to intimate partner violence. *Trauma, Violence, and Abuse, 22*(4), 728–738. https://doi.org/10.1177/1524838019881737

Samuelson, K. W., Krueger, C. E., & Wilson, C. (2012). Relationships between maternal emotion regulation, parenting, and children's executive functioning in families exposed to intimate partner violence. *Journal of Interpersonal Violence, 27*(17), 3532–3550. https://doi.org/10.1177/0886260512445385

Saunders, B. E. (2003). Understanding children exposed toward an integration of overlapping fields. *Journal of Interpersonal Violence, 18*(4), 356–376. https://doi.org/10.1177/0886260502250840

Scheff, T. J., & Retzinger, S. M. (1991). *Emotions and violence: Shame and rage in destructive conflicts*. Free Press.

Shen, A. C. (2009). Self-esteem of young adults experiencing interparental violence and child physical maltreatment: Parental and peer relationships as mediators. *Journal of Interpersonal Violence, 24*(5), 770–794. https://doi.org/10.1177/0886260508317188

Shonkoff, J. P., & Garner, A. S. (2012). The lifelong effects of early childhood adversity and toxic stress. *Pediatrics, 129*(1), E232–E246. https://doi.org/10.1542/peds.2011-2663

Silverman, J. G., Decker, M. R., Reed, E., & Raj, A. (2006). Intimate partner violence victimization prior to and during pregnancy among women residing in 26 U.S. states: Associations with maternal and neonatal health. *American Journal of Obstetrics and Gynecology, 195*(1), 140–148. https://doi.org/10.1016/j.ajog.2005.12.052

Silverman, J. G., Gupta, J., Decker, M. R., Kapur, N., & Raj, A. (2007). Intimate partner violence and unwanted pregnancy, miscarriage, induced abortion, and stillbirth among a national sample of Bangladeshi women. *BJOG: An International Journal of Obstertrics & Gynaecology, 144*(10), 1246–1252. https://doi.org/10.1111/j.1471-0528.2007.01481.x

Silvern, L., & Kaersvang, L. (1989). The traumatized children of violent marriages. *Child Welfare, 68*(4), 421–436.

Sitney, M. H., & Kaufman, K. L. (2021). A chip of the old block: The impact of fathers on sexual offending behavior. *Trauma, Violence, and Abuse, 22*(4), 961–975. https://doi.org/10.1177/1524838019898463

Slep, A. M. S., & O'Leary, S. G. (2001). Examining partner and child abuse: Are we ready for a more integrated approach to family violence? *Clinical and Family Psychology Review, 4*(2), 87–107. https://doi.org/10.1023/A:1011319213874

Smagur, K. E., Bogat, G. A., & Levendosky, A. A. (2017). Gender role and gender as predictors of behavior problems in children exposed to intimate partner violence. *Journal of Family Violence, 32*(2), 157–168. https://doi.org/10.1007/s10896-016-9890-3

Smokowski, P. R., & Evans, C. B. R. (2019). Bullying in intimate partner relationships: Teen dating violence and adult intimate partner violence as forms of bullying. In P. R. Smokowski & C. B. R. Evans (Eds.), *Bullying and victimization across thr lifespan: Playground politics and power* (pp. 167–182). Springer.

Sonego, M., Pichiuli, M., Gandarillas, A., Polo, C., & Ordobas, M. (2018). Mental health in girls and boys exposed to intimate partner violence. *Public Health, 164*, 26–29. https://doi.org/10.1016/j.puhe.2018.07.003

Sternberg, K. J., Baradaran, L. P., Abbott, C. B., Lamb, M. E., & Guterman, E. (2006a). Type of violence, age, and gender differences in the effects of family violence on children's behavior problems: A mega-analysis. *Developmental Review, 26*(1), 89–112. https://doi.org/10.1016/j.dr.2005.12.001

Sternberg, K. J., Rockville, M. D., Lamb, M. E., Guterman, E., & Abbott, C. B. (2006b). Effects of early and late family violence on children's behaviour problems and depression: A longitudinal multi-informant perspective. *Child Abuse and Neglect, 30*(3), 283–306. https://doi.org/10.1037/a0018787

Straus, M. A. (1979). Measuring intrafamily conflict and violence: The Conflict Tactics Scales. *Journal of Marriage and the Family, 41*(1), 75–88. https://doi.org/10.2307/351733

Straus, M. A. (1990). The conflict tactics scale and its critics: An evaluation and new data on validity and reliability. In M. A. Strauss & R. J. Gelles (Eds.), *Physical violence in American families: Risk factors and adaptations to violence in 8,145 families* (pp. 49–73). Transaction Publishing.

Straus, M. A. (2008). Dominance and symmetry in partner violence by male and female university students in 32 nations. *Children and Youth Services Review, 30*(3), 252–275. https://doi.org/10.1016/j.childyouth.2007.10.004

Straus, M., Hamby, S., Boney-McCoy, S., & Sugerman, D. (1996). The revised conflict tactics scales (CTS2): Development and preliminary psychometric data. *Journal of Family Issues, 17*(3), 283–316. https://doi.org/10.1177/019251396017003001

Supol, M., Satyen, L., Ghayour-Minaie, M., & Toumbourou, J. W. (2021). Effects of family violence exposure on adolescent academic achievement: A systematic review. *Trauma, Violence, and Abuse, 22*(5), 1042–1056. https://doi.org/10.1177/1524838019899486

Teicher, M. H., & Samson, J. A. (2016). Annual research review: Enduring neurobiological effects of childhood abuse and neglect. *Journal of Child Psychology and Psychiatry*, *57*(3), 241–266. https://doi.org/10.1111/jcpp.12507

Tjaden, P., & Thoennes, N. (2000). Prevalence and consequences of male-to-female and female-to-male intimate partner violence as measured by the national violence against women survey. *Violence Against Women*, *6*(2), 142–161. https://doi.org/10.1177/10778010022181769

Visser, M., Schoemaker, K., Schipper, C., Winkelman, F. L., & Finkenauer, C. (2016). Interparental violence and the mediating role of parental availability in children's trauma related symptoms. *Journal of Child and Adolescents Trauma*, *9*, 115–125. https://doi.org/10.1007/s40653-015-0071-y

Voisin, D. R., & Hong, J. S. (2012). A meditational model linking witnessing intimate partner violence and bullying behaviors and victimization among youth. *Educational Psychology Review*, *24*(4), 479–498. https://doi.org/10.1007/s10648-012-9197-8

Vu, N. L., Jouriles, E. N., McDonald, R., & Rosenfield, D. (2016). Children's exposure to intimate partner violence: A meta-analysis of longitudinal associations with child adjustment problems. *Clinical Psychology Review*, *46*, 25–33. https://doi.org/10.1016/j.cpr.2016.04.003

Wang, X., & Maguire-Jack, K. (2018). Family and environmental influences on child behavioral health. *Journal of Developmental and Behavioral Pediatrics*, *39*(1), 28–36. https://doi.org/10.1097/DBP.0000000000000506

Widom, C. S. (1989). *The intergenerational transmission of violence*. Harry Frank Guggenheim Foundation.

Widom, C. S., & Jay, J. (2017). Long-term impact of childhood abuse and neglect on crime and violence. *Journal of Clinical Psychology-Science and Practice*, *24*(2), 186–202. https://doi.org/10.1111/cpsp.12194

Winstok, Z. (2007). Toward an interactional perspective on intimate partner violence. *Aggression and Violent Behavior*, *12*(3), 348–363. https://doi.org/10.1016/j.avb.2006.12.001

Winstok, Z. (2008). Conflict escalation to violence and escalation of violent conflicts in intimate relationships. *Children and Youth Service Review*, *30*(3), 297–310. https://doi.org/10.1016/j.childyouth.2007.10.007

Winstok, Z. (2013). *Partner violence: A new paradigm for understanding conflict escalation*. Springer.

Winstok, Z., Eisikovits, Z., & Gelles, R. (2002). Structure and dynamics of escalation from the batterer's perspective. *Families in Society*, *83*(2), 129–141. https://doi.org/10.1606/1044-3894.37

Wolfe, D. A., Crooks, C. V., Lee, V., McIntyre-Smith, A., & Jaffe, P. G. (2003). The effects of children's exposure to domestic violence: A meta-analysis and critique. *Clinical Child and Family Psychology Review*, *6*(3), 171–187. https://doi.org/10.1023/A:1024910416164

Zolkoski, S. M., & Bullock, L. M. (2012). Resilience in children and youth: A review. *Children and Youth Services Review*, *34*(12), 2295–2303. https://doi.org/10.1016/j.2012.0

Chapter 2

Intervention with children exposed to interparental violence

The aim of this chapter is to examine the development of the body of knowledge on intervention with children exposed to violence. Through this examination, we will attempt to learn about the implications of research findings, in the field of exposure to violence, for shaping interventions and treatment policy regarding this population. Moreover, we will examine the role of the clinical field in building this body of knowledge.

2.1 The theoretical and empirical basis for shaping interventions for children exposed to interparental violence

It is very important to understand the nature of the process that lies behind the outcomes of exposure to violence when identifying potential goals of intervention and introducing adaptations for its improvement. In this context, cumulative knowledge of those factors that moderate and mediate the relationship between exposure to violence and its outcomes served as the basis for understanding and shaping the intervention (McDonald et al., 2011). In the following paragraphs, I will discuss the theoretical relationship between exposure to interparental violence and adjustment problems in children.

Researchers attempted to understand the process whereby exposure to violence affects children's adjustment from several theoretical perspectives, including social learning theory, cognitive theory, the theory of emotional security, family system theory, and trauma theory. It is important to note that none of these theories is considered the grand theory that explains how exposure to violence affects children (McDonald et al., 2011).

2.1.1 Social learning theory

According to social learning theory, children learn how to behave and think in relation to aggression by observation, by means of instructions given to them, or through case learning. For example, which behaviors their parents do or do not encourage in interactions with their children and how they explain away the existence of violence at home. Repeated exposure to violence, especially to aggression from individuals who are important to the children, influences the development of their set of internal beliefs, knowledge structures, expectations, and additional internal representations regarding relationships, which increase the children's likelihood of engaging in aggressive behavior (Fosco et al., 2007).

In keeping with the hypothesis derived from social learning theory, children exposed to serious interpersonal conflicts and violence tended to act aggressively and justify the aggression when their inner perception was related to high levels of aggression toward the peer group and intimate partners (Howell et al., 2012; Kinsfogel & Grych, 2004; Lee et al., 2022). Experiences of aggressive parenting were also found to be related to children's beliefs and knowledge surrounding aggression and aggressive behavior. (Fusco, 2017; Jouriles et al., 2008b; Vogel & Keith, 2015).

2.1.2 Cognitive-contextual theory

Cognitive-contextual theory by Grych and colleagues (Grych & Fincham, 1990; Fosco & Grych, 2008) explains how specific cognitive evaluations and emotional reactions to interpersonal conflict may influence children's psychological adjustment. The theory's main claim is that children's reactions to conflict are based on their evaluation of the significance and outcomes for themselves and their families. Specifically, the extent to which children feel threatened by the conflict (e.g., harm to the parent or the breakup of the family) and the extent to which they see themselves as responsible for starting or ending the violence will influence their adjustment.

A significant body of empirical research conducted in the community and with clinical samples produced results that were consistent with the theoretical claims, showing that children's perception of the threat and their evaluation of guilt (i.e., the children blame themselves for the abusive situation) mediated the relationship between exposure to violence and adjustment problems (McDonald & Grych, 2006; Benavides, 2015; Bender, 2022). Most of the research focused on school age and early adolescence, but the theoretical thinking regarding the relationship between exposure to violence and children's adjustment can be applied to younger age groups, taking into account that their evaluations will be less complicated and more concrete (McDonald et al., 2011; Hambrick et al., 2019).

2.1.3 The theory of emotional security

The theory of emotional security by Cummings and colleagues (Davies & Cummings, 1994, 1998) emphasizes the emotional reactions and emotion regulation in the relationship between the exposure to violence and children's adjustment. According to this theory, exposure to violence reduces the children's sense of emotional security, which is an important contributor to their psychological well-being. Emotions, emotion regulation, cognitive evaluations, and behaviors are perceived as intertwined in a relationship of mutuality. Nevertheless, the emotional reactions are perceived as a basis on which the children lean in their attempts to attain and preserve emotional security.

Research on the emotional security hypothesis focused mainly on emotional aspects of children's reactions to exposure to violence, thus contributing much to the researchers' understanding of the emotional functioning of children exposed to violence (Gewirtz & Edleson, 2007; Fogarty et al., 2019).

2.1.4 Family system theory

Family system theory links exposure to violence to problematic family functioning in the areas of family adjustment, connection among family members, and quality of family relationships (Owen et al., 2009; Fusco, 2017). Another problematic area which, according to the theory, is perceived as influencing the children's adjustment is the extent of their involvement in the conflict between their parents (Fosco & Grych, 2008; Callaghan et al., 2016). Each of the aforementioned variables was found to moderate the relationship between exposure to violence and the children's adjustment (Owen et al., 2009; Fusco, 2017).

2.1.5 Trauma theory

Trauma-inducing events, especially recurrent events, are linked to the absence of regulation of biological processes related to sensitivity to stress and the ability to react appropriately to stress (Cloitre et al., 2009; Margolin & Gordis, 2000; Van der Kolk, 2014; Teicher & Samson, 2016). With time and exposure to chronic stress, the emotion regulation mechanisms undergo long-term changes, which affect the organism's reactions to stress. This includes changes that lead to hyperarousal, related to PTSD symptoms, or changes that lead to a limited reaction to stress, related to depression (Cloitre et al., 2009; Schore, 2015).

The theory on children's reactions to interparental conflict and exposure to violence claims that the latter elevates the neurological aspects of trauma, thereby reducing the children's ability to regulate their reactions toward the stressors, which in turn leads to adjustment problems. Accordingly, empirical research, which evaluated the relationship between biology and psychological outcomes among children exposed to violence, found several biological symptoms and reactions to emotional functioning that were typical of these children (Cameranesi et al., 2022; Margolin & Gordis, 2000; Teicher & Samson, 2016).

It is important to note that trauma theory is consistent with the theory of emotional security, in that emotional security is associated with children's emotion regulation ability regarding perceived events, which in turn will affect their behavior. The empirical results show that emotion regulation indeed moderates the relationship between interpersonal conflict and children's adjustment (Davies & Cummings, 1998; Fogarty et al., 2019). Moreover, consistent with cognitive-contextual theory and the theory of emotional security, emotion regulation and cognitive evaluation were found to mediate the relationship between interpersonal conflict and exposure to violence and children's adjustment problems, when the mediators were analyzed simultaneously (Jouriles et al., 2008a; Wiese, 2013).

2.1.6 Dynamic perspectives and attachment theory

Based on these theories, it was acknowledged that children's internal representations of relationships with others are derived directly from their relationships with their primary caregivers and that the history, nature, and quality of these primary relationships are the key to children's psychological and social adjustment (Berdot-Talmeir et al., 2016; McDonald et al., 2011; McIntosh et al., 2021).

2.2 Interventions for children exposed to interparental violence

The theoretical principles that were raised in order to understand how exposure to violence affects children's adjustment and that were supported empirically constituted the basis for building interventions for these children. In this context, it is important to take note that since the various theories are directed toward understanding problems with different forms of adjustment (behavioral, cognitive, and emotional), the shaped interventions usually draw on several theoretical perceptions aimed at bringing about an improvement in the children (McDonald et al., 2011; Latzman et al., 2019).

Working with the mothers was chosen as an important component in some of the interventions since all these theories explicitly and implicitly perceive parenting as an important mediating variable for enhancing children's psychological adjustment (Katz, 2019). Thus, for example, in the theory of emotional security, even though no direct reference is made to the parenting component, since, in the early years, children depend on their parents for emotion regulation and later on them for guidance, it is inferred that an emotion regulation briefing by the non-abusive parent, in the context of trauma, will be helpful (Graham-Bermann, 2011; Fogarty et al., 2019).

Later interventions, which were shaped for children exposed to violence, drew on integrative approaches, such as developmental psychopathology (as well as normal development) and ecological theory (McDonald et al., 2011; Romano et al., 2021). Developmental psychopathological theory and resilience theory (Graham-Bermann, 1998; Gewirtz & Edleson, 2007) claim that development is a product of children's interactions with their environment, with risk potential and protective factors, which specifically affect development and psychological adjustment at any point in time. From the ecological theory perspective (Cicchetti & Lynch, 1993; Timmer & Urquiza, 2014), it is understood that risk factors and protective factors that influence children's development are derived from several sources: From the children themselves, from the parents or the family, from the neighborhood, school, or community, and from the wider culture. In addition, the theory recognizes the multidirectional influence of the aforementioned dimensions.

2.2.1 Interventions with children exposed to interparental violence and with their mothers: First wave of evaluation (mid-1980s to the beginning of the 2000s)

2.2.1.1 Intervention programs for children aged 0–3 years and their mothers

Intervention may be critical for infants exposed to domestic violence since cumulative studies in the field have shown that symptoms or developmental delays are not necessarily cured automatically (McTavish et al., 2016). In addition, research shows that mothers, who experienced abuse and their children, benefited from receiving services, especially home-based services for young mothers (Howell et al., 2015).

During this period, at least two successful home-based-service programs were developed for mothers at-risk with young children. These interventions provided a response to a wide variety of psychological symptoms including developmental disabilities, problems in the parental environment (such as intimate violence), problems in the children's living environment (such as poverty), and specific traumatic reactions (Rossman et al., 2004). One of the programs, called Home Visitation, is designed as a preventive intervention (Olds et al., 1997) and focuses on providing individual and parental support, as well as help with sources of livelihood. Another program, called Infant–Parent Psychotherapy Program, identifies problematic behavior in the infant–parent relationship and tries to construct new meaning in this relationship (Liberman et al., 2000).

Based on the common components of these two programs—providing individual and material support for the mothers and creating guided interactions so that the mothers and their young children would experience positive reactions in their relationship—a Home Visitation type program was shaped and evaluated for mothers who had experienced violence at the hands of their partners and for their children aged one to three years (Rossman et al., 2004). The program included attention to contextual components (siblings), parental and child-related components, and influences of the intervention. The following evaluation indices were constructed: Self-efficacy, parenting, mother–child relationship, attention to environmental deficit, and the possibility of support from within the community.

Since the intervention was evaluated only as a pilot intervention study, it was implemented with 20 low-income mothers who were exposed to violence and included 7 meetings spread over 3–5 months. The researchers were unable to determine the intervention's effectiveness in relation to objective indices, even though they controlled for the base variables (Rossman et al., 2004).

2.2.1.2 Intervention programs for kindergarten- and school-age children and their mothers

The first programs were developed for children staying in shelters (Hughes, 1982; Jaffe et al., 1990; Peled & Davis, 1995; Peled & Edleson, 1992). These group intervention programs included a ten-week psychoeducational treatment format offered to the children as well as (but not necessarily) to their mothers.

The first program developed for children in shelters and for their mothers was by Hughes (1982). This program served kindergarten-age and school-age children and their mothers. Its aim was to enhance parental skills, build the child's self-image, reduce anxiety, and improve coping behavior combined with changing attitudes to family violence. The initial evaluation of the intervention, performed with 12 children, showed a decrease in both the children's and the mothers' anxiety following the intervention (Hughes, 1982; Hughes & Barad, 1983).

Another program that included ten weekly meetings and was developed for preschool and elementary school children staying in battered women's shelters was by Jaffe et al. (1986). The program focused on changing children's attitudes to violence and was evaluated as successful (Jaffe et al., 1990).

The group program for children who had witnessed domestic violence, developed by Peled and Edleson (1992), attempted to evaluate whether children exposed to domestic violence were able to change their approach to violence, talk about their emotional reactions to violence (disclose their feelings about violence), and learn alternative strategies for coping with violence in a supportive environment. Children aged 4–12 years were accepted into the program if they were comfortable being separated from their mothers, if they had an appropriate attention span, and if they were able to interact socially in a small group. An evaluation study (Peled & Edleson, 1992; Peled & Davis, 1995) used qualitative methods to interview the 30 mothers at the end of the final intervention session. The results showed that mothers reported that their children were able to talk about the violence and to disclose their emotional reactions. However, the program did not improve the children's coping ability.

The intervention programs frequently offered in shelters were expanded to community frameworks (Rossman et al., 2004). At the same time, new intervention programs were developed for use in shelters and in the community. An intervention called The Storybook Club (Tutty & Wagar, 1994) was designed to teach problem-solving, conflict resolution, and safety skills to five- to seven-year-olds who had witnessed violence and were evaluated. Taking the children's developmental age into consideration, the program was based on introducing stories to children and reading to them. Cox (1995) evaluated this program for 13 children aged 5–7 years from low-income families and found that they experienced a significant reduction in anxiety following the intervention.

Another intervention, called Project Support, was designed by Jouriles et al. (2001). This program was intended for children assessed as having serious conduct problems following exposure to violence. The program is intended to offer the children alternative problem-solving models to develop and, later, to reinforce nonviolent conflict resolution strategies. Within the program framework, each individual child works with a therapist, who serves as a mentor providing support while serving as a model for the mother. In parallel, the mothers participate in a support group for parents aimed at helping them to develop parental skills in the context under discussion.

The program was evaluated with a sample of 36 children and their mothers at 3 time points, including a follow-up evaluation 8 months after the intervention (Jouriles et al., 2001). The families were allocated randomly to either the study group or the control group. The results showed a decrease in conduct problems and an improvement in parental skills in the group that received the intervention compared to the control group.

The Preschool Kids Club program is a ten-session intervention designed for young children who are exposed to violence (Graham-Bermann & Follett, 2000). The aim of the program is to enrich three- to six-year-olds' knowledge of family violence; their attitudes and beliefs about families in general and family violence in particular; their fears and anxieties, as well as their social behavior in a small-group setting.

An evaluation of 120 children in the School-Age Kids Club version of the program showed a significant change, compared to the starting point, in the children's thinking (they increased their knowledge of the violence and created plans to protect themselves), in their social interaction among themselves (enhanced their social skills and demonstrated emotion regulation), and in behavioral and emotional domains (reduced anxiety and behavioral symptoms; Graham-Bermann et al., 2002). When both the mothers and the children received the intervention, the effects in all the aforementioned domains were stronger than for children who had participated only in the group intervention or in comparison to the control group (Graham-Bermann, 2001). From this evaluation study, it was concluded that, to be effective, any intervention for the younger age must include the children's mothers.

The Preschool Kids Club program empowers women to identify their own and their children's needs when coping with stress induced by domestic violence. It helps them develop safety plans and to make contact with social services (Graham-Bermann & Levendosky, 1994). This program was developed and tested with three groups of preschool-age children, who had been exposed to severe violence. The support components and use of social services were found to be effective (Sullivan & Bybee, 1999).

2.2.1.3 Evaluating the results of the intervention

An analysis of the results of the interventions that have been developed, thus far, for the population of children exposed to violence showed: 1) A dearth of studies that evaluated interventions in the context of domestic violence and 2) that notwithstanding the tendency toward a positive change following the various interventions, the positive effect was not significant (Carlson, 2000). Several explanations for this have been proposed: Samples of children exposed to violence did not take into consideration the different degrees of their exposure to violence or of the presence or absence of specific symptoms; samples included a wide range of age groups; samples were too small to produce a significant effect; there was an absence of briefings that would raise the likelihood that those effects and results would be found also in additional evaluations that would be performed (Graham-Bermann, 2011); interventions were too short and insufficiently intensive to achieve improvement, also among children with a relatively low level of exposure to violence and manifestation of symptoms (Carlson, 2000); certain components of the intervention either did not facilitate or even stood in the way of improvement (Carlson, 2000). In the latter context, researchers and clinicians discussed the central component of most of the intervention programs—imparting self-protection skills to the children (developing safety plans with them and for them). Peled and Edleson (1992) reported that the children were troubled particularly by the aforementioned component. As a result, concern was expressed that placing responsibility on the children to find solutions for how to act in a domestic violence reality conveyed a double message to them regarding the legitimacy and illegitimacy of the violence (MacMillan et al., 2013; McTavish et al., 2016).

Following the analysis of the intervention programs, researchers were worried about the finding that their positive effect was not great, especially in light of the serious methodological limitations of existing studies (Rossman et al., 2004). In view of the range of problems that were documented in the professional literature and that will be described below, the researchers decided that no clear conclusion could be drawn as to whether the interventions that were shaped based on the variables that mediate the relationship between exposure to violence and its outcomes indeed led to change or not (Hockenhull et al., 2015).

The methodological limitations, as identified and documented, were as follows: 1) Heterogeneity in the aims of the intervention in the different programs. Some of them were designed for children, some for mothers, and some for both populations. Such heterogeneity does not provide a basis for comparing the outcomes of the interventions (in the absence of a large enough number of intervention evaluations). 2) Heterogeneity regarding the topics chosen for work within the program. In this context as well, the heterogeneity did not allow the creation of a basis for comparing the outcomes of the interventions (Hockenhull et al., 2015). 3) Samples were too small to enable an examination of the specific variable that is responsible for the positive correlation that was found (Rizo et al., 2011). This lack does not enable the development of programs specifically tailored to the field. 4) The absence of a comparison group is a methodological problem that does not allow an examination of whether these programs effectively reduce negative symptoms related to exposure and whether violence-focused interventions are more effective than general interventions. 5) Use of "convenience" samples (shelter samples), because of the high severity of violence against the mother within these samples, as well as a high percentage of direct abuse of the children, and a broad age range, does not allow generalization of the findings to the wider population of children exposed to violence. 6) An absence of follow-up studies. 7) Efficacy studies managed by the developers of the interventions themselves (Jaffe et al., 2004).

2.2.1.4 Summary and conclusions

The theoretical principles that were raised in the attempt to understand the way in which exposure to violence affects children's adjustment and were supported empirically constituted the basis for building intervention programs for them. Due to the fact that the different theories are directed toward understanding adjustment problems from different perspectives, the interventions shaped to achieve improvement among the children usually drew on several theoretical perceptions (McDonald et al., 2011). In fact, this led to a situation in which the various interventions addressed a wide range of topics and directed them toward a wealth of skills and capabilities (Graham-Bermann, 2011). Working with the mothers was chosen as an additional component in some of the interventions, based on the assumption shared by all the theories that parenting is an important mediating variable for improving the children's psychological adjustment.

The first stage of program evaluations proposed for interventions with children was characterized by a small number of evaluations, as well as by a small number of evaluations that examined the overall effectiveness of these programs (Jaffe et al., 2004). In light of the numerous methodological problems identified in these studies, assessing their effectiveness became especially difficult. This situation was explained as an outcome of several factors: The first was that this field of intervention was in its infancy compared to other fields of intervention; the second was the challenge of funding stringent evaluations, and the third was the difficulty of accessing samples from the community. In any case, this deficiency made the use of these programs problematic since it was impossible to know whether they were helpful, ineffective, or even harmful (Jaffe et al., 2004; Graham-Bermann, 2011). Following on from this, researchers in the field of exposure to violence suggested refining the writing of existing programs, improving the design of the modes of evaluation and proposing new interventions suitable for work in this field (Hockenhull et al., 2015; Rizo et al., 2011).

2.2.2 Interventions with children exposed to interparental violence and their mothers: Second wave of evaluation (from the beginning of the 2000s to the present)

In light of the various criticisms that have been voiced regarding the effectiveness of the first wave of interventions that were designed for children exposed to violence, a limited number of interventions have undergone more stringent evaluation (McDonald et al., 2011; Romano et al., 2021). In this chapter, I will provide an update on interventions that were previously found to be potentially successful and describe the outcomes of additional interventions that have been evaluated in the meantime.

2.2.2.1 Intervention programs for children aged 0–3 years and their mothers

Two studies compared interventions for mothers and infants in times of crisis (outreach interventions) with nurse case management interventions (McFarlane et al., 2005a, 2005b). The aim of outreach interventions was to improve the children's behavior by raising the mothers' awareness of safety planning within the home and by enhancing their knowledge of community sources of support. The aim of the nurse case management intervention was to provide the mothers with knowledge about sources for safety planning via an instruction booklet and an hour-long conversation with a nurse.

Two additional outreach interventions that were designed for mothers of infants included broader interventions with the mothers (Blodgett et al., 2008; Ernst et al., 2008). The main aim of these interventions was improving the children's behavior, but they both had other goals as well: Improving the mother's safety at home (feeling of self-protection); improving parental coping skills; increasing the mother's sense of emotional security; and connecting the families to sources of support in the community. The structure of the intervention was different in each program. While one intervention program provided intervention 24/7 at a time of crisis (Blodgett et al., 2008), the other intervention provided individual treatment for the mothers once a week. Despite their different structure, both interventions attempted to provide a response to the needs of the mothers and their children.

All four studies that examined the aforementioned interventions found them to be effective, i.e., both the children's behavior and the mothers' knowledge and emotional state had improved. Nevertheless, the four studies differed in the strength and weakness of their methodology. Even though they all used samples that were considered as medium to large (58–270 participants), the two that compared outreach interventions with nurse case management interventions made use of meticulous planning, which included an experimental group and a control group, as well as a follow-up study (McFarlane et al., 2005a, 2005b). In contrast, the two other studies on outreach interventions (Blodgett et al., 2008; Ernst et al., 2008) included neither meticulous planning nor follow-up. In addition, the interventions offered to the mothers differed in duration, and the absence of a detailed written plan meant that they could not be precisely repeated.

2.2.2.2 Intervention programs for kindergarten- and school-age children and their mothers

In the context of preschool and elementary school, consulting and therapeutic intervention programs were developed, focusing on children or on children and mothers. The programs that were directed toward children only as well as those directed to children and mothers were intended to improve the children's functioning (Rizo et al., 2011). In other words, the goal of the intervention was achieving a change in the children's perception, feelings, and behavior.

Interventions focused only on children were designed to improve the children's functioning by developing skills for coping, self-protection, communication, conflict resolution, and problem-solving (e.g., Kot et al., 1998; McWhirter, 2008; Sudermann et al., 2000; Tyndall-Lind et al., 2001). They also attempted to improve the children's functioning by increasing their understanding of domestic violence. (In this context, the intention is breaking myths about violence and reducing the sense of guilt; e.g., Pepler et al., 2000; Sudermann et al., 2000; Wagar & Rodway, 1995). These consultation and therapeutic interventions had a distinct structure: Some of them were designed as individual therapy (Kot et al., 1998), some were designed as sibling play therapy (Tyndall-Lind et al., 2001), and others were designed as group interventions (McWhirter, 2008; Pepler et al., 2000; Sudermann et al., 2000; Wagar & Rodway, 1995). In addition, the duration of the interventions was different; while the individual therapy was planned for periods of between 12 days and 3 weeks, the group therapy was planned for between 5 and 12 weekly sessions.

The consultation and therapeutic programs directed toward both mothers and children also had the goal of improving the children's functioning but had different goals regarding the mothers (McDonald et al., 2011; Rizo et al., 2011). Some of the programs focused on improving parent–child interaction (Liberman et al., 2005; Liberman et al., 2006; Smith & Landreth, 2003; Timmer et al., 2010), whereas others tried to impart behavior management skills (Timmer et al., 2010) to raise the mothers' awareness of the effects on children of exposure to violence, to relieve the children's distress, and to help children understand their thoughts and emotions better (Johnston, 2003; Marshall et al., 1995). In addition, the programs varied in their distribution of the different components among the children and the mothers. The variations were as follows: 1) 12 parental coaching sessions in addition to parent–child therapy (Smith & Landreth, 2003); 2) 10 weeks of parallel therapy for mothers and children (Marshall et al., 1995); 3) 50 weekly sessions for mothers and children together (Liberman et al., 2005; Liberman et al., 2006); 4) 14–20 weekly sessions for mothers and children (Timmer et al., 2010); and 5) 10–15 weekly meetings of group therapy for children in parallel to feedback sessions for the parents, in addition to a psychoeducational group for the mothers (Johnston, 2003).

Evaluation studies of the aforementioned consultation and therapeutic intervention programs were limited (Hockenhull et al., 2015; Howarth et al., 2016 McDonald et al., 2011; Rizo et al., 2011). In addition, most of them involved small samples (31–33 participants, on average), which were not randomized and did not include meticulous planning with an experimental group, a comparative treatment, or a control. Only two out of the limited number of evaluation studies included a follow-up study. Therefore, despite the fact that the evaluation research outcomes showed an improvement in the children's behavioral problems, it was impossible to conclude that they were effective. A small number of interventions received more stringent evaluation. Characteristic of these studies was a stringent experimental procedure and a follow-up a long time after the treatment. Details of these intervention programs are outlined below.

2.2.2.3 Project support

This program belongs to the first wave of interventions that were shaped for children exposed to violence and that were evaluated (Jouriles et al., 2001; see Section 2.2.1). It was designed for four- to nine-year-olds with clinical levels of externalized behavioral problems, who lived in the shelter with their mothers (McDonald et al., 2011). Project Support includes two components: 1) Providing alternative problem-solving models for children and 2) parental coaching as well as social and instrumental support for mothers. In the second evaluation study of the project, the specific role of the parental variable was examined (McDonald et al., 2011; Jouriles et al., 2009). The sample comprised 66 families with children aged between 4 and 9 years with different levels of clinical behavioral problems whose mothers were staying in battered women's shelters. In this case, more accurate measurement strategies were used, in an attempt to learn whether the mothers' improved parenting mediated the effectiveness of the intervention with the children. The results supported the findings of the first evaluation, that behavioral problems in the experimental group reduced significantly compared to the control group. The follow-up study conducted 20 months after the end of the intervention found that the experimental group continued to show improvement, in that 74% of the children and mothers who had undergone the intervention entered the normal range compared to 48% in the control group. Thus, motherhood was found to be a significant mediating variable, even though what was found specifically to be responsible for the change was the acquisition of parental skills and not a reduction of the mother's psychological distress.

2.2.2.4 Kids' Club Program

This program also belongs to the first wave of interventions that were designed for children exposed to violence and were evaluated (Graham-Bermann & Follet, 2000; see Section 2.2.1). The program was developed in the United States and published as a handbook in 1992, and in 1994 it was recognized by the social service department as specifically mediating the prevention of domestic violence (Graham-Bermann, 2011). Following on from this, facilitation of the program began in the protection center in Ann Arbor, Michigan, with continuous stringent evaluation for the next 19 years. Since the protection center in Ann Arbor serves both women and children in the shelter as well as families who live in the vicinity, the program was directed toward families who live in the shelter and those who do not (Graham-Bermann, 2011). A version was adapted for preschool children and was written as a handbook in 2001 (Preschool Kids' Club Program, 2001). Since then, this program has undergone evaluation that was completed in the last decade (Graham-Bermann, 2011) and was proven to be effective.

The Kids' Club Program was adopted as a specific work program for the population of children exposed to violence in 26 states throughout the United States, as well as in Canada, Australia, Sweden, Mexico, and Israel (Graham-Bermann, 2011). The goals of the program are to help children understand that the violence between their parents is neither their fault nor their responsibility, to help the children identify and express a wide range of emotions toward violence, to enable them to talk about the violence and to help them cope better, and to acquire specific coping skills, namely, to plan safety strategies. The psychoeducational component of the program provides practical and factual information related to exposure to violence. Therefore, this program takes into consideration cognitive, social, and emotional needs of children exposed to violence (Graham-Bermann et al., 2007).

Planning the facilitation of the program within a small-group structure was chosen based on the rationale of creating relationships between children during the weekly meetings over ten weeks (Graham-Bermann et al., 2007). The assumption is that two types of interaction help in the process of creating the relationship, especially for children who undergo this type of trauma: Adult–child interaction and child–child interaction. The relationships are built both by the program facilitators and by the children themselves (Graham-Bermann et al., 2007). In addition to providing the children with information about how to cope with exposure to violence in their families, the group facilitators have an important role to play in providing support and empowerment to the children (Graham-Bermann et al., 2011).

In parallel to working with the children, the mothers, most of whom are in the process of separating from their partners, participate in a support group (Graham-Bermann & Levendosky, 1994). The aim of the program was to empower the mothers to support their parental capabilities, as well as to discuss the violent influences on different areas of the children's development and to create a safe place for fears and worries that arise surrounding these subjects.

The Kids' Club program was evaluated through an experimental procedure that compared three groups under three different conditions (Graham-Bermann, 2000; Graham-Bermann et al., 2007). In the first group, only the children received intervention; in the second group, intervention was for mother and child; and the third group was put on a waiting list for treatment. Overall, 211 families were evaluated. The results were measured using the Child-Behavior Check List based on teachers' reports. In addition, the children's attitudes toward violence in the family were examined on a scale completed by the children (Graham-Bermann, 2000; Graham-Bermann et al., 2007).

The three groups were compared over time in relation to the base measures, and the analysis revealed that, compared to the waiting-list group, the children whose mothers also participated in the parenting program showed the most positive results. Not only were their externalized behavioral problems reduced, but their attitudes toward violence also changed. The researchers reported a small improvement in the group that received child intervention and a medium improvement in the group that received intervention for mother and child (Graham-Bermann et al., 2011).

A long-term change was evaluated for the two groups that received treatment eight months later. Here, the changes that were found for the two groups were more pronounced when the effect of the change on externalized behavioral problems and on attitudes toward violence was defined as high in the group of children whose mothers also received treatment. The change for the better in the non-intervention group, over time, was explained by the fact that children with less severe problems (who were not included in the clinical sample) received help with their recovery and coping (Graham-Bermann et al., 2011).

2.2.2.5 Evaluating the results of the intervention

A systematic review, based on a range of studies that are comparable through meta-analysis, is essential for creating a scientific body of knowledge available for use (Hockenhull et al., 2015). Three such overall reviews were conducted, in the last two decades, to evaluate the effectiveness of interventions for children exposed to violence (Hockenhull et al., 2015; Howarth et al., 2016; Rizo et al., 2011).

The results of these reviews reveal several problematic focal areas: 1) Even though the interventions in the different programs had identical goals—developing self-protection, communication, conflict resolution, and problem-solving skills, as well as increasing the children's understanding of domestic violence, and most of them were designed as group interventions—they were different, both in the *group structure* (sibling play therapy or psychoeducational group), in the *focus of the intervention* (children/mothers or both), and in the *duration of the intervention* (the group therapy was designed for 5–12 weekly sessions). Given the heterogeneity in the contexts mentioned above and because the number of evaluations performed in the second wave (in the last two decades) was also limited, it was impossible to determine which intervention was the most effective (Howarth et al., 2016; Hockenhull et al., 2015). 2) Several intervention programs used medium-to-large random samples, which included a stringent experimental procedure incorporating experimental and control groups and a follow-up study (Graham-Bermann et al., 2007; Jouriles et al., 2009). Nevertheless, the researchers hold that even if a study is well-structured and is proven to have medium-to-high effectiveness, it needs to be repeated to ensure generalizability (Graham-Bermann, 2011; Hockenhull et al., 2015; Howarth et al., 2016). 3) Most of the research evaluations performed in the last two decades still have serious methodological problems: Small samples that are not randomized, no control group, and the absence of a detailed program evaluation plan that will enable accurate repetition during facilitation of the program. In addition, these studies lack adequate reports of the effectiveness of the interventions. Therefore, although some of the studies were conducted on *community samples*, all the aforementioned deficiencies make it impossible to answer important questions such as: Which of the existing programs are the most effective? What is the required amount and type of treatment? Which positive effects last for more than a year? Which intervention programs are suitable for work in the community? (Hockenhull et al., 2015; Howarth et al., 2016; Rizo et al., 2011). 4) Another problematic focus addressed by researchers was that the samples were too small to enable an examination of the specific variable that is responsible for the positive correlation that was found. Since many of the intervention programs draw on different theoretical approaches, which are directed toward similar components but claim that different mechanisms are responsible for them (e.g., the theory of emotional safety, cognitive-contextual theory, and trauma theory are all directed toward achieving emotional security, but each theory sees this security as an outcome of different factors), it is necessary to examine the specific mechanisms that will enable the change, namely improving children's adjustment (Hockenhull et al., 2015; Rizo et al., 2011).

Based on the ongoing dearth of evaluation studies and their methodological problems that were revealed, as well as the wide heterogeneity that characterizes the professional literature in the field of intervention programs for children exposed to violence, the researchers concluded that the scientific literature cannot attune itself to an appropriate focus in the field. Following on from this, two options were proposed as alternative solutions: 1) Adopting key topics that are suitable for working with trauma in general, i.e., evidence-based intervention programs for children who experience abuse and 2) writing new intervention programs that place other subjects for work at their base (Hockenhull et al., 2015; McTavish et al., 2016).

Just as the first wave of evaluation studies raised concern about the results of the intervention regarding the issue of strategies to improve the child's safety, the present wave of evaluations raised similar concern. This is in light of the centrality of developing self-protection plans within the framework of the different programs offered as intervention for children exposed to violence, and in the absence of a clearly empirical answer regarding the effectiveness of safety planning for mothers and children (Anderson, 2017; MacMillan et al., 2013).

In the aforementioned context, clinicians raised the concern that, in the absence of clear evidence that specific protection strategies are suitable for exposure to violence, safety plans for the children might expose them to greater harm (Anderson, 2017; Howarth et al., 2016; McTavish et al., 2016). Moreover, in situations likely to create tension between the safety strategies offered to women and those offered to children (surrounding the woman's desire to leave, for example, or her choice to remain at home), the danger posed to the children is likely to increase (Douglas & Walsh, 2015; Howarth et al., 2016). Following on from this, many clinicians expressed concern that the position of children exposed to violence might be even more serious when the situation at home does not require reporting. This is because, when the child protection authorities are involved, there is, at least, a professional group that focuses specifically on thinking about the safety needs of the child (Black et al., 2020; Douglas & Walsh, 2015; MacMillan et al., 2013).

The scarcity of research alongside the question marks raised by the clinical field led researchers to create a new, general conceptualization of the term: Protectiveness. Although protectiveness was conceptualized for intervention programs thus far as a protection strategy to attain physical security, it was reconceptualized (MacMillan et al., 2013) from the subjective dimension of feeling safe, based on the relationship that was found between exposure to violence and the range of difficult, intense emotions including anxiety, insecurity, and uncertainty. Such a conceptualization transfers the responsibility for finding a solution from the child to the adult (McTavish et al., 2016).

An examination of the continued development in the knowledge field since 2016 shows that researchers have adopted evidence-based interventions for children who experience abuse as a solution for children who experience exposure to violence (D'Andrea & Graham-Bermann, 2017; Cameranesi & Piotrowski, 2020). At the same time, new intervention programs with the same central focus as previously were built: For children, exposing difficult experiences, managing complex emotions, and imparting coping strategies (Fellin et al., 2019); and for mothers, developing healthy coping strategies and attachment behaviors (Katz, 2019, 2022).

2.2.2.6 Summary and conclusions

The knowledge built in the field of intervention programs for children exposed to violence was characterized in the last two decades: 1) By writing additional programs dealing with subjects that were found to be relevant to exposure to violence based on the mediating variables and 2) by attempting to increase the number and the accuracy of evaluation programs. Nevertheless, a review of the existing intervention programs and their evaluation shows that most of the evaluations performed continued to lack stringency regarding their research design, had deficiently small samples, and an absence of adequate detail that would allow precise repetition of the studies that were conducted. The few programs that did meet the required research criteria and were implemented with community samples did not deal with precise examination of the specific mechanism responsible for the change that was found. In addition, these programs did not continue with further evaluations, leading to limited generalizability of the findings of these interventions. In light of this problematic situation, which exposed ongoing absence of complex evaluations that were able to prove effectiveness, researchers proposed the use of evidence-based program interventions that were written for children who had experienced abuse (programs relating to key variables in the field of abuse) or, alternatively, the examination of new intervention programs. The first option—of evidence-based interventions—was chosen.

2.2.3 Critical learning of knowledge building in the field of intervention for children exposed to violence

The first 15 years (from the mid-1980s until the 2000s) of building the knowledge field of interventions for children exposed to violence were characterized by interventions that drew on variables that were found to mediate the impact of violence, in accordance with knowledge that had begun to accumulate in the field. The limited evaluation of these programs, their small positive effect, and the doubt raised in regard to it as well as the serious methodological problems typical of the research designs led the researchers to suggest two directions for continuation: First, refining the existing programs for greater accuracy, while improving the planning of the study designs for the purpose of evaluating the programs, and second, proposing new programs that would be suitable for work in the field.

An analysis of the knowledge field in the two subsequent decades (from the 2000s until the present) reveals that the researchers chose to focus only on the first direction. Several of the existing studies were refined, and their accuracy was improved for the purpose of a more stringent new evaluation. Others were not changed and underwent further evaluations. Even though new interventions were written, the innovation was manifest in the program structure (one type of therapy or another) and not in the chosen topics on which to work. (The same topics remained: Imparting self-protection strategies and coping skills to the children; communication; conflict resolution; and problem-solving and understanding the children's attitudes toward domestic violence.) Even though the choice to focus on this direction is understandable in view of the deficiencies that characterized the previous evaluations, disregard for the additional direction is surprising. This is for two reasons: 1) The development of new knowledge regarding the understanding of the way in which the risk plays out in practice (i.e., understanding the essence of the process; Eisikovits & Winstok, 2001; McGee, 2000; Peled, 1998) and 2) the reservations expressed by researchers and clinicians who reported problems in imparting self-protection strategies to the children, which is the central component in the intervention programs (Carlson, 2000; Peled & Edleson, 1992). The children's behaviors and fears expressed in relation to this component, over the years, reinforced these reservations (e.g., MacMillan et al., 2013; McTavish et al., 2016). An example is the intervention by Graham-Bermann (2007), designed exclusively for children whose mothers had separated from their violent partners.

The way the field has developed over the last two decades should be even more astonishing because of the revelation of additional knowledge during that period (e.g., Arai et al., 2021; Noble-Carr et al., 2019; Goldblatt & Eisikovits, 2005; Mullender et al., 2002). This knowledge indicates the serious harm caused to the children, not only because of their presence at the scene of the confrontation but also as a result of what they experience (Buckley et al., 2007; Callaghan & Alexander, 2015; Callaghan et al., 2018; Carmel, 2010; Øverlien, 2016; Rogers & Berger, 2022). This empirical knowledge should have channeled the writing of interventions that place central focus on the phenomenology of the experience of the children exposed to violence, with special emphasis on the awareness component that is responsible for shaping their perception of reality.

Meta-analyses that were performed regarding evaluation of the various interventions in the last two decades showed that most of the evaluations still do not meet the requirements of stringent research designs. Therefore, they cannot be used as a basis on which to establish an appropriate focus for the nature of work with these children (Hockenhull et al., 2015; Howarth et al., 2016; Rizo et al., 2011). Following on from this, two directions were suggested: First, adopting evidence-based intervention programs for children who have experienced abuse, and second, writing new interventions. Corresponding to the first proposed direction, researchers in the field of intervention programs called for a critical, comparative review of theories that can be applied on the basic assumption level and on the empirical level, regarding the study of adjustment problems among children exposed to violence (D'Andrea & Graham-Bermann, 2017). A new, comprehensive study that attempted to fill the gap in the scientific literature, in the aforementioned context (Cameranesi & Piotrowski, 2020), showed that trauma theory has great potential to explain the mechanisms involved in the development of symptoms (validated also by immunology and neuroscience studies), despite limited application of the theory in the field to date.

Despite the logic in adopting the former proposed direction, this choice is still astonishing in view of the knowledge which, although in need of an additional, broader examination, points specifically to the complexity of the experience of children exposed to violence. Knowledge learned in context is considered essential for shaping effective intervention programs for specific populations (Arai, 2021; Latzman et al., 2019; Romano et al., 2021), which is why the lack of use or disregard of this information is unclear. In this context, the use of evidence-based programs, which are suitable for a wide variety of traumas, might be the direction to pursue instead of new context-focused programs if the effectiveness of the latter will not be proved.

Another point worthy of attention is the assumption that the situation of children in the shelter is more difficult than that of children living in the community (who, otherwise, would have been referred to a shelter) and that the symptoms manifest in both populations would differ in their severity, with the children in the shelter being worse off. Latent reservations regarding this axiom can be identified when researchers in the field note that the situation of children exposed to violence, who do not belong to the category in which reporting is obligatory, might be more difficult than that of children within this category and who are therefore under the scrutiny of the child protection authorities. Indeed, the involvement of the child protection authorities means, at least, that a professional group is focused specifically on thinking about the child's safety needs (Douglas & Walsh, 2015; McTavish et al., 2016). This point may indicate the complexity and difficulty of many children's situations, not only of those who are referred to a shelter (Katz, 2022; Rogers & Berger, 2022). Therefore, innovative thinking is warranted regarding the nature of the specific kind of work required for this population. The knowledge in the field of exposure to violence points in the direction of ongoing, in-depth cognitive-phenomenological work.

2.3 Adolescents' experiences of interparental violence and its implications for intervention

A large body of research knowledge has accumulated in the field of reactions to exposure to violence in early and middle childhood. Nonetheless, a parallel body of research knowledge is still terribly lacking in the field of adolescents exposed to domestic violence (McCloskey, 2011; Miranda et al., 2022). The reasons for this are essentially practical: 1) Middle childhood is an age group that is considered trustworthy for reporting and 2) shelters do not usually accept children above the ages of 12 or 13, especially boys (DeBoard-Lucas & Grych, 2011). Since most empirical research is based on shelter samples, it is understandable why the adolescent population of children exposed to violence is underrepresented in this field. The implications of this lack for the field of intervention with adolescents are critical, since inadequate knowledge of the nature of the process on the basis of the exposure findings makes it difficult to tailor intervention that will achieve some improvement (Cunningham & Baker, 2011; Hielscher et al., 2021; Muir et al., 2022).

In light of the above, a developmental framework for understanding the needs of adolescents exposed to violence was adopted for the purpose of adapting the types of services that would be helpful to them. This developmental framework takes into consideration the age of the adolescents and the age of the exposure and is based on clinical work with adolescents and empirical studies (Cunningham & Baker, 2011; Hines, 2015; Ravi & Casolaro, 2018).

Goldblatt (2003) found that adolescents who live in a violent reality in the present differ from their younger siblings and from the peer groups of younger children who are exposed to violence. They are more active outside the home, are capable of considering problems from several different perspectives, are aware of social values that are opposed to violence, and are more capable of expressing their opinions. Since they are stronger, they are able to intervene physically and may confront the abuser emotionally.

Data gathered in 2008 regarding 911 applications by adolescents (Gewirtz & Medhanie, 2008) suggested that older children tended to be more directly involved in violent incidents, their interpretation of the causes and outcomes of exposure to violence had become more sophisticated, and they revealed a broad repertoire of coping reactions. These may include healthy reactions such as seeking the help of a friend or more worrying options such as involvement in violence, physical avoidance by leaving home, or emotional escapes (e.g., using drugs).

Baker and Cunningham (2004) spoke about the potential influence of exposure to violence on adolescents' development. In their view, during this important transition stage, adolescents living in a reality of violence might not experience stability and guidance from the significant adult figures in their lives, which are necessary conditions for their optimal development. In this context, they addressed central aspects of development that might be damaged: Distorted self-perception; difficulty in creating healthy intimate relationships (avoidance of intimacy or early pregnancy as a means of escape for the adolescent and of creating a self-support system); "all or nothing" (black or white) interpretations as well as assimilation of attitudes and values that connect to violence and/or victimization; and violent behavior and gender stereotypes.

Based on the empirical studies and clinical analysis of working with adolescents, the mechanisms behind the negative impact of exposure to violence were learned: Exposure to abusive masculine models as men and fathers; damaged mother–child attachment; negative beliefs about the self; isolation from necessary support; unhealthy family roles; perceiving the world as unsafe; possibility of the appearance of additional vulnerabilities; adopting problematic coping means; adopting attitudes that justify violence in intimate relationships; and adopting myths relating to victimization (Chanmugam, 2009, 2015; Hines; 2015; Ravi & Casolaro, 2018; Miranda et al., 2022). In relation to each of the mechanisms, implications were written for interventions including the following topics: Repairing distorted perceptions; encouraging coping strategies; building skills such as problem-solving; and helping with managing intense emotions (Cunningham & Baker, 2011; Fellin et al., 2019).

As can be learned, as regards interventions that were prepared for children exposed to violence as well as for adolescents, the basis suggested for intervention is mainly psychoeducational and is directed toward exposure of fundamental beliefs, reconceptualization of the phenomenon/situation, support for mothers to strengthen the adolescent's self-image, encouraging a sense of control by acquiring self-protection skills, and use of the peer group to teach new communication skills.

In the absence of an evaluation of the proposed intervention, researchers (Hielscher et al., 2021; Muir et al., 2022) suggest that professionals collect information about the use of intervention surrounding the encounter with a variety of cases of exposure to violence among adolescents. These include domestic violence, adolescents who have experienced direct abuse, have abused a dating partner, have experienced victimization in a romantic relationship during adolescence, or all of the above. It should be noted that this situation will recreate the problem of heterogeneity in evaluation.

2.4 Evidence-based intervention for treating children who have experienced maltreatment

The transition to the direction of evidence-based intervention helped researchers to ensure that the treatments would have a theoretical basis, focused clinical literature, a high level of acceptance among practitioners in the field of abuse, low likelihood of causing harm, and empirical support of the effectiveness of its use among victims of abuse (Cameranesi & Piotrowski, 2020; Forte et al., 2014). Nevertheless, research on evidence-based treatment in psychology illuminated the fact that interventions are not always context-based, i.e., based on characteristics of a specific population (Forte et al., 2014).

2.4.1 The ecological-transaction model of development

The ecological-transaction model of development (Cicchetti & Lynch, 1993) was established based on the understanding that different qualities of children's different environments (their cultural environments, social resources, family environments, and individual differences) altogether shape the way in which children react to the world around them. Specifically, the characteristics of these environments will affect the way in which the children will come into contact with the developmental tasks and will provide the foundations of the way in which one developmental time point will affect development later on.

Cicchetti and Lynch (1993) suggested that the different environments contain potentiating factors—conditions that raise the likelihood that the abuse will harm the child—and compensatory factors—conditions that reduce the negative impact of abuse and its deleterious effects. Thus, the relationship between the negative and positive factors in each of the environments and weighting them together will either increase or decrease the likelihood of adjustment problems in the children. Nevertheless, the theoreticians noted (Alink et al., 2009; Cicchetti & Toth, 2000) that the strength of those factors promotes either risk or resilience, which, at any point in time, changes in relation to: 1) The child's developmental stage and 2) what happened to the child in earlier stages. In other words, in their opinion, the same negative event that happens at two different time points when the child is at two different developmental stages can have different outcomes for the child's mental health. This is because of the difference in their cognitive ability to understand the event and its meaning at the time point at which it occurred, as well as its meaning from the point of view of the child's ability to adjust positively and to "collect" protective factors from the environment (such as a supportive and enriching teacher).

While cognitive maturity, in the theoreticians' perception, either limits or shapes the children's understanding of their world, according to this approach, each developmental step contains different "tasks" that are considered central to the children's ability to negotiate successfully at that stage. The extent to which the tasks will be resolved positively will determine the quality of the reorganization and integration of the various systems (neurological, cognitive, social, and emotional) at that stage (O'Connor, 2003). The network of the integrated systems will provide a basis, according to which developmental constructs will be built later on. In this manner, the different developmental tasks always maintain their meaning long-term (O'Connor, 2003).

The assumption that development of psychopathology is possible and not unavoidable and that this possibility is shaped and reshaped constantly through experiences is the most important assumption of the ecological theory for researchers and clinicians who are interested in prevention and intervention for children who experience trauma. The intention is that a change of direction in development is always possible when the option of accumulating new positive experiences exists (Timmer & Urquiza, 2014).

Effective interventions for improving mental health, according to the ecological approach, need help to change the negative effects of primary trauma on future functioning (Timmer & Urquiza, 2014). This is by placing emphasis on the following elements: Attachment (Sroufe, 2005), parenting (Martorell & Bugental, 2006), and cognition (Luciana et al., 2005). Specifically, according to the ecological approach, effective interventions need to include imparting strategies for managing negative emotions; supporting healthy decision-making; controlling impulses; and involving parents and providing support to parents in order to create support and guidance for children and adolescents (Timmer & Urquiza, 2014).

2.4.2 Trauma-focused cognitive-behavioral therapy

Trauma-focused cognitive-behavioral therapy (TF-CBT) was originally developed for children who had undergone sexual abuse and for their non-abusive caregivers (Cohen et al., 2006). Additional contemporary studies show that intervention is effective for many areas of trauma (Cohen et al., 2010). In fact, in a meta-analysis of evidence-based psychological therapies for children and adolescents who had been exposed to traumatic events, TF-CBT was the only intervention that achieved well-established criteria for effectiveness (Silverman et al., 2008).

The model is based on different theoretical approaches, including family system theory, the neurobiological model, developmental theory, attachment theory, and postulates of client-based humanistic therapy. Nevertheless, the fundamental theoretical components of TF-CBT are cognitive-behavioral principles, specifically, the ability to reflect, to connect things, and to change maladaptive traumatic thoughts, emotions, and behaviors (Mannarino et al., 2014).

TF-CBT is based on the theoretical perception of gradual exposure. Children are exposed gradually to a frightening reality to help them overcome their avoidance of traumatic events that they have experienced. This is a therapeutic approach designed for short-term use of 8–16 sessions (Cohen et al., 2006). However, the model was used for adolescents with complex trauma with 25 treatment sessions (Kliethermes & Wamser, 2012).

According to the intervention protocol, the model contains several components, and each component constitutes the basis for establishing the next components. In fact, this is a three-stage model that includes the following stages: 1) Constructing and stabilizing the acquired skills; 2) the story and narrative stage, and 3) merging with the parent and closure (Mannarino et al., 2014).

The skill-building stage includes psychoeducational components of relaxation, emotion regulation, and cognitive coping. The use of relaxation was designed to reduce hyperarousal related to symptoms of traumatic stress when the relaxation strategies are tailored to the individual child. Effective emotion regulation includes strategies such as problem-solving and targeting troublesome thoughts. It is important to note that gradual exposure is integrated into the psychoeducational stage, so that, with time, the children begin gradually to talk about the traumatic events that they have experienced (Cohen et al., 2006; Mannarino et al., 2014). Through cognitive coping that includes thinking reconstruction, the children learn to create a link between thoughts, emotions, and behavior.

The second stage includes the story and narrative of the trauma and its cognitive processing. The aim of this stage is to help the children gain control of the traumatic memories since they describe the trauma as a personal experience (Deblinger et al., 2011). The methods of developing a trauma narrative include writing a book, having a conversation, being interviewed on media programs, text messaging, drama, and drawing with young children (Grosso, 2012).

The final stage includes joint parent–child sessions and increasing the child's security. The goal of this stage is to merge skills acquired in previous treatment sessions for integration into the therapeutic experience as well as enhancing positive attachment and communication. These components are learned in parallel therapeutic processes for the children and the mothers (Mannarino et al., 2014).

2.4.3 The question of tailoring the evidence-based intervention programs to the context of children exposed to violence: A critical analysis

An observation of the components at the basis of both the models described above—the ecological-transaction model of development and TF-CBT—shows that they both perceive emotion regulation as critical for healthy decision-making. Nevertheless, whereas the ecological-transaction model of development places emphasis on managing negative emotions, the TF-CBT model emphasizes the cognitive coping that is required with increasing exposure to the threatening reality. Therefore, the TF-CBT model can be suitable for working with children exposed to violence whose parents have separated (i.e., the child does not live in the same house as the abuser) but can be very problematic for children whose parents continue to live in a violent situation. In this context, the concrete threat to the child's safety may impair the therapeutic process. Elevating the safety component by imparting protection strategies for use in the home (in order to neutralize the threatening situation) returns us to the same problematic points raised by researchers and clinicians that are discussed at length in this chapter: The absence of proof of the strategies' effectiveness for children and the incompatibility of the mother's self-protection strategies to those required by the children (e.g., McTavish et al., 2016). Furthermore, the assumption that the threatening situation comes to an end with the parents' separation is erroneous. Many clinicians and researchers have addressed the violence that the women and their children continue to experience because of the man's difficulty in accepting the separation. The man's inability to come to terms with the fact that his wife has left him is reflected in the visitation arrangements, especially during the initial post-separation stage, which is accompanied by tension, violence, and use of the children against the mother (e.g., Barnett, 2014; Black et al., 2020; Jenney & Alaggia, 2012; Macdonald, 2017).

The ecological-transaction model of development that places central focus on managing negative emotions and is intended for work with the mothers for emotional support and guidance for the children, may therefore, accordingly, be more appropriate for working with children exposed to violence. The more indirect and less threat-focused direction might facilitate work from a less confrontational stance. Moreover, in this context, the work with the mothers may be perceived by the children as designed to support them emotionally. This type of work may be compatible with the new conceptualization of protectiveness proposed by MacMillan et al. (2013): Emotional protectiveness, rather than the nature of the work that was acceptable until now, which was focused on physical protectiveness. Still, the context-focused intervention may be more effective if it were based on in-depth understanding of how the problematic situation is formed and of how the risk (the clinical symptoms) is expressed in practice. An additional point to consider is feminist researchers' criticism of intervention focused on mother–child relationships (Guille, 2004). These researchers suggest that this approach could be interpreted as blaming the mothers for inadequate parenting, specifically in the context of domestic violence.

2.5 Summary and conclusions

The inability to prove the effectiveness of programs developed for exposure to violence (e.g., Howarth et al., 2016; Rizo et al., 2011; Romano et al., 2021) as well as the increasing criticism voiced by clinicians and researchers regarding the central component of these programs (imparting self-protection strategies within the home; e.g., MacMillan et al., 2013) arouse astonishment at the disregard by those occupied with this field of the obvious need to create new context-based programs based on findings relating to the phenomenology of the children's experience. This astonishment might be even greater because of clinicians' and researchers' concern (Douglas & Walsh, 2015; McTavish et al., 2016) that the situation of children exposed to violence might be more serious than was thought until now, even in situations that were considered more moderate, because of the mothers' fluctuations in the decision as to whether to separate from her partner or to remain at home.

An explanation for this odd state of affairs, in which those involved in the field either avoid or stop themselves from continuing to build knowledge in the required directions, should lead us to seek an explanation for the phenomenon. Since the level of intervention has a direct influence on *the level of policy*, the analysis of the nature of the work that was adopted for the population of children exposed to violence may well provide us with an answer. Therefore, in the next chapter, I address the policy for treating the phenomenon.

References

Alink, L., Cicchetti, D., Kim, J., & Rogosch, F. (2009). Mediating and moderating processes in the relation between maltreatment and psychopathology: Mother-child relationship quality and emotion regulation. *Journal of Abnormal Psychology, 37*(6), 831–843. https://doi.org/10.1007/s10802-009-9314-4

Anderson, K. (2017). Children's protective strategies in the context of exposure to domestic violence. *Journal of Human Behavior in the Social Environment, 27*(8), 835–846. https://doi.org/10.1080/19011359.2017.1339654

Arai, L., Shaw, A., Feder, G., Howarth, E., MacMillan, H., Moore, T. H. M., Stanley, N., & Gregory, A. (2021). Hope, agency, and the lived experience of violence: A qualitative systematic review of children's perspectives on domestic violence and abuse. *Trauma, Violence, and Abuse, 22*(3), 427–438. https://doi.org/10.1177/1524838019849582

Baker, L. L., & Cunningham, A. J. (2004). *Helping children thrive/supporting women abuse survivors as mothers: A resource to support parenting.* Centre for Children & Families in the Justice System.

Barnett, A. (2014). Contact at all costs? Domestic violence and children's welfare. *Child and Family Law Quarterly, 26*(4), 439–462. https://bura.brunel.ac.uk/handle/2438/10241

Benavides, L. E. (2015). Protective factors in children and adolescents exposed to intimate partner violence: An empirical research review. *Child and Adolescent Social Work Journal, 32*(2), 93–107. https://doi.org/10.1007/s10560-014-0339-3

Bender, A. E. (2022). *An exploration of sibling relationships in middle childhood among children exposed to intimate partner violence* (Unpublished doctoral dissertation). Case Western Reserve University.

Berdot-Talmeir, A. C., Pierrehumbert, B., & Gaudron, C. Z. (2016). Attachment representations in children exposed to domestic violence, aged 3 to 7 years old. *Devenir, 28*(1), 21–42. https://doi.org/10.3917/dev.161.0021.

Black, T., Fallon, B., Nikolova, K., Tarshis, S., Baird, S., & Carradine, J. (2020). Exploring subtypes of children's exposure to intimate partner violence. *Children and Youth Services Review, 118,* Article 105375. https://doi.org/10.1016/j.childyouth.2020.105375

Blodgett, C., Behan, K., Erp, M., Harrington, R., & Souers, K. (2008). Crisis intervention for children and caregivers exposed to intimate partner violence. *Best Practices in Mental Health: An International Journal, 4*(1), 74–91.

Buckley, H., Holt, S., & Whelan, S. (2007). Listen to me! Children's experiences of domestic violence. *Child Abuse Review, 16*(5), 296–310. https://doi.org/10.1002/car.995

Callaghan, J. E. M., & Alexander, J. H. (2015). *Understanding agency and resistance strategies (UNARS): Children's experiences of domestic violence.* European Commission project JUST/2012/DAP/AG/3461. University of Northampton.

Callaghan, J. E. M., Alexander, J. H., Sixsmith, J., & Fellin, L. C. (2016). Children's experiences of domestic violence and abuse: Siblings' accounts of relational coping. *Clinical Child Psychology and Psychiatry, 21*(4), 649–668. https://doi.org/10.1177/1359104515620250

Callaghan, J. E., Alexander, J. H., Sixsmith, J., & Fellin, L. C. (2018). Beyond "witnessing": Children's experiences of coercive control in domestic violence and abuse. *Journal of Interpersonal Violence, 33*(10), 1551–1581. https://doi.org/10.1177/0886260515618956

Cameranesi, M., & Piotrowski, C. C. (2020). Critical review of theoretical frameworks elucidating the mechanisms accounting for the adverse developmental outcomes observed in children following exposure to intimate partner violence. *Aggression and Violent Behavior, 55,* Article 101455. https://doi.org/10.1016/j.avb.2020.101455

Cameranesi, M., Shooshtari, S., & Piotrowski, C. C. (2022). Investigating adjustment profiles in children exposed to intimate partner violence using a biopsychosocial resilience framework: A Canadian population-based study. *Child Abuse and Neglect, 125,* 105453.

Carlson, B. (2000). Children exposed to intimate partner violence: Research findings and implications for intervention. *Trauma, Violence, and Abuse, 1*(4), 321–342. https://doi.org/10.1177/1524838000001004002

Carmel, Y. (2010). *Escalation of interparental conflicts from the children's perspective* (Unpublished doctoral dissertation). University of Haifa, Israel (Hebrew).
Chanmugam, A. (2015). Young adolescents' situational coping during adult intimate partner violence. *Child and Youth Services, 36*(2), 98–123. https://doi.org/10.1080/0145935X.2014.990627
Chanmugam, A. G. (2009). *Perspectives of young adolescent and mother dyads residing in family violence shelters: A qualitative study using life story methods* (Unpublished doctoral dissertation). University of Texas.
Cicchetti, D., & Lynch, M. (1993). Toward an ecological/transactional model of community violence and child maltreatment: Consequences for children's development. *Psychiatry, 56*(1), 96–118. https://doi.org/10.1080/00332747.1993.11024624
Cicchetti, D., & Toth, S. L. (2000). Developmental processes in maltreated children. In D. Hansen (Ed.), *Nebraska symposium on motivation: Vol. 46. Motivation and maltreatment* (pp. 85–160). University of Nebraska Press.
Cloitre, M., Stolbach, B., Herman, J. L., Van der Kolk, B., Pynoos, R., Wang, J., & Petkova, E. (2009). A developmental approach to complex PTSD: Childhood and adult cumulative trauma as predictors of symptom complexity. *Journal of Traumatic Stress, 22*(5), 399–488. https://doi.org/10.1002/jts.20444
Cohen, J. A., Mannarino, A. P., & Deblinger, E. (2006). *Treating trauma and traumatic grief in children and adolescents*. The Guilford Press.
Cohen, J. A., Mannarino, A. P., & Deblinger, E. (2010). Trauma-focused cognitive behavioral therapy for traumatized children. In J. A. Weiss & A. E. Kazdin (Eds.), *Evidence-based psychotherapies for children and adolescents* (pp. 295–311). The Guilford Press.
Cox, G. M. (1995). *Changes in self-esteem and anxiety in children in a group program for witnesses of wife assault* (Unpublished master's thesis). School of Social Work, University of Calgary, Alberta, Canada.
Cunningham, A. J., & Baker, L. L. (2011). The adolescent's experience of intimate partner violence and implications for intervention. In S. Graham-Bermann & A. A. Levendosky (Eds.), *How intimate partner violence affects children* (pp. 247–272). American Psychological Association.
D'Andrea, W., & Graham-Bermann, S. (2017). Social context and violence exposure as predictors of internalizing symptoms in mothers and children exposed to intimate partner violence. *Journal of Family Violence, 32*(2), 145–155. https://doi.org/10.1007/s10896-016-9869-0
Davies, P. T., & Cummings, E. M. (1994). Marital conflict and child adjustment: An emotional security hypothesis. *Psychological Bulletin, 116*(3), 387–411. https://doi.org/10.1037/0033-2909.116.3.387
Davies, P. T., & Cummings, E. M. (1998). Exploring children's emotional security as a mediator of the link between marital relations and child adjustment. *Child Development, 69*(1), 124–139. https://doi.org/10.2307/1132075
Deblinger, E., Mannarino, A. P., Cohen, J., Runyon, M. K., & Steer, R. A. (2011). Trauma-focused cognitive-behavioral therapy for children: Impact of the trauma narrative and treatment length. *Depression and Anxiety, 28*(1), 67–75. https://doi.org/10.1002/da.20744
DeBoard-Lucas, R. L., & Grych, J. H. (2011). The effects of intimate partner violence on school-age children. In S. Graham-Bermann & A. A. Levendosky (Eds.), *How intimate partner violence affects children* (pp. 155–178). American Psychological Association.

Douglas, H., & Walsh, T. (2015). Mandatory reporting of child abuse and marginalized families. In B. Mathews & D. C. Bross (Eds.), *Mandatory reporting laws and the identification of severe child abuse and neglect* (pp. 491–512). Springer.

Eisikovits, Z., & Winstok, Z. (2001). Researching children's experience of interparental violence: Towards a multidimensional conceptualization. In J. L. Edleson & S. A. Graham-Bermann (Eds.), *Domestic violence in the lives of children* (pp. 203–218). American Psychological Association.

Ernst, A. A., Weiss, S. J., Enright-Smith, S., & Hansen, J. P. (2008). Positive outcomes from an immediate and ongoing intervention for child witnesses of intimate partner violence. *The American Journal of Emergency Medicine, 26*(4), 389–394. https://doi.org/10.1016/j.ajem.2007.06.018

Fellin, L. C., Callaghan, J. E. M., Alexander, J. H., Harrison-Breed, C., Mavrou, S., & Papthanassiou, M. (2019). Empowering young people who experienced domestic violence and abuse: The development of a group therapy intervention. *Clinical Child Psychology and Psychiatry, 24*(1), 170–189. https://doi.org./10.1177/1359104518794783

Fogarty, A., Giallo, R., Wood, C., Kaufman, J., & Brown, S. (2019). Emotional-behavioral resilience and competence in preschool children exposed and not exposed to intimate partner violence in early life. *International Journal of Behavioral Development, 44*(2), 97–106. https://doi.org/10.1177/0165025419830241

Forte, L. A., Timmer, S., & Urquiza, A. (2014). A brief history of evidence-based practice. In S. Timmer & A. Urquiza (Eds.), *Evidence-based approaches for the treatment of maltreated children* (pp. 13–18). Springer.

Fosco, G. M., DeBoard, R. L., & Grych, J. H. (2007). Making sense of family violence: Implications of children's appraisals of interparental aggression for their short-and long-term functioning. *European Psychologist, 12*(1), 6–16. https://doi.org/10.1027/1016-9040.12.1.6

Fosco, G. M., & Grych, J. H. (2008). Emotional, cognitive, and family system mediators of children's adjustment to interparental conflict. *Journal of Family Psychology, 22*(6), 843–854. https://doi.org/10.1037/a0013809

Fusco, R. A. (2017). Socioemotional problems in children exposed to intimate partner violence: Mediating effects of attachment and family supports. *Journal of Interpersonal Violence, 32*(16), 2515–2532. https://doi.org/ 10.1177/0886260515593545

Gewirtz, A. H., & Edleson, J. L. (2007). Young children's exposure to intimate partner violence: Towards a developmental risk and resilience framework for research and intervention. *Journal of Family Violence, 22*(3), 151–163. https://doi.org/10.1007/s10896-007-9065-3

Gewirtz, A. H., & Medhanie, A. (2008). Proximity and risk in children's witnessing of intimate partner violence incidents. *Journal of Emotional Abuse, 8*(1–2), 67–82. https://doi.org/10.1080/10926790801982436

Goldblatt, H. (2003). Strategies of coping among adolescents experiencing interparental violence. *Journal of Interpersonal Violence, 18*(2), 532–552. https://doi.org/10.1177/0886260503251071

Goldblatt, H., & Eisikovits, Z. (2005). Role taking of youth in a family context: Adolescents exposed to interparental violence. *American Journal of Orthopsychiatry, 75*(4), 644–657. https://doi.org/10.1037/ 0002-9432.75.4.644

Graham-Bermann, S. A. (1998). The impact of women abuse on children's social development: Research and theoretical perspectives. In G. W. Holden, R. Geffner, & E. N. Jouriles (Eds.), *Children exposed to marital violence: Therapy, research and applied issues* (pp. 21–54). American Psychological Association.

Graham-Bermann, S. A. (2000). Evaluating interventions for children exposed to family violence. *Journal of Aggression, Maltreatment and Trauma, 4*(1), 191–215. https://doi.org/10.1300/J146v04n0109

Graham-Bermann, S. A. (2001). Designing intervention evaluations for children exposed to domestic violence: Applications of research and theory. In S. A. Graham-Bermann & J. Edleson (Eds.), *Domestic violence in the lives of children: The future of research, intervention, and social policy* (pp. 237–267). American Psychological Association.

Graham-Bermann, S. A. (2011). Evidence-based practices for school-age children exposed to intimate partner violence and evaluation of the kids' club program. In S. A. Graham-Bermann & A. A. Levendosky (Eds.), *How intimate partner violence affects children* (pp. 179–206). American Psychological Association.

Graham-Bermann, S. A., & Follett, C. (2000). *The preschool kids' club: A preventive intervention program for children of battered women*. University of Michigan, Department of Psychology.

Graham-Bermann, S. A., & Levendosky, A. A. (1994). *The moms' group: A parenting support and intervention program for battered women who are mothers*. University of Michigan, Department of Psychology.

Graham-Bermann, S. A., Lynch, S., Banyard, V., DeVoe, E., & Halabu, H. (2007). Community based intervention for children exposed to intimate partner violence: An efficacy trial. *Journal of Consulting and Clinical Psychology, 75*, 99–209. https://doi.org/10.1037/fam0000091

Graham-Bermann, S. A., Lynch, S., & Halabu, H. (2002). *Testing models of effects of interventions to reduce anxiety, depression and aggression in children of battered women*. Unpublished Manuscript.

Grosso, C. A. (2012). Children with developmental disabilities. In J. A. Cohen, P. Mannarino, & E. Deblinger (Eds.), *Trauma-focused CBT for children and adolescents: Treatment applications* (pp. 149–174). The Guilford Press.

Grych, J. H., & Fincham, F. D. (1990). Marital conflict and children's adjustment: A cognitive-contextual framework. *Psychological Bulletin, 108*(2), 267–290. https://doi.org/10.1037/0033-2909.108.2.267

Guille, L. (2004). Men who batter and their children: An integrated review. *Aggression and Violent Behavior, 9*(3), 129–163. https://doi.org/10.1016/s1359-1789(02)00119-2

Hambrick, E. P., Brawner, T. W., Perry, B. D., Brandt, K., Hofmeister, C., & Collins, J. O. (2019). Beyond the ACE score: Examining relationships between timing of developmental adversity, relational health and developmental outcomes in children. *Archives of Psychiatric Nursing, 33*(3), 238–247. https://doi.org/10.1016/j.apnu.2018.11.001

Hielscher, E., Moores, C., Blenkin, M., Jadambaa, A., & Scott, J. G. (2021). Intervention programs designed to promote healthy romantic relationships in youth: A systematic review. *Journal of Adolescence, 92*, 194–236. https://doi.org/10.1016/j.adolescence.2021.08.008

Hines, L. (2015). Children's coping with family violence: Policy and service recommendations. *Child and Adolescent Social Work Journal, 32*(2), 109–119. https://doi.org/10.1007/s10560-014-0333-9

Hockenhull, J. C., Cherry, M. G., Whittington, R., Dickson, R. C., Leitner, M., Barr, W., & McGuire, J. (2015). Heterogeneity in interpersonal violence research: An investigation and discussion of clinical and research implications. *Aggression and Violent Behavior, 22*, 18–25. https://doi.org/10.1016/j.avb.2015.02.005

Howarth, E., Moore, T., Welton, N., Lewis, N., Stanley, N., MacMillan, H., Shaw, S., Hester, M., Bryden, P., & Feder, G. (2016). Improving Outcomes for children exposed to domestic violence (IMPROVE): An evidence synthesis. *Public Health Research, 4*(10). https://doi.org/10.3310/ phr04100

Howell, K. H., Lilly, M. M., Burlaka, V., Grogan-Kaylor, A., Graham-Bermann, S. (2015). Strengthening positive parenting through intervention: Evaluating the moms' empowerment program for women experiencing intimate partner violence. *Journal of Interpersonal Violence, 30*(2), 232–252. https://doi.org/10.1177/0886260514533155

Howell, K. H., Miller, L. E., & Graham-Bermann, S. A. (2012). Evaluating preschool children's attitudes and beliefs about intimate partner violence. *Violence and Victims, 27*(6), 941–956. https://doi.org/10.1891/0886-6708.27.6.941

Hughes, H. (1982). Brief interventions with children in a battered women's shelter: A model program. *Family Relations, 31*(4), 495–502.

Hughes, H., & Barad, S. (1983). Psychological functioning of children in a battered women's shelter: A preliminary investigation. *American Journal of Orthopsychiatry, 53*(3), 525–531. https://doi.org/10.1111/j.1939-0025.1983.tb03396.x

Jaffe, P. G., Baker, L., & Cunningham, A. J. (2004). Purpose and overview. In P. G. Jaffe, L. L. Baker, & A. J. Cunningham (Eds.), *Protecting children from domestic violence* (pp. 3–7). The Guilford Press.

Jaffe, P. G., Wilson, S. K., & Wolfe, D. A. (1986). Promoting changes in attitudes and understanding of conflict resolution among child witnesses of family violence. *Canadian Journal of Behavioral Sciences, 18*(4), 356–366. https://doi.org/10.1037/h0079969

Jaffe, P. G., Wolfe, D. A., & Wilson, S. K. (1990). *Children of battered women*. Sage.

Jenney, A., & Alaggia, R. (2012). Children's exposure to domestic violence: Integrating policy, research, and practice to address children's mental health. InR. Alaggia & C. Vine (Eds.), *Cruel but not unusual: Violence in Canadian families* (pp. 303–336). Wilfrid Laurier University Press.

Johnston, J. R. (2003). Group interventions for children at-risk from family abuse and exposure to violence: A report of a study. *Journal of Emotional Abuse, 3*(3), 203–226. https://doi.org/10.1300/j135v03n03-03

Jouriles, E. N., Brown, A., McDonald, R., Rosenfield, D., Leahy, M. M., & Silver, C. (2008a). Intimate partner violence and preschoolers' explicit memory functioning. *Journal of Family Psychology, 22*(3), 420–428. https://doi.org/10.1037/0893-3200.22.3.420

Jouriles, E. N., McDonald, R., Rosenfield, D., Stephens, N., Corbitt-Shindler, D., & Miller, P. C. (2009). Reducing conduct problems among children exposed to intimate partner violence: A randomized clinical trial examining effects of project support. *Journal of Consulting and Clinical Psychology, 77*(4), 705–717. https://doi.org/10.1037/a0015994

Jouriles, E. N., McDonald, R., Slep, A. M., Heyman, R. E., & Garrido, E. (2008b). Child abuse in the context of domestic violence: Prevalence, explanations, and practice implications. *Violence and Victims, 23*(2), 221–235. https://doi.org/10.1891/0886-6708.23.2.221

Jouriles, E. N., McDonald, R., Spiller, L., Norwood, W. D., Swank, P. R., Stephens, N., ... Buzy, W. M. (2001). Reducing conduct problems among children of battered women. *Journal of Consulting and Clinical Psychology, 69*(5), 774–785. https://doi.org/10.1037/0022-006X.69.5.774

Katz, E. (2019). Coercive control, domestic violence, and a five-factor framework: Five factors that influence closeness, distance, and strain in mother–child relationships. *Violence Against Women, 25*(15), 1829–1853. https://doi.org/10.1177/1077801218824998

Katz, E. (2022). *Coercive control in children's and mothers' lives*. Oxford University Press.

Kinsfogel, K. M., & Grych, J. H. (2004). Interparental conflict and adolescent dating relationships: Integrating cognitive, emotional, and peer influences. *Journal of Family Psychology, 18*(3), 505–515. https://doi.org/10.1037/0893-3200.18.3.505

Kliethermes, M., & Wamser, S. (2012). Adolescents with complex trauma. In J. A. Cohen, A. P. Mannarino, & E. Deblinger (Eds.), *Trauma-focused CBT for children and adolescents: Treatment applications* (pp. 175–196). The Guilford Press.

Kot, S., Landreth, G. L., & Giordano, M. (1998). Intensive child-centered play therapy with child witnesses of domestic violence. *International of Play Therapy, 7*(2), 17–36. https://doi.org/10.1037/h0089421

Latzman, N. E., Casaneuva, C., Brinton, J., & Forman Hoffman, V. L. (2019). The promotion of well-being among children exposed to intimate partner violence: A systematic review of interventions. *Campbell Systematic Reviews, 15*(3), e1049. https://doi.org/10.1002/cl2.1049

Lee, H., Russell, K. N., O'Donnell, K. A., Miller, E. K., Bender, A. E., Scaggs, A. L., Harris III, L. A., Holmes, M. R., & Berg, K. A. (2022). The effect of childhood intimate partner violence (IPV) exposure on bullying: A systematic review. *Journal of Family Violence*, 1–8. https://doi.org/10.1007/s10896-021-00299-w

Liberman, A. F., Ippen, C. G., & Van Horn, P. (2006). Child-parent psychotherapy: 6-month follow-up of a randomized controlled trial. *Journal of the American Academy of Child and Adolescent Psychiatry, 45*(8), 913–918. https://doi.org/10.1097/01.chi.0000222784.03735.92

Liberman, A. F., Silverman, R., & Pawl, J. H. (2000). Infant-parent psychotherapy: Core concepts and current approaches. In C. H. Zeanah Jr. (Ed.), *Handbook of infant mental health* (2nd ed., pp. 472–484). The Guilford Press.

Liberman, A. F., Van Horn, P., & Ippen, C. G. (2005). Toward evidence-based treatment: Child-parent psychotherapy with preschoolers exposed to marital violence. *Journal of the American Academy of Child and Adolescent Psychiatry, 44*(12), 1241–1248. https://doi.org/10.1097/01.chi.0000181047.59702.58

Luciana, M., Conklin, H. M., Cooper, C. J., & Yarger, R. S. (2005). The development of nonverbal working memory and executive control processes in adolescents. *Child Development, 76*(3), 697–712. https://doi.org/10.1111/j.1467-8624.2005.00872.x

Macdonald, G. S. (2017). Hearing children's voices? Including children's perspectives on the experiences of domestic violence in welfare reports prepared for the English courts in private family law proceedings. *Child Abuse and Neglect, 65*, 1–13. https://doi.org/10.1016/j.chiabu.2016.12.013

MacMillan, H. L., Wathen, C. N., & Varcoe, C. M. (2013). Intimate partner violence in the family: Considerations for children's safety. *Child Abuse and Neglect, 37*(12), 1186–1191. https://doi.org/10.1016/j.chiabu. 2013.05.005

Mannarino, A. P., Cohen, J. A., & Deblinger, E. (2014). Trauma-focused cognitive-behavioral therapy. In S. Timmer & A. Urquiza (Eds.), *Evidence-based approaches for the treatment of maltreated children* (pp. 165–185). Springer.

Margolin, G., & Gordis, E. B. (2000). The effects of family and community violence on children. *Annual Review of Psychology, 51*, 445–479. https://doi.org/10.1146/annurev.psych.51. 1.445

Marshall, L., Miller, S., Miller-Hewitt, S., Sudermann, M., & Watson, L. (1995). *Evaluation of groups for children who have witnessed violence.* London Family Court Clinic and Centre for Research and Violence Against Women and Children at University of Western Ontario.

Martorell, G. A., & Bugental, D. B. (2006). Maternal variations in stress reactivity: Implications for harsh parenting practices with young children. *Journal of Family Psychology, 20*(4), 641–647. https://doi.org/10.1037/0893-3200.20.4.641

McCloskey, L. A. (2011). The impact of intimate partner violence on adolescents. In S. Graham-Bermann & A. A. Levendosky (Eds.), *How intimate partner violence affects children* (pp. 225–246). American Psychological Association.

McDonald, R., & Grych, J. H. (2006). Young children's appraisals of interparental conflict: Measurement and links with adjustment problems. *Journal of Family Psychology, 20*(1), 88–99. https://doi.org/10.1037/ 0893-3200.20.1.88

McDonald, R., Jouriles, E. N., & Minze, L. (2011). Intervention for young children exposed to intimate partner violence. In S. Graham-Bermann & A. A. Levendosky (Eds.), *How intimate partner violence affects children* (pp. 109–131). American Psychological Association.

McFarlane, J. M., Groff, J. Y., O'Brien, J. A., & Watson, K. (2005a). Behaviors of children exposed to intimate partner violence before and 1 year after a treatment program for their mother. *Applied Nursing Research, 18*(1), 7–12. https://doi.org/10.1016/j.apnr.2004.06.011

McFarlane, J. M., Groff, J. Y., O'Brien, J. A., & Watson, K. (2005b). Behaviors of children following a randomized controlled treatment program for their abused mothers. *Issues in Comprehensive Pediatric Nursing, 28*(4), 195–211. https://doi.org/10.1080/01460860500396708

McGee, C. (2000). *Childhood experiences of domestic violence.* Jessica Kingsley.

McIntosh, J. E., Tan, E. S., Levendosky, A. A., & Holtzworth-Munroe, A. (2021). Mothers' experience of intimate partner violence and subsequent offspring attachment security ages 1–5 years: A meta-analysis. *Trauma, Violence, and Abuse, 22*(4), 885–899. https://doi.org/10.1177/1524838019888560

McTavish, J. R., MacGregor, C. D., Wathen, C. N., & MacMillan, H. L. (2016). Children's exposure to intimate violence: An overview. *International Review of Psychiatry, 28*(5), 505–518. https://doi.org/10.1080/ 09540261.2016. 1205001

McWhirter, P. T. (2008). An empirical evaluation of a collaborative child and family violence prevention and intervention program. In G. R. Walz, J. C. Bleuer, & R. K. Yep (Eds.), *Compelling counseling interventions: Celebrating VISTAS fifth anniversary* (pp. 221–227). American Counseling Association.

Miranda, J. K., Olivares, N., & Crockett, M. A. (2022). Growing up with intimate partner violence at home: Adolescents' narratives on their coping strategies. *Journal of Family Violence.* https://doi.org/10.1007/s10896-021-00345-7

Muir, C., Adams, E. A., Evans, V., Geijer-Simpson, E., Kaner, E., Phillips, S. M., Salonen, D., Smart, D., Winstone, L., & McGovern, R. (2022). A systematic review of qualitative studies exploring lived experiences, perceived impact, and coping strategies of children and young people whose parents use substances. *Trauma, Violence, and Abuse.* https://doi.org/10.1177/15248380221134297

Mullender, A., Hague, G., Imam, U., Kelly, L., Malos, E., & Regan, L. (2002). *Children's perspectives on domestic violence.* Sage.

Noble-Carr, D., Moore, T. H., & McArthur, M. (2019). Children's experiences and needs in relation to domestic and family violence: Findings from a meta-synthesis. *Child and Family Social Work, 25*(1), 182–191. https://doi.org/10.1111/cfs.12645

O'Connor, T. G. (2003). Early experiences and psychological development: Conceptual questions, empirical illustrations, and implications for intervention. *Development and Psychopathology, 15*(3), 671–690. https://doi.org/10.1017/S0954579403000336

Olds, D., Kitzmann, H., Cole, R., & Robinson, J. (1997). Theoretical foundations of a program of home visitation for pregnant women and parents of young children. *Journal of Community Psychology, 25*(1), 9–25. https://doi.org/10.1002/(SICI)1520-6629(199701)25:1<9::AID-JCOP2>3.0.CO;2-V

Øverlien, C. (2016). "Do you want to do some arm wrestling?" Children's strategies when experiencing domestic violence and the meaning of age. *Child and Family Social Work, 22*(2), 680–688. https://doi.org/10.1111/cfs.12283

Owen, A. E., Thompson, M. P., Shaffer, A., Jackson, E. B., & Kaslow, N. J. (2009). Family variables that mediate the relation between intimate partner violence (IPV) and child adjustment. *Journal of Family Violence, 24*(7), 433–445. https://doi.org/10.1007/s10896-009-9239-2

Peled, E. (1998). The experience of living with violence for preadolescent children of battered women. *Youth and Society, 29*(4), 395–430. https://doi.org/10.1177/0044118X98029004001

Peled, E., & Davis, D. (1995). *Groupwork with children of battered women.* Sage.

Peled, E., & Edleson, J. (1992). Multiple perspectives on groupwork with children of battered women. *Violence and Victims, 7*(4), 327–346. https://doi.org/10.1891/0886-6708.7.4.327

Pepler, D. J., Catallo, R., & Moore, T. E. (2000). Consider the children: Research informing interventions for children exposed to domestic violence. *Journal of Aggression, Maltreatment and Trauma, 3*(1), 37–57. https://doi.org/10.1300/j146v03n01_04

Ravi, K. E., & Casolaro, T. E. (2018). Children's exposure to intimate partner violence: A qualitative interpretive meta-synthesis. *Child and Adolescent Social Work Journal, 35*(3), 283–295. https://doi.org/10.1007/s10560-017-0525-1

Rizo, C. F., Macy, R. J., Ermentrout, D. M., & Johns, N. B. (2011). A review of family interventions for intimate partner violence with a child focus or child component.

Aggression and Violent Behavior, 16(2), 144–166. https://doi.org/10.1016/j.avb.2011.02.004

Rogers, K., & Berger, E. (2022). A systematic review of children's perspectives of fathers who perpetrate intimate partner violence. *Trauma, Violence, and Abuse*, 1–20. https://doi.org/10.1177/15248380221124268

Romano, E., Weegar, K., Gallitto, E., Zak, S., & Saini, M. (2021). Meta-analysis on interventions for children exposed to intimate partner violence. *Trauma, Violence, and Abuse, 22*(4), 728–738. https://doi.org/10.1177/1524838019881737

Rossman, B. R., Rea, J. G., Graham-Bermann, S., & Butterfield, P. M. (2004). Young children exposed to adult domestic violence. In P. G. Jaffe, L. Baker, & A. L. Cunningham (Eds.), *Protecting children from domestic violence* (pp. 30–48). The Guilford Press.

Schore, A. N. (2015). Plenary address, Australian childhood foundation conference childhood trauma: Understanding the basis of change and recovery early right brain regulation and the relational origins of emotional wellbeing. *Children Australia, 40*(2), 103–113.

Silverman, W. K., Ortiz, C. D., Viswesvaran, C., Burns, B. J., Kolko, D., Putnam, F. W., & Amaya-Jackson, L. (2008). Evidence-based psychosocial treatments for children and adolescents exposed to traumatic events. *Journal of Clinical Child and Adolescent Psychology, 37*(1), 156–183. https://doi.org/10.1080/15374410701818293

Smith, N., & Landreth, G. (2003). Intensive filial therapy with child witnesses of domestic violence: A comparison with individual and sibling group play therapy. *International Journal of Play Therapy, 12*(1), 67–88. https://doi.org/10.1037/h0088872

Sroufe, L. A. (2005). Attachment and development: A prospective study from birth to adulthood. *Attachment and Human Development, 7*(4), 349–367. https://doi.org/10.1080/14616730500365928

Sudermann, M., Marshall, L., & Loosely, S. (2000). Evaluation of the London (Ontario) community group treatment program for children who have witnessed women abuse. *Journal of Aggression, Maltreatment and Trauma, 3*(1), 127–146. https://doi.org/10.1300/j146v03n01_09

Sullivan, C. M., & Bybee, D. L. (1999). Reducing violence using community-based advocacy for women with abusive partners. *Journal of Consulting and Clinical Psychology, 67*(1), 43–53. https://doi.org/10.1037//0022-006x.67.1.43

Teicher, M. H., & Samson, J. A. (2016). Annual research review: Enduring neurobiological effects of childhood abuse and neglect. *Journal of Child Psychology and Psychiatry, 57*(3), 241–266. https://doi.org/10.1111/jcpp.12507

Timmer, S. G., Ware, L. M., Urqiza, A. J., & Zebell, N. M. (2010). The effectiveness of parent-child interaction therapy for victims of interparental violence. *Violence and Victims, 25*(4), 486–503. https://doi.org/10.1891/0886-6708 25. 4.486

Timmer, S., Urquiza, A., (2014). Why we think we can make things better with evidence-based practice: Theoretical and developmental context. In S. Timmer & A. Urquiza (Eds.), *Evidence-based approaches for the treatment of maltreated children* (pp. 19–39). Springer.

Tutty, L. M., & Wagar, J. (1994). The evolution of a group for young children who have witnessed family violence. *Social Work with Groups, 17*(1/2), 89–104. https://doi.org/10.1300/J009v17n01_06

Tyndall-Lind, A., Landreth, G. L., & Giordano, M. A. (2001). Intensive group play therapy with child witnesses of domestic violence. *International Journal of Play Therapy*, *10*(1), 53–83. https://doi.org/10.1037/ h0089443

Van der Kolk, B. (2014). *The body keeps the score: Brain, mind and body in the healing of trauma*. Viking.

Vogel, M., & Keith, S. (2015). Vicarious peer victimization and adolescent violence: Unpacking the effects of social learning, general strain, and peer group selection. *Deviant Behavior*, *36*(10), 834–852. https://doi.org/10.1080/01639625.2014.977187

Wagar, J. M., & Rodway, M. R. (1995). An evaluation of a group treatment approach for children who have witnessed wife abuse. *Journal of Family Violence*, *10*(3), 295–306. https://doi.org/10.1007/ BF02110994

Wiese, E. (2013). Psychology of trauma: Vulnerability and resilience. In T. Van Leeuwen & M. Brouwer (Eds.), *Psychology of trauma* (pp. 225–236). Nova Science Publisher.

Chapter 3

Treatment policy for the phenomenon of exposure to interparental violence

3.1 Historical review

Increasing awareness of the complexity of domestic violence and its related damage during the first two decades of research on this phenomenon (from the 1970s to the 1990s) has deepened researchers', practitioners', and policymakers' understanding of the negative effects that exposure to violence has on children. The result was the introduction of intervention programs designed to protect children in centers for the prevention and treatment of family violence, based on the understanding that the children's protection needs to be an integral part of protecting the victimized parent. These programs were based on the wish to form a coherent intervention strategy that takes into consideration the needs of children who are exposed to violence as part of an **overall policy regarding family violence** that is in keeping with the research and practice in the field (Berg et al., 2020; Jenney & Alaggia, 2012).

In this context, the underlying principles guiding the policy for treating the phenomenon of exposure to violence were as follows:

1. Exposure to violence and harm to children are correlated—this population is sometimes at-risk for developing clinical problems. In addition, these children are at high risk for direct abuse (Berg et al., 2020; Edleson, 2004; Finkelhor et al., 2011; Wathen & MacMillan, 2013).
2. Child abuse and neglect, to one degree or another, characterizes *all* violent men who are fathers—hence their fatherhood requires critical attention (e.g., Haddix, 1996; Harne & Radford, 1994).
3. Women victims of violence must be seen as mothers at-risk since they function as mothers in conditions of severe distress, which make motherhood difficult and could potentially harm the children (Howell et al., 2017; Peled & Perel, 2010; Stover et al., 2009; Van Parys et al., 2014). Nevertheless, the children's relationship with the mother who cares for them can be the most significant reparative factor for healing and recovery (Hollin, 2016; Jenney & Alaggia, 2012; Peled & Perl, 2010).

DOI: 10.4324/9781003364221-4

Based on these assumptions, by the 1990s, a response was developed, tailored to the children's needs and to the needs of the mother, the victim of violence: Laws were passed in the criminal and civic fields, influencing the responses by child protection agencies, the criminal justice system, and the treatment programs for domestic violence and exposure to violence (Edleson, 2004; Macy et al., 2010; Panzer et al., 2000; Zweig & Burt, 2007). On the practical level, 1) introduction of intervention programs strengthened women's economic, social, and personal resources. In this context, two evidence-based programs were found to be suitable for working with children's and mothers' trauma caused by exposure to violence: Child–parent psychotherapy, intended for children up to age 7, and project support, intended for ages 4 to 9. 2) Treatment for men was offered as an alternative to incarceration or as part of a contract to consent to participate in a group for violent men (the proposed treatment was and continues to be short term: Psychoeducational groups designed to stop the violence). 3) Introduction of programs for treating children's trauma (Banks et al., 2008; Kracke & Cohen, 2008; Shlonsky et al., 2007).

A dispute arose surrounding the question of whether children who are exposed to violence need to be defined as children who experience abuse. This was in response to an additional wave of research that established the correlation between exposure to violence and harm to children, as well as qualitative studies that helped in understanding contextual variables and studies that showed that domestic violence may indicate risk for child abuse and vice versa (the 1990s to the beginning of the 2000s; Artz et al., 2014; Holt et al., 2008; Irwin et al., 2006; Jenney & Alaggia, 2012; Øverlien, 2010). As a result, child protection agencies gradually included domestic violence in their definitions of abuse (Black et al., 2020; Clarke & Wydall, 2015; Davies & Krane, 2006). In this context, Edleson (2004) claimed that even if opinions for and against defining exposure to violence as abuse are valid (the main claim against automatic definition being that a large number of children are not clinically damaged), if this field is placed in the abuse category, many families may be left without suitable treatment. In fact, the child protection system has only a limited number of placements, and therefore only high-risk cases are actually treated. In light of this, if exposure to violence is not included in the abuse category, it can be interpreted as failing to safeguard the children. Therefore, Edleson suggested an additional direction for observing and managing the phenomenon: An approach that still protects the children while remaining sensitive to the family situation. According to this approach, exposure to domestic violence will not be defined automatically as a subfield of child abuse. This will serve to avoid legal procedures and thus spare the children from police inquiries and interventions against family members, which could be damaging to the entire family. Instead, assessment and intervention will take place within the community. In cases where children are at high risk for harm as a result of the male partner's violence, the child protection system will engage in assessing and intervening with the family as a whole (Edleson, 2004).

Although Edleson's proposed direction was adopted as policy in cases of exposure to violence in the United States and Canada (in the first decade of the 2000s), at the same time, these countries saw an increase in legislative initiatives related to domestic violence, including legal initiatives that entailed defining children exposed to violence as requiring legal protection (Berg et al., 2020; Clarke & Wydall, 2015; Henry, 2017). The justice system in the United States, Canada, and the United Kingdom criminalized domestic violence by making arrests, initiating actions and operating courts that specialize in the field. Children's exposure to domestic violence as a type of abuse comes under the category of child protection laws (Black et al., 2020; Henry, 2017; Kim, 2013; Richardson-Foster et al., 2012; Shields, 2008). Abuse in this context is defined as damage caused by repeated exposure to domestic violence and includes a declaration demanding child protection from the authorities in cases where either the parent or the guardian refuses services for intervention, therapy, or reducing violence (Jenney & Alaggia, 2012).

The definition is problematic since it might be interpreted to mean that both the abusive parent and the victimized parent are responsible for the child's exposure to violence. Furthermore, the child protection system is designed to intervene mainly with the parent who is the child's primary caregiver, when, in cases of domestic violence, it is frequently the mother who is the victim of the violence. These two variables created tensions between the child protection services and agencies dealing with violence against women, since the rights of the children received preference over the rights of women (Coulter & Mercado-Crespo, 2015; Hazen et al., 2007; Jenney & Alaggia, 2012). To reduce tension between the different service provider sectors and to improve outcomes for children and their mothers, several initiatives were developed to encourage cooperation. Joint training for child protection and domestic violence agencies (multi-agency risk assessment and management) became a basic component in the education of workers in many child protection agencies throughout Canada and the United States (Berg et al., 2020; Stanley & Humphreys, 2014).

Initiatives took the form of community collaborations; a foundation of experts in domestic violence within the child protection organizations; intersectoral trust with workers in the field of child protection and workers in the field of violence against women; development of programs for men who expose children to violence; constructing models for differential, apparently promising, responses in child protection, and the development of skills for reaching out to abusers with the aim of safeguarding the children and mothers (Alaggia et al., 2007; Berg et al., 2020; Edleson et al., 2006; Humphreys et al., 2018; Laing et al., 2013; Stanley, 2015).

In fact, despite the documented initiatives, many of the collaborations are still in their initial stages. Most of the service providers currently offer services to children exposed to violence **external to and without the involvement of** child protection agencies. The services and programs developed as a solution for children exposed to violence, as part of the response for past and present women victims of violence, and simultaneously involve both mothers and children in intervention (Appel & Kim-Appel, 2006; Holmes et al., 2019; Rogers & Parkinson, 2018).

Mandatory reporting of child abuse in the domestic violence context raises several complex issues: 1) For example, while the abusive parent is indeed an abuser from the child protection approach, the victimized parent may also be perceived as an abuser as a result of the inability to protect the child from exposure to violence. This perception of the failure to protect is derived from the assumption that parents are obligated to protect their children from harm. The perception is misguided insofar as it disregards the fact that the possibilities available to domestic violence victims are very often limited, and some women remain in the violent situation in the belief that leaving would place themselves and their children at even higher risk (Carter et al., 1999; Davies & Krane, 2006; Langenderfer-Magruder et al., 2019; Peled & Perel, 2010). 2) Evidence from the field shows that the involvement of child protection authorities is very troubling for women victims of violence. Questions regarding their ability to protect breeds fear of losing custody of the children (Black et al., 2020; Edleson et al., 2006). 3) There is also a risk that the child protection approach will focus narrowly on the immediate protection of the children instead of performing long-term assessment that takes into consideration the needs of the children and the victimized parent (the mother; Jenney & Alaggia, 2012). 4) In addition, since the child protection approach demands that **all** suspected cases be reported, it limits community services' involvement in determining the degree to which the situation either does or does not require child protection intervention (Carter et al., 1999; Edleson et al., 2006; Shlonsky et al., 2007).

A historical review of intervention policy in the field of exposure to violence may, therefore, show that defining children who are exposed to violence as children who experience abuse has created a conflictual and complex reality. The reality that obligates intervention in the shadow of the law, on one hand, frequently places the children's and women's interests at odds with each other, and on the other hand, shows that women's and children's protection cannot be reasonably separated. Nonetheless, the reality in which these children live and their exposure to violence demands that they be treated as children at-risk. As can be seen, the solution is actually theoretical since, according to the definition, these children require enactment of protection laws, but in practice, the way in which they are dealt with does not enact these laws.

The situation described above led to a "regression" from the viewpoint of the rights of the child, in the sense that exposure to domestic violence as a distinct type of child abuse was removed from the definition of "child maltreatment" in the Youth Law in most of the United States (Henry, 2017). The implications of this legal change on the policy level was the search for a paradigm that would not give preference either to child protection or to domestic violence. In other words, the interests of children and women alike would be maintained. This paradigm was defined as creating safe environments for children, in which their primary caregivers would support them to improve their lives (Buckley, 2018).

From the aforementioned material, we learn of three key issues that were central to involvement under the law: 1) How can protection of the victimized parent remain central if the mother's safety and her ability to protect her children is undermined by exclusively child-focused interventions that potentially accuse the mother of exposing the children to violence? 2) What is the best way to intervene with children in this process, in the knowledge that exposure to domestic violence has a negative influence on the children and that their relationship with the mother, who cares for them, can be the most significant reparative factor in healing and recovery? 3) How can violent men be held responsible for the violence as part of the child protection intervention approach (Jenney & Alaggia, 2012)?

In the context under discussion, three possible solutions were proposed: First, the harm reduction (HR) approach following exposure to violence (Shlonsky et al., 2007); second, the approach that entails learning about the subjective experience of the mothers living in circumstances of domestic violence (Davies & Krane, 2006); and third, the family group conference (FGC) model (Rogers & Parkinson, 2018).

The following premises lie behind the HR approach as a result of exposure to violence: 1) Only limited evidence points to the effectiveness of interventions for violent men. Meta-analysis in the field revealed particularly low effectiveness of the interventions (Babcock et al., 2004; Burnette et al., 2015; Eckhardt et al., 2013; Stover et al., 2022; Whitaker et al., 2008). 2) The removal of children to foster care may improve the lives of some of the children by distancing them from the abuser. However, the ways of examining the advantages are limited. It is difficult to predict which children will undergo abuse again in the out-of-home placement, not to mention the parents' right to raise their own children (Courtney et al., 2005; Macdonald, 2016, 2017; Shlonsky & Wagner, 2005). 3) Many women victims of violence are either unable or unwilling to leave their abusive partners, and hence the option of the shelter is not relevant for them (Howell et al., 2017; Shlonsky et al., 2007; Van Parys et al., 2014). Based on these assumptions, the shapers of this approach (Shlonsky et al., 2007) claim that even though everyone who deals with the field of violence would like to see the eradication of child and women abuse, it is unrealistic to define success of the treatment in terms of complete elimination of the phenomenon, and a more practical approach is needed. In their opinion, idealism leads to missed opportunities.

In view of this, the HR approach proposes a range of possibilities to **reduce the harm** to the clients involved (women and children), including the mother taking responsibility despite the known difficulties while giving her optimal support in all domains—economic, social, and cultural; introducing home-based treatments, e.g., in cases where the violent man returns home following a restraining order or incarceration. In cases where child protection is relevant, stricter responses or possibilities may be considered, which take into account standards to ensure the children's welfare. In other words, the proposed model suggests tailoring solutions to each family. The leading principle, according to this approach, is weighing up the potential advantages and harm of each action, while acknowledging that the chosen solution might need to be changed. In the theoreticians' view, the proposed approach will encourage definition of a range of key goals, including the use of aids regarding validated guidelines.

The approach of learning about the motherhood experience of women victims of violence (motherhood from a subjective perspective) suggests that the gap between the child protection and women protection contexts derives from a lack of assessment of the women's experience as mothers (Davies & Krane, 2006). According to the shapers of this approach (Davies & Krane, 2006), researchers indicate that, despite the fact that men are present in child protection cases, the tendency is to disregard them and to focus on the women (Humphreys et al., 2019; Stanley & Goddard, 2002). In such a context, not feeling strong enough to leave the violent relationship may evoke women's resistance to child protection interventions. With time, the mothers' relationship with the professionals might be experienced as antagonistic or even as hostile (Alaggia et al., 2007; Langenderfer-Magruder et al., 2019).

This complex situation, which places *responsibility for protection mainly on the woman*, drew researchers' attention to two central problems: First, the disregard of the complexity of child protection in the context of violence and the context of captivity, in which the woman is unable to make decisions from a position of free will. Second, a situation in which the mothers may stop cooperating with the child protection authorities (Black et al., 2020; Davies & Krane, 2006). In this situation, the solution for understanding them may be to learn about the subjective perspective of mothers in the context of violence. Such understanding may open a window to identifying strategies that **the women** perceive as the right ones for protecting their children and hence enable a redefinition of the concept of "protection" as a term that, in the context of women victims of violence, relates to the perception of safety in survival contexts (Davies & Krane, 2006). Katz (2022) broadens the understanding of this approach, suggesting that mothers and children be seen as co-victims of the same perpetrator. In such a context, the mothers can be seen as implementing a survival-oriented protection strategy in the domestic dynamics.

The FGC model suggests possibilities for a coherent and integrative response, which takes into consideration the children's and the mothers' interests together, as a holistic approach for the safety and welfare of the family (Rogers & Parkinson, 2018). The model places risk management at the center when the families are involved in making the decisions for the family with the professionals. In this manner, the model entails more democratic decision-making, offering the families an opportunity to develop their self-confidence and to support a program that protects and cares for their children while recognizing the family's inner strengths.

Even though the use of FGC in circumstances of domestic violence has become a subject of concern among professionals because of bringing the family together in circumstances where violence is present, the shapers of this approach in the context of domestic violence claim that research evidence does not indicate a cause for concern but quite the opposite. A consultation situation in which both the man and the woman are present may empower the woman and give her a sense of control in light of the need for abusers to take responsibility for their behavior and to advance toward change. The shapers of this approach emphasize that this is not an attempt to mediate between abuser and victim but to develop a protection program for the children (Rogers & Parkinson, 2018).

In addition to the three approaches that were developed as an attempt to provide an innovative response for child protection and women's rights within the framework of domestic violence, another attempt was made to use the original differential response model (Edleson, 2004), this time through emphasizing cooperation between the different agencies that were involved in domestic violence (Bushinski, 2017; Humphreys et al., 2018; Macvean et al., 2018; Murray et al., 2020): Child protection, domestic violence, and family courts. In this context, the researchers emphasize the importance of collaboration between the agencies to channel the treatment into the right context in the early stages, as well as the need to create differential work of agencies based on risk assessment. In addition, the researchers stress that, despite the lack of effectiveness of elements that might make cooperation easier, all components found relevant in the research literature for developing integrative practice may be used.

3.2 Critical learning of the history of treatment policy for the phenomenon of exposure to interparental violence

An analysis of the intervention strategies for the exposure to violence phenomenon through the years may reveal attempts by policy shapers in the field to preserve distinct treatment for children within an overall family violence policy. Researchers in the field of children exposed to violence established the correlation between living in a violent reality and the development of clinical symptoms in children in various domains. This correlation was continuously strengthened by the accumulation of quantitative, clinical, and qualitative studies that revealed the complexity and intensity of child harm. In addition, researchers increasingly raised the need to relate domestic violence as a form of abuse. Nonetheless, policy shaping in this field was still guided by the claim that large numbers of children are not clinically harmed by this reality, implying that many children, under recovery conditions, will overcome the trauma. In other words, claiming that children's exposure to violence and the domestic violence itself do not need to be treated separately. This works on the assumption that if members of the family system (the parents) receive appropriate assistance and treatment, most children will receive adequate protection and rehabilitation as long as they receive suitable intervention.

Thus, based on the explanations of differential harm to children and owing to the inability of child protection agencies to provide services to very large numbers of children, policy shapers in the field of exposure to violence have attempted to keep the children's treatment in an overall family framework. However, they have been less and less able to ignore research assessments and clinical findings from the field. Effectiveness evaluations of the intervention programs that were developed for violent men showed a weak positive effect at best and a modest effect at worst. Reports regarding women showed that many of them either were unable or did not wish to leave the captivity circumstances in which they were living, for a wide variety of reasons. Therefore, it was necessary to reexamine the assumption that appropriate assistance to the family system as a whole—men and women—would change the children's reality and facilitate intervention programs for children in the framework of recovery conditions. If, to the above, we add the evaluations of the various child intervention programs, evaluations that have not succeeded in proving effectiveness according to the required scientific criteria, as well as the concern about the interventions' key component—a child protection strategy (see Chapter 2)—then we have reached a situation in which it is essential to define the situation of these children as either abuse or neglect, in the absence of an appropriate solution for them.

This situation, as presented by the above review, led to collaboration attempts between agencies responsible for the treatment of violence against women and child protection agencies, collaborations that could have reflected the attempt to shape a new policy line for treating the population of children exposed to violence (that recognizes them as children at-risk, and thus their risk assessment and interventions need to be distinct from the general family procedure but performed sensitively, taking into account all the family system components). I use the expression "could have reflected" because, **in actual fact**, these attempts came to nothing, creating a bizarre situation, which should be noted as unique to the field of exposure to violence: **In theory**, these children were included under the category of enacting protection laws (i.e., the obligation to report), but **in practice**, they are not treated as cases defined as abuse since the assessment and intervention take place within the community. In other words, in the vast majority of cases, reports are made on children, but the intervention that they receive does not involve police inquiries and interventions against family members.

In this context under discussion, it is worth noting the explanations for this "neither-here-nor-there" policy, in which the children fall between two stools. As opposed to the explanations behind the general policy line regarding the risk involved in leaving numerous families without suitable treatment and in view of the large number of children who do not develop psychopathology,[1] the explanations behind the new policy line were issues related specifically to protecting the victimized parent. That is to say, whereas the first group of explanations related specifically to the nature of the child harm, the second group of explanations moved on to child harm context—the mother's captivity—and not to the issue of the harm to the children themselves. This context is extremely relevant to the issue of the children, both morally, regarding who cared for them in the situation of captivity, and practically, regarding who could, in certain conditions, become stronger and help the children's recovery. However, these arguments, in fact, concerning the protection of the victimized parent within the children's context, distance the focus from the children themselves. The mother is in the center as a victim, and the child is less of a victim. (As mentioned above, including the mother in the children's recovery is, nonetheless, very relevant for their healing).

An observation of the solutions that were proposed for this situation in which the children fall between two stools might shed additional light on the line of thinking that guided the attempt to shape new policy in the field of exposure to violence, a policy that takes into consideration the children's difficult situation as well as protection of the mother as victim of violence.

The HR approach (Shlonsky et al., 2007) proposes changing the assumption that the abuse must be stopped, which is the basis of intervention in situations of abuse through exposure to violence. In this context, it is important to note that changing the ideal goal to a goal of minimal damage actually makes it possible to 1) leave the definition of exposure to violence under the category of abuse; 2) find solutions that do not insist on removing children from parents, but reduce the damage (obviously not in situations in which children are assessed as severely harmed and cannot be left with the parents), through work that takes into consideration also the range of existing possibilities and the specific timing for all members of the family. In other words, changing the goal of intervention enables transfer of emphasis from the actual argument as to whether exposure to violence should be defined as abuse in order to find realistic solutions to that situation. With this in mind, the shapers of this approach achieve the following: 1) Recognition of the children's difficult situation; 2) placing responsibility on the perpetrator for creating the abusive circumstances; 3) consideration of the mother's rights as victim and involving her in the children's rehabilitation; and 4) where possible, working with the men, mainly to minimize the damage caused by the violence.

The approach to learning how women victims of violence subjectively perceive their motherhood (Davies & Krane, 2006) suggests learning about the term "protection" in the specific context of captivity. This learning will expose the strategies used by women to protect the children and to reduce the damage caused by the violence to a minimum. This perspective may throw light on how the shapers of this approach understand the solution of how to refer to exposure, not by redefining the "failure to protect" concept in the context of exposure to violence, but by removing the women from this context as the providers of concrete protection for their children in the situation of captivity. (Again, except in situations of direct child abuse or in situations that may put the children at-risk as a result of the father's violence against the mother.)

Analysis of the proposed solution may teach us that emphasizing the mothers' situation of captivity immediately draws attention also to the children's difficult situation, thus legitimizing the definition of exposure to violence as abuse. At the same time, the perpetrator is held responsible for creating these circumstances. In addition, the mothers are simultaneously perceived as the ones most likely to provide relatively good protection for the children in most of the complex situations of captivity.

The FGC model for exposure to domestic violence (Rogers & Parkinson, 2018) places risk management at the center. As such, it enables immediate definition of exposure to violence as creating child abuse circumstances. Nevertheless, the model is directed toward creating protection plans for the children while involving their primary caregivers and emphasizing their strengths, thereby turning the spotlight on finding a solution within the family rather than elsewhere. Specifically emphasizing the perpetrators' need to take responsibility for their behavior and actually change it is a clear declaration as to whom this approach perceives as responsible for creating the state of captivity.

As can be learned, the three proposed solutions define the children's situation as abuse in light of the complex circumstances of captivity and in parallel suggest adopting realistic solutions for the children within the home framework. It is important for us to note, in this context, that even though the proposed solutions recognize the severity of the harm to children and solve the issue of placing responsibility on the perpetrator as well as of blaming the mother for the exposure to violence, they perpetuate the absence of a solution for the children. None of these approaches suggests a different intervention for the children's situation, which changes from "difficult sometimes" to a situation that demands their definition as "children at risk." Furthermore, not one of the approaches offers a method that, in practice, proposes how to deal with the families in a way that is different than previously suggested. In fact, it means returning to a solution that was proposed by Edleson (2004) through the differential response model. According to the model, it is necessary to perform assessments and implement interventions in the community and to use discretion regarding the introduction of child protection agencies depending on the specific family's circumstances. The expansion of the model later on (Humphreys et al., 2018), through emphasizing cooperation between child protection agencies, domestic violence agencies, and the family courts, advocates the same type of solution.

The actual significance of this is that the treatment of the children is included within an overall policy framework toward family violence, but in the context of the new policy that is in formation, more attention is given to the child protection issue. In this context, the rights of women, as victims of violence, are at the center rather than the rights of children, even though it officially leaves room for both aspects. Even though the issue of women victims of violence must be taken into account within the children's treatment framework (and relevant suggestions have been made as to how this can be solved), the children's difficult situation must be recognized as an issue in itself that demands differential thinking and attention to the children who are caught in circumstances of captivity (i.e., in themselves victims of the state of captivity in which they live). Without such recognition, the children's treatment may be parallel to their situation of captivity and preserve it. In other words, the perception that attempts to preserve the mother's position as victim and to recognize that she is an important part of the healing process does not take into account that, because of the actual circumstances of captivity, the children's situation requires special attention. Without this special attention, the message conveyed to the children will be that society recognizes that they are captive in abusive circumstances, but since there is no realistic possibility of rescue, they are expected to continue to survive in this dangerous reality. The mother's efforts to care for them in these circumstances cannot change their captivity status, as long as the mother continues to be exposed to them. She, too, as captive, is part of this dynamics. It must be taken into account that the situation may worsen if she changes her survival behavior in accordance with external therapeutic or judicial instructions. This is because the man may perceive any change in the woman's or the children's behavior as a change in the behavioral script in the home that he might experience as a loss of control and as a threat. In continuation to the proposed thesis, I suggest that the following question be placed at the focus of researching the children's experience: How are children affected by violent domestic dynamics that create a space in which the woman is subject to her abuser's control? This differs from Katz's suggestion to place the following question at the focus of study: How are children affected by the abusive man's campaign of coercive control? The first question takes into consideration the cognitive filter of the woman as captive.

Current research points to apparent gaps in the new policy that claims to place emphasis on child protection through legislation and the obligation to report while not creating either a legal or a practical response. Specifically, three gaps come to light: 1) Between the growing number of child exposure investigations based on reports to child protection agencies and the large number of closed cases and absence of follow-up by the relevant services (Black et al., 2020); 2) between the increasing awareness among professionals dealing with child abuse and the trauma of exposure to violence and prioritization of children's needs and existing interventions for this particular type of abuse (Clarke & Wydall, 2015); and 3) between the acknowledgment by directors of agencies dealing (either directly or indirectly) with domestic violence of the children's need for trauma-focused therapy and the responses offered to them in practice (Berg et al., 2020).

The women's problematic situation was created by the absence of a solution for the men. That is to say, exercising power and performing arrests enabled a temporary break in the captivity situation, but in the absence of effective programs for working with the men, the state of violence became an ongoing, sustained reality. At this point, the question must arise as to what happens in cases of separation—when women victims of violence decide to leave the violent relationship? One would think that this was an ideal opportunity for the woman to rehabilitate herself and for her children to recover.

A study of violent men's behavior following separation from their partners revealed a high rate of woman abuse after the separation, which the children are likely to witness (Eriksson et al., 2005; Fleury et al., 2000; Heward-Belle, 2015; Humphreys & Thiara, 2003; Hay et al., 2021; Katz et al., 2020; Maglinte et al., 2016; Perel & Peled, 2008; Thiara & Gill, 2012; Woodlock, 2017). The risk of sexual abuse by the man increases after separation, as well as the risk of murder (Bancroft et al., 2012; Brandon et al., 2009; Katz, 2022; Kelly et al., 2014; Sharp-Jeffs et al., 2018; Walby & Allen, 2004). Besides the risk of threats or violent acts toward the mother, researchers and clinicians exposed a whole array of risks and harm toward the children by the abusive man, in the context of his separation from their mother (Campbell, 2017; Coy et al., 2012; Coy et al., 2015; Feresin et al., 2019; Hester & Radford, 1996; Jaffe et al., 2003; Katz et al., 2020; Katz, 2022; Lee et al., 2009; Peled, 2000; Women's Aid National Survey, 2016): Undermining of the mother's parental authority and creating tension between mother and child (Bancroft & Silverman, 2004; Coy et al., 2015; Katz, 2022); psychological and manipulative abuse using visitation as an opportunity to control the mother via the children (Bancroft & Silverman, 2004; Beeble et al., 2007; Galántai, 2019; Stambe & Meyer, 2022); increased risk of physical and sexual abuse of the children because of the mother's inability to supervise the father's parenting and due to the men's tendency to take revenge (Bancroft et al., 2012; Bidarra et al., 2016; Lee et al., 2009; Salter, 1995); strict and authoritative parenting (Bancroft & Silverman, 2002; Burnette et al., 2015; Margolin et al., 1996; Rogers & Berger, 2022); and neglectful parenting, expressed through difficulty in focusing on the children's needs as a result of selfish and narcissistic tendencies. In addition, these men sometimes deliberately use neglectful behaviors (e.g., in issues of food, discipline, watching television programs with violent or sexual content) in order to win the children's loyalty (Burnette et al., 2015; Coy et al., 2012; Leberg, 1997; Lee et al., 2009; Hay et al., 2021). Neglectful behaviors were observed also among violent fathers who showed an apparent interest in their children but afterward, either neglected or ignored them for long periods. Men with this type of parenting style tend to keep visitation arrangements and then stop them, which disturbs the children's daily routine and is extremely hurtful to their feelings. These fathers are problematic role models (Bancroft & Silverman, 2002; Bancroft et al., 2012; Rogers & Berger, 2022; Stambe & Meyer, 2022).

Studying the risks that separation from the abusive man creates for the woman and her children demands a review of the legal, political, and social contexts that were created for the sake of the children's mental health.

The guiding principle in custody is the benefit of the child, relating to the best interests of the children, such as parental management, maximum contact with each parent, and legal authorities. In the context of violence against women, it was found essential to balance the tension surrounding maximizing contact with both parents (e.g., Harrison, 2008) and reducing conflict to the minimum (e.g., Thiara & Gill, 2012) in order to protect the children (Birnbaum, 2012; Coy et al., 2015; Macdonald, 2017; Perrin, 2017). For this purpose, toward the end of the 2000s, the examination of five priorities was proposed for cases of custody assessment (Jaffe et al., 2008): First priority, protecting the child from a violent, abusive, and neglectful parental environment; second priority, protecting the safety and mental health of the victimized parent, for his or her ability to protect the children better; third priority, empowering and simultaneously respecting the parents for them to find a direction in their lives and make appropriate choices for their children; fourth priority, placing responsibility on the abusive parent in the context of past and future violent acts; and fifth priority, enabling and advancing a less limiting relationship between the parent and child and creating a parental program from which the child will benefit.

In addition, a model was proposed (Bancroft & Silverman, 2004) that is especially suitable for assessing risk following separation from the abusive man. This model determined points in relation to which information needed to be gathered by the professional authorities: The degree of physical risk to the mother; the history of physical abuse of the children; the history of sexual abuse of the children; modes of psychological abuse of either the mother or the children (the degree of emotional abuse at home is an important variable, according to the shapers of the model, in determining the severity of the difficulties demonstrated by the children); the degree of control and manipulation throughout the relationship; the degree of egocentrism and narcissism; the history of using the child as a weapon through which to hurt the mother; refusal to accept the end of a relationship or the woman's decision to begin a new relationship; degree of risk of abduction; and history of mental illness. Information about the history of the perpetrator's behavior and his perceptions needs to be collected from several sources (since the men's reports were found to be untrustworthy): From the mother, the children, and previous partners; police and courtroom reports; child protection and medical reports; and school staff and anyone else who witnessed relevant incidents (Bancroft & Silverman, 2004). Since then, research in the field of domestic violence and children's exposure to this type of violence has constantly established the body of knowledge in the context of the woman's separation from her violent partner (e.g., Beeble et al., 2007; Galántai et al., 2019; Rogers & Berger, 2022). Following on from this, researchers strengthened the proposal that draws on the need to work according to the model that prioritizes the protection of the child and the woman surrounding visitation arrangements (Humphreys et al., 2020; Stambe & Meyer, 2022; Turhan, 2021).

Despite the various criteria proposed for determining custody and visitation arrangements, there is still inconsistency in the way different judges approach the subject of violence against women, with the issue of custody at the center (Birchall & Choudhry, 2022; Macdonald, 2016; Meier, 2020; Neilson, 2018; Perrin, 2017). The custodial parent (usually the mother) is required to provide evidence of the violence, which makes the children invisible at the most vulnerable time for them (Birnbaum, 2012; Birchall & Choudhry, 2022). Even though a large body of scientific literature presented the "quiet" nature of this kind of abuse (domestic violence) that happens behind closed doors, the obligation to prove is still placed on the victim (Jaffe et al., 2004; Meier, 2020). In other words, psychological abuse, threats, suicidal fantasies, access to a weapon, obsessions, and control all take place in private and therefore are perceived as requiring proof.

The victim, usually the mother, is presented/interpreted as a hysterical personality trying to limit contact with the father and is not perceived as someone who, through her behavior, is reacting to the dynamics of control. The reality is that, often, the judge does not take the issue of the woman's victimization seriously enough and attributes everything to the confrontation between the partners **and not to the specific characteristics of violence** (Barnett, 2014; Birnbaum, 2012; Halperin-Kaddari & Zafran, 2022; Jackman-Ladani, 2020; Ministry of Justice UK, 2020; Perrin, 2017; Silberg & Dallam, 2019; Thiara & Harrisson, 2016; Webb et al., 2021). One common behavior by the violent partner (usually the father) is threatening to gain custody as a way of leaving the partner in the relationship and continuing to hurt her. Recognition of this dynamics is the basis for understanding why custody in the context of domestic violence is more complex (Birchall & Choudhry, 2022; Casas Vila, 2020; Feresin, 2020; Macdonald, 2016; Mackenzie et al., 2020; Perrin, 2017; Thiara & Gill, 2012). In this context, some researchers note the unsuitability of shared custody in cases of domestic violence (Perrin, 2017; Rogers & Berger, 2022), whereas others go even further and suggest supervised visitation arrangements (Macdonald, 2016; Stambe & Meyer, 2022).

The criticism heard regarding the current management is that it is unclear how to take the violence into consideration (Birnbaum, 2012) and that legal approaches to violence in the family throughout the United States and Canada continue to be inconsistent still today (Perrin, 2017). Following on from this, experts in the field of exposure to violence agree on the need for a structured and integrative strategy to provide conditions suitable for intervention with children and their families, after the separation (Rogers & Berger, 2022; Stambe & Meyer, 2022).

The existence of criteria for custody assessment, as well as a model for assessing the man's level of risk to the woman and her children, shows clear recognition by those dealing with the domestic violence field regarding the need to shape circumstances that allow the woman and her children to live outside of the shadow of violence, once the woman has separated from her violent partner. In this context, the reticence in taking the next step forward to define clearly what is the strategy to adopt in cases of custody and visitation arrangements in the context of violence against women, including exerting pressure on legislating laws that will enable clear conduct in these contexts, is unfathomable. In other words, leaving the criteria at a general level rather than taking them to a practical, legal level (determining custody and the nature of visitation arrangements in these situations) is incomprehensible and astonishing.

Examining the field of men's rights in the parental context may shed light on the nature of the chosen conduct. Lawyers from the domestic violence field are worried about an ongoing pattern of abusive behavior by the violent man even after the separation. Contrary to this, some lawyers are concerned about the rights of the men. Lawyers in this field and their supporters claim that current approaches and laws discriminate against men, also from the point of view of accessibility to their children (as noncustodial parents) and of their ability to care for the children, namely to demonstrate emotional involvement and to be full partners in their education. Regarding their view, given the high percentage of divorce, alongside the reality in which custody is invariably given to mothers, and considering the high percentage of children born to unmarried parents, the question of meaningful, serious parental encouragement and support of children by fathers becomes especially relevant. Following on from this, these lawyers are interested in giving men emotional confidence and helping them take responsibility for the lives of their children. They encourage the men to spend time with their children and to provide for their emotional and economic needs (Barnett, 2020; Doherty et al., 1996; McDermott, 2019, personal communication, as cited in Birchall & Choudhry, 2022; Sheeran & Hampton, 1999).

Regarding the discussion in hand, it is noteworthy that fatherhood as a movement developed in the context of changing social norms. That is to say, attention was drawn to historical processes that limited men's place in their children's lives inter alia against a background of a complex, changing social reality in which the role of fathers changed. Changes in gender relations, fathers' greater participation in childrearing, and women's presence in the work force led to the shaping of a perception of egalitarian fatherhood, with involvement in all the family domains (Lamb, 2000; Macdonald, 2017). Following on from this, programs and organizations for fathers' involvement encourage men to find suitable employment and to reorganize their lives in order to take responsibility for their children (Johnson et al., 1998).

In general, fatherhood groups perceive partner violence as a result of conflict and negative interaction between men and women. For some, violence is the natural outcome of conflict. In other words, the groups differ in their willingness to acknowledge and react to masculine violence (Williams et al., 2004).

While responsible fatherhood groups acknowledge the fact of domestic violence but blame its occurrence on the **society** and the movement away from traditional family values (Blankenhorn, 1995), fathers' rights groups **deny** the existence of domestic violence and claim that the responsibility for it lies equally with the man and the woman (Braver & O'Connell, 1998). Following on from this, since the responsible fatherhood groups claim that men are naturally aggressive and when the family breaks down and the society allows them to move away (thereby releasing them from responsibility for the family's well-being), they become more violent; these groups suggest that contact with the family will give men meaning and will immediately reduce the level of violence (Blankenhorn, 1995). This differs from the fathers' rights groups, whose claim of partners' equal responsibility for the violence led them to suggest that when women blame men for the violence, they deliberately intend to deny the men their rights (Braver & O'Connell, 1998).

Analysis of the two approaches reveals an essential difference between them. The responsible fatherhood groups take into account a social context that recognizes that domestic violence exists whereas the fathers' rights group blurs the context and takes into account only the characteristics of the negative gender conflict. Despite these differences, both these approaches advocate a solution based on placing equal responsibility on the man in family life in situations of domestic violence. The responsible fatherhood group does not place responsibility for the domestic violence on the father, as the one who exposes his children to violence because of some problem or deficit of his own. This group holds the society responsible for creating violent circumstances by distancing men from their families (not demanding that they take an active part in caring for the family after the separation). As mentioned above, the basic approach of fathers' rights groups does not acknowledge any deficit in the men and denies that domestic violence exists (calling it mutual violence). It can be observed, therefore, that neither approach accepts the "deficit paradigm" as a basic principle (Lupton & Barclay, 1997) in the context of domestic violence. This paradigm assumes that violent fathers have a dangerous side (Perel & Peled, 2008; Peled, 2000). Contrary to this, the two fatherhood approaches see violence as fundamental human behavior, part of human nature expressed in dysfunctional couple conflicts. Such an approach is directed toward perceiving domestic violence in a partner confrontation context and negates the possibility of taking the woman's victimization and control dynamics seriously in the context of domestic violence.

In the context outlined here, two questions must be asked: First, why did fatherhood, as a movement, not see fit to allocate a place for irregular situations such as men's violence against women? Why did it not create and enable a distinction between normative and deviant situations? Second, why did the feminist approach to understanding violence against women, in general, and within the family system, in particular, not rise against the fatherhood movement in the specific context of violence against women?

I would like to suggest some possible answers to my questions presented above. The answer to the first question might be that, for many years, men were in a sensitive position to which they were afraid to return. The deficit paradigm that, until recently, was dominant in the academic and public discourse on fathers and fatherhood (Lupton & Barclay, 1997) described fatherhood from a remote and pathological viewpoint. The professional literature wrote about the less rich culture of fatherhood, the problematic nature of men and fathers (unaware and emotionally detached), and their lack of involvement in home life (Hawkins & Dollahite, 1997). An additional aspect of this paradigm is the prevalent use of a matricentric approach to fathers, according to which motherhood is a benchmark for good parenting (Doherty et al., 1998). The generative fathering paradigm (Hawkins & Dollahite, 1997), which developed as an antithesis of the deficit paradigm, is part of a relatively new trend for understanding fatherhood in its social context while acknowledging the uniqueness of the fathers' role. Today, fathers appear to experience a gradually increasing space for maneuver in constructing their fatherhood, and the "new father" is perceived as equal and involved in all areas of childcare (Lamb, 2000; Marsiglio et al., 2000). In the newly forming context, the men's recognition of the existence of a large group of men (indeed, the domestic violence dimensions have been shown and continue to be shown to reach epidemic proportions) with deficient and pathological behavior, might, from their point of view, pose a threat. The recognition that they are suitable and obligated to take an active part in their children's lives in general and in situations in which they have separated from their spouse, in particular, may undergo a regression. That is to say, the men preferred a situation where their "cleanliness" was assured and the question of their suitability as parents was not in jeopardy.

The answer to the second question may be more complicated. It would seem that the feminist approach to understanding violence against women, which perceives the gender inequality in relationships between women and men as the source of violence against women, should have strongly opposed approaches that are based on the conflict theory and that completely disregard the gender context of domestic violence. Furthermore, one would have thought that the feminist approach, which sees improvement in fathers' functioning and their increased involvement in their children's upbringing as a feminine interest (Peled, 2000), would have needed to make sure to emphasize and distinguish between most men, **who have the basic desire and moral obligation to care for and educate their children** (e.g., Gerson, 1997) and a **certain group** of men which, despite being large, is still a small percentage of the general population, who put their children at-risk and pose a danger to them from a wide range of aspects. If that is the case, why were these steps not taken?

Cautiously, I wish to draw attention to the hidden reason that may be at the base of this behavior: The woman's "fragile" situation in the context of child protection. Bringing the men's role to the fore and emphasizing their responsibility for the children's difficult situation may necessitate affirming the difficult situation and setting stringent, limiting conditions, including reducing the father's visitation rights to the minimum. Thus, in cases where the woman finds herself subject to insurmountable stress (either economic or psychological) and prefers to return to the situation of captivity rather than coping with an unbearably hard reality, she will immediately become the guilty one, as the one who has had an opportunity and yet has failed to rebuild a new life for herself with her children, or as one who might have deliberately acted against her ex-husband. Either way, the complex reality shows that the woman's state of captivity affects her behavior in the context of attempting to separate from her husband, which directly projects onto her decisions regarding her conduct toward her children. Although this complex situation must be taken into consideration in the child protection context, realistically, it places the woman in a problematic position and again may create a situation in which the question of the woman's ability to protect her children will be discussed, maybe intensively. Given these complex conditions, it would appear that a "win-win-situation" has been created, in which the fatherhood movement, which places men's rights at the center, and the feminist approach, which places women's rights at the center, enable reduced complexity of child abuse by violent men.

3.3 Interventions with violent men and with women victims of domestic violence reflected in the treatment policy for the phenomenon of exposure to interparental violence

As is apparent from the critical analysis above, women's rights as victims and men's rights as abusers in the fatherhood context have become central surrounding the policy of how to treat children exposed to violence. In earlier stages of treating the exposure to violence phenomenon, the way to create a healthier environment for the children was through interventions focused on an attempt to reduce it significantly and eventually to stop the man's violent behavior altogether while creating conditions for the mother's healthy reattachment to her children and for strengthening parental skills that were impossible under conditions of captivity. With time (toward the end of the 2000s), intervention with men made space for the parental dimension and intervention with mothers made space for the subjective motherhood experience as well as for the feminine dimension. Thus, placed in the center was the view that children's best interests depended, first and foremost, on maximizing the contact with both parents.

3.3.1 Intervention with violent men as fathers

At the basis of these interventions is the assumption that, despite the significant deficits in violent men's fatherhood, there is no way of working with these fathers without acknowledging the violating parts of their fatherhood and relating to them (Perel & Peled, 2008; Baker et al., 2004). Therefore, the interventions include components for improving parental skills, confronting the violent child abuse, and attempting to cope with it, as well as listening to the fathers' experience (that they perceive as positive and good, but with deviances) and their longing to be warm fathers, who are significant figures for their children and close to them (Burnette et al., 2015; Perel & Peled, 2008; Rogers & Berger, 2022).

3.3.2 Intervention with mothers who are victims of domestic violence

The interventions with women are based on two central aims: Empowerment and enhanced attachment in the mother–child dyad. In addition, they work on the split in the women's experience between their victimhood and their motherhood (Katz, 2019, 2022; Van den Hoeven et al., 2022; Peled et al., 2000; Peled & Perel, 2010). Despite the different approaches and emphases, researchers agree that women who have been violently abused by their partners require intervention that is empowering on a variety of dimensions, including skills, knowledge, and emotional and material resources, as well as their choices.

Note

1 These explanations are interdependent since the assumption of differential harm is the basis for the claim that many children may gain from the absence of the obligation to report.

References

Alaggia, R., Jenney, A., Mazzuca, J., & Redmond, M. (2007). In whose best interest? A Canadian case study of the impact of child welfare policies in cases of domestic violence. *Journal of Brief Therapy and Crisis Intervention*, 7(4), 275–290. https:///doi.org/10.1093/brief-treatment/mhm018

Appel, J. K., & Kim-Appel, D. (2006). Child maltreatment and domestic violence: Human services issues. *Journal of Health and Human Services Administration*, 29(2), 228–244. http://www.jstor.org/stable/25790689

Artz, S., Jackson, M. A., Rossiter, K. R., Nijdam-Jones, A., Géczy, I., & Porteous, S. (2014). A comprehensive review of the literature on the impact of exposure to intimate partner violence for children and youth. *International Journal of Child, Youth and Family Studies*, 5(4), 493–587. https:///doi.org/10.1016/j.chiabu.2007.10.002

Babcock, J., Green, C., & Robie, C. (2004). Does batterers' treatment work? A meta-analytic review of domestic violence treatment. *Clinical Psychology Review*, 23(8), 1023–1053. https://doi.org/10.1016/j.cpr.2002.07.001

Baker, L. L., Cunningham, A. J., & Jaffe, P. G. (2004). Future directions in ending domestic violence in the lives of children. In P. Jaffe, L. Baker, & A. Cunningham (Eds.), *Protecting children from domestic violence: Strategies for community intervention* (pp. 221–230). The Guilford Press.

Bancroft, L., & Silverman, G. (2002). *The batterer as parent: Addressing the impact of domestic violence on family dynamics*. Sage.

Bancroft, L., & Silverman, G. (2004). Assessing abusers' risks to children. In P. G. Jaffe, L. L. Baker, & A. J. Cunningham (Eds.), *Protecting children from domestic violence: Strategies for community intervention* (pp. 101–119). The Guilford Press.

Bancroft, L., Silverman, J. G., & Ritchie, D. (2012). *The batterer as parent: Addressing the impacts of domestic violence on family dynamics* (2nd ed.). Sage.

Banks, D., Dutch, N., & Wang, K. (2008). Collaborative efforts to improve system response to families who are experiencing child maltreatment and domestic violence. *Journal of Interpersonal Violence*, *23*(7), 876–902. https://doi.org/10.1177/0886260508314690

Barnett, A. (2014). Contact at all costs? Domestic violence and children's welfare. *Child and Family Law Quarterly*, *26*(4), 439–462. https://bura.brunel.ac.uk/handle/2438/10241

Barnett, A. (2020). A genealogy of hostility: Parental alienation in England and Wales. *Journal of Social Welfare and Family Law*, *42*(1), 18–29. https://doi.org/10.1080/09649069.2019.1701921

Beeble, M. L., Bybee, D., & Sullivan, C. M. (2007). Abusive men's use of children to control their partners and ex-partners. *European Psychologist*, *12*(1), 54–61. https://doi.org/10.1027/1016-9040.12.1.54

Berg, K. A., Bender, A. E., Evans, K. E., Holmes, M. R., Davis, A. P., Scaggs, A. L., & King, J. A. (2020). Service needs of children exposed to domestic violence: Qualitative findings from a statewide survey of domestic violence agencies. *Children and Youth Services Review*, *18*, 105414. https://doi.org/10.1016/j.childyouth.2020.105414

Bidarra, Z. S., Lessard, G., & Dumont, A. (2016). Co-occurrence of intimate partner violence and sexual abuse: Prevalence, risk factors and related issues. *Child Abuse and Neglect*, *55*, 10–21. https://doi.org/10.1016/j.chiabu.2016.03.007

Birchall, J., & Choudhry, S. (2022). "I was punished for telling the truth: "How allegations of parental alienation are used to silence, sideline and disempower survivors of domestic abuse in family law proceedings. *Journal of Gender-Based Violence*, *6*(1), 115–131. https://doi.org/10.1332/239868021X16287966471815

Birnbaum, R. (2012). Rendering children invisible: The forces at play during separation and divorces in the context of family violence. In R. Alaggia & C. Vine (Eds.), *Cruel but not unusual: Violence in Canadian families* (pp. 371–412). Wilfrid Laurier University Press.

Black, T., Fallon, B., Nikolova, K., Tarshis, S., Baird, S., & Carradine, J. (2020). Exploring subtypes of children's exposure to intimate partner violence. *Children and Youth Services Review*, *118*, 105375. https://doi.org/10.1016/j.childyouth.2020.105375

Blankenhorn, D. (1995). *Fatherless America: Confronting our most urgent social problem*. Beacon Press.

Brandon, M., Bailey, S., Belderson, P., Gardner, R., Sidebotham, P., Dodsworth, J., Warren, C., & Black, J. (2009). *Understanding serious case reviews and their impact: A biennial analysis of serious case reviews 2005–07* (Research Report DCSF-RR129). Department for Children, Schools and Families.

Braver, S., & O'Connell, D. (1998). *Divorced dads: Shattering the myths*. Tarcher Putnam.

Buckley, H. (2018). Editorial. *Australian Social Work, 71*(2), 131–134. https://doi.org/10.1080/0312407x.2018.1438029

Burnette, C. E., Ferreira, R. J., & Buttell, F. (2015). Male parenting attitudes and batterer intervention: Assessing child maltreatment risk. *Research on Social Work Practice, 27*(4), 468–477. https://doi.org/10.1177/1049731515579202

Bushinski, C. (2017). Handling kids in crisis with care. *Educational Leadership, 75*(4), 66–67. https://www.ascd.org/el/articles/handling-kids-in-crisis-with-care

Campbell, E. (2017). How domestic violence batterers use custody proceedings in family courts to abuse victims, and how courts can put a stop to it. *UCLA Journal of Gender and Law, 24*(1), 41–66. http://dx.org/10.5070/L3241036415

Carter, L. S., Weithorn, L. A., & Behrman, R. E. (1999). Domestic violence and children: Analysis and recommendations. *The Future of Children, 9*(3), 4–20. https://doi.org/10.2307/1602778

Casas Vila, G. (2020). Parental alienation syndrome in Spain: Opposed byt the government but accepted in courts. *Journal of Social Welfare and Family Law, 42*(1), 45–55. https://doi.org/10.1080/09649069.2019.1701923

Clarke, A., & Wydall, S. (2015). From 'Rights to Action': Practitioners' perceptions of the needs of children experiencing domestic violence. *Child and Family Social Work, 20*(2), 181–190. https://doi.org/10.1111/cfs.12066

Coulter, M. L., & Mercado-Crespo, M. C. (2015). Co-occurrence of intimate partner violence and child maltreatment: Service providers' perceptions. *Journal of Family Violence, 30*(2), 255–262. https://doi.org/10.1007/s10896-014-9667-5

Courtney, M., Dworsky, A., Ruth, A., Keller, T., Havlicek, J., & Bost, J. (2005). *Midwest evaluation of the adult functioning of former foster youth: Outcomes at age 19*. Chapin Hall Center for Children.

Coy, M., Perks, K., Scott, E., & Tweedale, R. (2012). *Picking up the pieces: Domestic violence and child contact*. Rights of Women.

Coy, M., Scott, E., Tweedale, R., & Perks, K. (2015). "It's like going through the abuse again": Domestic violence and women and children's (un)safety in private law contact proceedings. *Journal of Social Welfare and Family Law, 37*(1), 53–69. https://doi.org/10.1080/09649069.2015.1004863

Davies, L., & Krane, J. (2006). Collaborate with caution: Protecting children, helping mothers. *Critical Social Policy, 26*(2), 412–425. https://doi.org/10.1177/0261018306062592

Doherty, W. J., Kouneski, E. F., & Erickson, M. F. (1996). Responsible fathering: An overview and conceptual framework. *Report for the Administration for Children and Families and the Office of the Assistant Secretary for Planning and Evaluation of the United States Department of Health and Human Services*, (pp. 1–55). Washington, DC.

Doherty, W. J., Kouneski, E. F., & Erickson, M. F. (1998). Responsible fathering: An overview and conceptual framework. *Journal of Marriage and the Family, 60*(2), 277–292. https://doi.org/10.2307/353848

Eckhardt, C. I., Murphy, C. M., Whitaker, D. J., Sprunger, J., Dykstra, R., & Woodard, K. (2013). The effectiveness of intervention programs for perpetrators and victims of intimate partner violence. *Partner Abuse, 4*(2), 196–231. https://doi.org/10.1891/1946-6560.4.2.196

Edleson, J. (2004). Should childhood exposure to adult domestic violence be defined as child maltreatment under the law? In P. Jaffe, L. Baker, & A. Cunningham (Eds.), *Protecting children from domestic violence: Strategies for community intervention* (pp. 8–29). The Guilford Press.

Edleson, J. L., Gassman-Pines, J., & Hill, M. B. (2006). Defining child exposure to domestic violence as neglect: Minnesota's difficult experience. *Social Work, 51*(2), 167–174. https://doi.org/10.1093/sw/51.2.167

Eriksson, M., Hester, M., Keskinen, S., & Pringle, K. (2005). *Tackling men's violence in families: Nordic issues and dilemmas*. Policy Press.

Feresin, M. (2020). Parental alienation (syndrome) in child custody cases: Survivors' experiences and the logic of psychosocial and legal services in Italy. *Journal of Social Welfare and Family Law, 42*(1), 56–67. https://doi.org/10.1080/09649069.2019.1701924

Feresin, M., Bastiani, F., Beltramini, L., & Romito, P. (2019). The involvement of children in postseparation intimate partner violence in Italy: A strategy to maintain coercive control? *Affilia, 34*(4), 481–497. https://doi.org/10.1177/0886109919857672

Finkelhor, D., Turner, H. A., Hamby, S. L., & Ormrod, R. K. (2011). Poly-victimization: Children's exposure of multiple types of violence, crime and abuse. *OJJDP- juvenile justice bulletin – NCJ235504* (pp. 1–12). US Government Printing Office.

Fleury, R. E., Sullivan, C. M., & Bybee, D. I. (2000). When ending the relationship does not end the violence: Women's experiences of violence by former partners. *Violence Against Women, 6*(12), 1363–1383. https://doi.org/10.1177/10778010022183695

Galántai, J., Ligeti, A. S., & Wirth, J. (2019). Children exposed to violence: Child custody and its effects in intimate partner violence related cases in Hungary. *Journal of Family Violence, 34*(5), 399–409. https://doi.org/10.1007/s10896-019-00066-y

Gerson, K. (1997). An institutional perspective on generative fathering: Creating social supports for parenting equality. In A. J. Hawkins & D. C. Dollahite (Eds.), *Generative fathering: Beyond deficit perspectives* (pp. 36–51). Sage.

Haddix, A. (1996). Unseen victims: Acknowledging the effects of domestic violence on children through statutory termination of parental rights. *California Law Review, 84*(3), 757–815. https://doi.org/10.2307/3480965

Halperin-Kaddari, R., & Zafran, R. (2022). Bothersome alienation. *Haruv Institute, Nekudat Mifgash Journal, 22*, 50–55. (Hebrew).

Harne, L., & Radford, J. (1994). Reinstating patriarchy: The politics of the family and the new legislation. In A. Mullender & R. Morley (Eds.), *Children living with domestic violence: Putting men's abuse of women on the child care agenda* (pp. 68–85). Whiting & Birch.

Harrison, C. (2008). Implacably hostile or appropriately protective? Women managing child contact in the context of domestic violence. *Violence Against Women, 14*(4), 381–405. https://doi.org/10.1177/1077801208314833

Hawkins, A. J., & Dollahite, D. C. (Eds.). (1997). *Generative fathering: Beyond deficit perspectives*. Sage.

Hay, C., Grobbelaar, M., & Guggisberg, M. (2021). Mothers' post-separation experiences of male partner abuse: An exploratory study. *Journal of Family Issues, 0*(0). https://doi.org/10.1177/0192513X211057541

Hazen, A. L., Connelly, C. D., Edleson, J. L., Kelleher, K. J., Landverk, J. A., Coben, J. H., Barth, R. P., McGeehan, J., Rolls, J. A., & Nuszkowski, M. A. (2007). Assessment of intimate partner violence by child welfare services. *Children and Youth Services Review, 29*(4), 490–500. https://doi.org/10.1016/j.childyouth.2006.10.004

Henry, C. (2017). Expanding the legal framework for child protection: Recognition of and response to child exposure to domestic violence in California law. *Social Service Review, 91*(2), 203–232. https://doi.org/10.1086/692399

Hester, M., & Radford, L. (1996). *Domestic violence and child contact arrangements in England and Denmark.* Policy Press.

Heward-Belle, S. (2015). The diverse fathering practices of men who perpetrate domestic violence. *Australian Social Work, 69*(3), 323–337. https://doi.org/10.1080/0312407X.2015.1057748

Hollin, C. R. (2016). *The psychology of interpersonal violence* (pp. 77–89). John Wiley & Sons.

Holmes, M. R., Bender, A. E., Crampton, D. S., Voith, L. A., & Prince, D. M. (2019). Research foundations of GreenBook interventions to address the co-occurrence of child maltreatment and adult domestic violence. *Juvenile and Family Court Journal, 70*(4), 11–36. https://doi.org/10.1111/jfcj.12150

Holt, S., Buckley, H., & Whelan, S. (2008). The impact of exposure to domestic violence on children and young people: A review of the literature. *Child Abuse and Neglect, 32*(8), 797–810. https://doi.org/10.1016/j.chiabu.2008.02.004

Howell, K. H., Miller-Graff, L. E., Hasselle, A. J., & Scrafford, K. E. (2017). The unique needs of pregnant, violent-exposed women: A systematic review of current interventions and directions for translational research, 128–138. https://doi.org/10.1016/j.avb.2017.01.021

Humphreys, C., Diemer, K., Bornemisza, A., Spiteri-Staines, A., Kaspiew, R., & Horsfall, B. (2019). More present than absent: Men who use domestic violence and their fathering. *Child and Family Social Work, 24*(2), 321–329. https://doi.org/10.1111/cfs.12617

Humphreys, C., Healey, L., Kirkwood, D., & Nicholson, D. (2018). Children living with domestic violence: A differential response through multi-agency collaboration. *Australian Social Work, 71*(2), 162–174. https://doi.org/10.1080/0312407X.2017.1415366

Humphreys, C., & Thiara, R. (2003). Mental health and domestic violence: 'I call it symptoms of abuse'. *The British Journal of Social Work, 33*(2), 209–226. https://doi.org/10.1093/bjsw/33.2.209

Irwin, J., Waugh, F., & Bonner, M. (2006). The inclusion of children and young people in research on domestic violence. *Communities, Children and Families, 1*(1). https://search.informit.org/doi/10.3316/informit.370827115003727

Jackman-Ladani, O. (2020). *Custody and child support: Chaos and judicial activism in the family courts* [Unpublished master's thesis]. Tel Aviv University (Hebrew).

Jaffe, P. G., Baker, L. L., & Cunningham, A. J. (Eds.). (2004). *Protecting children from domestic violence: Strategies for community intervention.* The Guilford Press.

Jaffe, P. G., Johnston, J. R., Crooks, C. V., & Bala, N. (2008). Custody disputes involving allegations of domestic violence: The need for differentiated approaches to parenting plans. *Family Court Review*, *46*(3), 500–522. https://doi.org/10.1111/j.1744-1617.2008.00216.x

Jaffe, P. G., Lemon, N. K. D., & Poisson, S. E. (2003). *Child custody & domestic violence: A call for safety and accountability*. Sage.

Jenney, A., & Alaggia, R. (2012). Children's exposure to domestic violence: Integrating policy, research, and practice to address children's mental health. In R. Alaggia & C. Vine (Eds.), *Cruel but not unusual: Violence in Canadian families* (pp. 303–336). Wilfrid Laurier University Press.

Johnson, E., Levin, A., & Doolittle, F. C. (1998). *Father's fair share: Helping poor men manage child support and fatherhood*. Russell Sage Foundation.

Katz, E. (2019). Coercive control, domestic violence, and a five-factor framework: Five factors that influence closeness, distance, and strain in mother–child relationships. *Violence Against Women*, *25*(15), 1829–1853. https://doi.org/10.1177/1077801218824998

Katz, E. (2022). *Coercive control in children's and mothers' lives*. Oxford University Press.

Katz, E., Nikupeteri, A., & Laitinen, M. (2020). When coercive control continues to harm children: Post-separation fathering, stalking and domestic violence. *Child Abuse Review*, *29*(4), 310–324. https://doi.org/10.1002/car.2611

Kelly, L., Sharp, N., & Klein, R. (2014). *Finding the costs of freedom: How women and children rebuild their lives after domestic violence*. Solace Women's Aid.

Kim, M. E. (2013). Challenging the pursuit of criminalization in the era of mass incarceration: The limitations of social work responses to domestic violence in the USA. *British Journal of Social Work*, *43*(7), 1276–1293. https://doi.org/10.1093/bjsw/bcs060

Kracke, K., & Cohen, E. P. (2008). The safe start initiative: Building and disseminating knowledge to support children exposed to violence. *Journal of Emotional Abuse*, *8*(1–2), (1–2). https://doi.org/10.1080/10926790801986031

Laing, L., Humphreys, C., & Cavanagh, K. (2013). *Social work and domestic violence: Critical and reflective practice*. Sage.

Lamb, M. E. (2000). The history of research on father involvement: An overview. In H. E. Peters, G. W. Peterson, S. K. Steinmetz, & R. D. Day (Eds.), *Fatherhood: Research, interventions and policies* (pp. 23–42). Haworth.

Langenderfer-Magruder, L., Alven, L., Wilke, D. J., & Spinelli, C. (2019). "Getting everyone on the same page": Child welfare workers' collaboration challenges on cases involving intimate partner violence. *Journal of Family Violence*, *34*(1), 21–31. https://doi.org/10.1007/s10896-018-0002-4

Leberg, E. (1997). *Understanding child molesters: Taking charge*. Sage.

Lee, S. J., Bellamy, J. L., & Guterman, N. B. (2009). Fathers, physical child abuse, and neglect: Advancing the knowledge base. *Child Maltreatment*, *14*(3), 227–231. https://doi.org/10.1177/1077559509339388

Lupton, D., & Barclay, L. (1997). *Constructing fatherhood: Discourses and experiences*. Sage.

Macdonald, G. S. (2016). Domestic violence and private family court proceedings: Promoting child welfare or promoting contact? *Violence Against Women*, *22*(7), 832–852. https://doi.org/10.1177/1077801215612600

Macdonald, G. S. (2017). Hearing children's voices? Including children's perspectives on their experiences of domestic violence in welfare reports prepared for the English courts in private family law proceedings. *Child Abuse and Neglect*, *65*, 1–13. https://doi.org/10.1016/j.chiabu.2016.12.013

Mackenzie, D., Herbert, R., & Robinson, L. (2020). 'It's not OK'. But 'it' never happened: Parental alienation accusations undermine children's safety in the New Zealand family court. *Journal of Social Welfare and Family Law*, *42*(1), 106–117. https://doi.org/10.1080/09649069.2020.1701942

Macvean, M. L., Humphreys, C., & Healey, L. (2018). Facilitating the collaborative interface between child protection and specialist domestic violence services: A scope review. *Australian Social Work*, *71*(2), 148–161. https://doi.org/10.1080/0312407X.2017.1415365

Macy, R. J., Giattina, M. C., Parish, S. L., & Crosby, C. (2010). Domestic violence and sexual assault services: Historical concerns and contemporary challenges. *Journal of Interpersonal Violence*, *25*(1), 3–32. https://doi.org/10.1177/0886260508329128

Maglinte, J. A., Reyes, M. E. S., & Balajadia, H. A. (2016). "I choked her but I did not punch her": Constructions of intimate partner violence among men in the Philippines. *Psychological Studies*, *61*(4), 321–330. https://doi.org/10.1007/s12646-016-0376-4

Margolin, G., John, R., Ghosh, C., & Gordis, E. (1996). Family interaction process: An essential tool for exploring abusive relationships. In D. Cahn & S. Lloyd (Eds.), *Family violence from a communication perspective* (pp. 37–58). Sage.

Marsiglio, W., Amato, P., Day, R. D., & Lamb, M. E. (2000). Scholarship on fatherhood in the 1990s and beyond. *Journal of Marriage and Family*, *62*(4), 1173–1191. https://doi.org/10.1111/j.1741-3737.2000.01173.x

Meier, J. S. (2020). U.S. custody outcomes in cases involving parental alienation and abuse allegations: What do the data show? *Journal of Social Welfare and Family Law*, *42*(1), 92–105. https://doi.org/10.1080/09649069.2020.1701941

Ministry of Justice, UK. (2020). *Assessing risk of harm to children and parents in private law children cases* (Final Report). https://assets.publishing.service.gov.uk/government/uploads/system/uploads/attachment_data/file/895173/assessing-risk-harm-children-parents-pl-childrens-cases-report_.pdf

Murray, C., Wyche, B., & Johnson, C. (2020). The community-level impact of a family justice center: Indicators from the Guilford County Family Justice Center. *Journal of Aggression, Conflict and Peace Research*, *12*(1), 1–20. https://doi.org/10.1108/JACPR-10-2019-0444

Neilson, S. C. (2018). *Parental alienation empirical analysis: Child best interests or parental rights?* Muriel McQueen Fergusson Centre for Family Violence Research and Vancouver: The FREDA Centre for Research on Violence Against Women and Children.

Øverlien, C. (2010). Children exposed to domestic violence: Conclusions from the literature and challenges ahead. *Journal of Social Work*, *10*(1), 80–97. https://doi.org/10.1177/1468017309350663

Panzer, P. G., Philip, M. B., & Hayward, R. A. (2000). Trends in domestic violence service and leadership: Implications for an integrated shelter model. *Administration and Policy in Mental Health*, *27*(5), 339–352. https://doi.org/10.1023/A:1021941129326

Peled, E. (2000). The parenting of men who abuse women: Issues and dilemmas. *British Journal of Social Work*, *30*(1), 25–36. https://doi.org/10.1093/bjsw/30.1.25

Peled, E., Eisikovits, Z., Enosh, G., & Winstok, Z. (2000). Choice and empowerment for battered women who stay: Towards a constructivist model. *Social Work*, *45*(1), 9–25. https://doi.org/10.1093/sw/45.1.9

Peled, E., & Perel, G. (2010). The mothering of women abused by their partner: An outcome evaluation of a group intervention. *Research on Social Work Practice*, *20*(4), 391–402. https://doi.org/10.1177/1049731510362225

Perel, G., & Peled, E. (2008). The fathering of violent men: Constriction and yearning. *Violence Against Women*, *14*(4), 457–482. https://doi.org/10.1177/1077801208314846

Perrin, R. L. (2017). Overcoming biased views of gender and victimhood in custody evaluations when domestic violence is alleged. *American University Journal of Gender, Social Policy and & the Law*, *25*(2), 155–177. Retrieved from https://digitalcommons.wcl.american.edu/jgspl/vol25/iss2/2/?utm_source=digitalcommons.wcl.american.edu%2Fjgspl%2Fvol25%2Fiss2%2F2&utm_medium=PDF&utm_campaign=PDFCoverPages

Richardson-Foster, H., Stanley, M., Miller, P., & Thomson, G. (2012). Police intervention in domestic violence incidents where children are present: Police and children's perspectives. *Policing and Society*, *22*(2), 220–234. https://doi.org/10.1080/10439463.2011.636815

Rogers, K., & Berger, E. (2022). A systematic review of children's perspectives of fathers who perpetrate intimate partner violence. *Trauma, Violence, and Abuse*, 1–20. https://doi.org/10.1177/15248380221124268

Rogers, M. M., & Parkinson, K. P. (2018). Exploring approaches to child welfare in contexts of domestic violence and abuse: Family group conferences. *Child and Family Social Work*, *23*(1), 105–112. http://doi.org/10.1111/cfs.12389

Salter, A. (1995). *Transforming trauma: A guide to understanding and treating adult survivors of child sexual abuse*. Sage.

Sharp-Jeffs, N., Kelly, L., & Klein, R. (2018). Long journeys toward freedom: The relationship between coercive control and space for action—Measurement and emerging evidence. *Violence Against Women*, *24*(2), 163–185. https://doi.org/10.1177/1077801216686199

Sheeran, M., & Hampton, S. (1999). Supervised visitation in cases of domestic violence. *Juvenile and Family Court Journal*, *50*(2), 13–26. https://doi.org/10.1111/j.1755-6988.1999.tb00796.x

Shields, J. P. (2008). An evaluation of police compliance with domestic violence documentation policy reform: Improving the identification of exposed children. *Best Practices in Mental Health*, *4*(1), 65–73.

Shlonsky, A., Friend, C., & Lambert, L. (2007). From culture clash to new possibilities: A harm reduction approach to family violence and child protection services. *Brief Treatment and Crisis Intervention*, *7*(4), 345–363. https://doi.org/10.1093/brief-treatment/mhm015

Shlonsky, A., & Wagner, D. (2005). The next step: Integrating actuarial risk assessment and clinical judgment into an evidence-based practice framework in CPS case management. *Children and Youth Services Review*, *27*(4), 409–427. https://doi.org/10.1016/j.childyouth.2004.11.007

Silberg, J., & Dallam, S. (2019). Abusers gaining custody in family courts: A case series of overturned decisions. *Journal of Child Custody, 16*(2), 140–169. https://doi.org/10.1080/15379418.2019.1613204

Stambe, R. M., & Meyer, S. (2022). Police and duty lawyer perceptions of domestic violence protection order proceedings involving parents: Towards greater system accountability and family-centred decision-making. *Journal of Family Violence*. https://doi.org/10.1007/s10896-022-00449-8

Stanley, J., & Goddard, C. (2002). *In the firing line: Violence and power in child protection work*. John Wiley & Sons.

Stanley, N. (2015). *Moving towards integrated domestic violence services for children and families*. Jessica Kingsley.

Stanley, N., & Humphreys, C. (2014). Multi-agency risk assessment and management for children and families experiencing domestic violence. *Children and Youth Services Review, 47*, 78–85. https://doi.org/10.1016/j.childyouth.2014.06.003

Stover, C. S., Meadows, A. L., & Kaufman, J. (2009). Interventions for intimate partner violence: Review and implications for evidence-based practice. *Professional Psychology: Research and Practice, 40*(3), 223–233. https://doi.org/10.1037/a0012718

Stover, C. S., Tobon, A. L., McFaul, C., & Gorio, M. C. F. (2022). A conceptual understanding of intimate partner violence behaviors in men: Implications for research and intervention. *Aggression and Violent Behavior, 65*, 1–9. https://doi.org/10.1016/j.avb.2022.101763

Thiara, R. K., & Gill, A. (2012). *Domestic violence, child contact, post-separation violence: Issues for South Asian and African-Caribbean women and children: A report of finding*. NSPCC.

Thiara, R., & Harrison, C. (2016). *Safe not sorry: Supporting the campaign for safer child contact*. Women's Aid.

Turhan, Z. (2021). Safe father–child contact postseparation in situations of intimate partner violence and positive fathering skills: A literature review. *Trauma, Violence, and Abuse, 22*(4), 856–869. https://doi.org/10.1177/1524838019888554

Van den Hoeven, M. L., Widdershoven, G. A. M., Van Duin, E. M., Hein, I. M., & Lindauer, R. J. L. (2022). A resilience enhancing trauma-informed program for children and mothers in domestic violence shelters: A qualitative study. *Child and Family Social Work*. https://doi.org/10.1111/cfs.12981

Van Parys, A.-S., Verhamme, A., Temmerman, M., & Verstraelen, H. (2014). Intimate partner violence and pregnancy: A systematic review of interventions. *PLOS ONE, 9*(1), Article e85084. https://doi.org/10.1371/journal.pone.0085084

Walby, S., & Allen, J. (2004). *Domestic violence, sexual assault and stalking: Findings from the British Crime Survey* (Home Office Research Study 276). Home Office.

Wathen, C. N., & MacMillan, H. L. (2013). Children's exposure to intimate partner violence: Impacts and interventions. *Paediatrics and Child Health, 18*(8), 419–422. https://doi.org/10.1093/pch/18.8.419

Webb, N., Moloney, L. J., Smyth, B. M., & Murphy, R. L. (2021). Allegations of child sexual abuse: An empirical analysis of published judgements from the family court of Australia 2012–2019. *Australian Journal of Social Issues, 56*(2), 1–22. https://doi.org/10.1002/ajs4.171

Whitaker, D. J., Baker, C. K., & Arias, I. (2008). Interventions to prevent intimate partner violence. In L. S. Doll, S. E. Bonzo, J. A. Mercy, D. A. Sleet, & E. N. Haas (Eds.), *Handbook of injury and violence prevention* (pp. 203–221). Springer.

Williams, O. J., Boggess, J., & Carter, J. (2004). Fatherhood and domestic violence: Exploring the role of abusive men in the lives of their children. In P. Jaffe, L. Baker, & A. Cunningham (Eds.), *Protecting children from domestic violence: Strategies for community intervention* (pp. 120–137). The Guilford Press.

Women's Aid National Survey. (2016). https://www.womensaid.org.uk/evidence-hub/research-and-publications/annual-survey-2016/

Woodlock, D. (2017). The abuse of technology in domestic violence and stalking. *Violence Against Women, 23*(5), 584–602. https://doi.org/10.1177/1077801216646277

Zweig, J. M., & Burt, M. R. (2007). Predicting women's perceptions of domestic violence and sexual assault agency helpfulness: What matters to program clients? *Violence Against Women, 13*(11), 1149–1178. https://doi.org/10.1177/1077801207307799

Chapter 4

The phenomenology of the experience of exposure to interparental violence

An overall analysis of the literature reviews presented in the previous chapters—relating to the field of exposure to violence, the field of intervention with the children, and the treatment policy—indicates that the knowledge field centered on "children exposed to violence" has developed differently from other knowledge fields dealing with child abuse and neglect. This is because the phenomenon of exposure to violence is related to a core phenomenon—men's violence against women, which, in a sense, underlies the phenomenon of children exposed to violence. This phenomenon within a phenomenon not only increases the children's vulnerability in view of their exposure to a variety of abusive behaviors by their fathers toward their mothers and toward them but, in actual fact, also obscures their vulnerability. This is partly because they are, supposedly, secondary victims and outside the direct spotlight of abuse, but it is mainly due to the complex nature of their state of captivity, which generally does not allow a change to take place for the children in the violent reality while demanding consideration of the special circumstances of the context of men's violence against women. In the woman's context, I am referring to the fact that it is morally impossible to disregard her ongoing state of being a victim of abuse, and we must take into account the way she can or cannot function in this situation. In the man's context, I am referring to the generalized statement that "a large number of men are involved in violence against women," a statement which, if not placed in a specific context, is threatening to the perception that men both need and are capable of taking an active part in their children's lives.

This situation of duality that has developed (intensifying and yet obscuring the children's vulnerability and abuse) has led to the formation of solutions which, albeit unintentionally, have not focused, first and foremost, on the children's needs. These solutions were successful in dealing with the phenomenon externally, by recognizing that these children are at risk and, for a while, categorizing exposure to violence as a subfield of child abuse, exactly like other subfields (although since then, it has been removed from the definition in most of the United States). However, they did not provide a genuine response to the children's distress, given the constant need to consider the sensitive status of all the sides involved—the perpetrating man and the victimized woman, and an in-depth investigation of the complexity of the experience of the children's exposure to violence was laid aside. Had such an investigation been performed, the child abuse would have been more starkly apparent, promptly accentuating the man's perpetrating role while simultaneously turning the spotlight on the circumstances of captivity in which the children are living and on the urgent need for change. (As mentioned above, responsibility for bringing about the change would fall more heavily on the mother.)

This special structure of the phenomenon of exposure to violence, of child abuse in the context of women abuse, demands creative solutions to deal with the problem as a whole. The complexity cannot be used as an excuse to continue to leave the children in a place that does not expose how its depth and diversity were formed. Although this learning may expose larger dimensions of abuse than have previously come to light and may place the circumstances of captivity as well as the one responsible for them in a more problematic place than has been learned to date, our moral obligation is, first and foremost, to the children, as those forced to live in these circumstances with no opportunity to choose. The creative solutions as to the best way to act in view of these data will be found. The direction of obscuring the phenomenon, which places in-depth learning about the children's experience in a kind of limbo, has not been proven as helpful for any of the sides involved. On the contrary, it seems that the absence of in-depth learning has reinforced and tightened the captivity circumstances without providing a solution for any of those involved in this complex family system—neither for the abusers, nor the women victims, nor for the child victims. Therefore, it seems that the time is ripe to change direction and to attempt to create new solutions, for the children as well as for the women and the men.

In this chapter, I will present the findings of a nationwide research that I conducted in Israel (Carmel, 2010). It was an in-depth study of the experience of exposure to violence, relating to the broad dimensions of the phenomenon against a background of core processes anchored within it, namely the escalation of interparental confrontations to all-out violence. In fact, this was an important qualitative study for three reasons: 1) Its scope, comprising 27 in-depth interviews with children exposed to violence—a large number for qualitative research, allowing good sampling of criteria. Even though qualitative research does not profess to generalize, sampling according to a sampling table that presents each criterion well enables better validity of the data. 2) The study was conducted in violence prevention centers and not among a participant sample from shelters. Research in the field of exposure to violence is lacking because of the difficulty in locating sample populations outside shelters and the resulting inability to generalize the findings. 3) The participants were sampled from centers in all areas of the country, north, south, east, and center. In addition, the study has theoretical implications for understanding the huge number of cases of direct (physical and sexual) abuse among children who are exposed to violence, and they will be discussed as part of understanding the overall phenomenon of exposure to violence.

In order to achieve a coherent, clear, and integrative presentation of the research findings, which will enable the readers a smooth transition to the implications of the findings for the new interventions proposed (see Chapters 5 and 6), I have written them in two separate sections referring, in fact, to two separate studies with the same research method. That is to say, in Study 2, to avoid repetition of the method, in the parts relating to the sample and participants, research tool, data collection, and data analysis, I refer the reader to Study 1, while emphasizing the content areas relevant to the analysis in each separate study. Each section addresses different research questions that were raised during the study, and Study 2 (Section 4.2) integrates the study findings to show how they project onto the characteristics of direct abuse of the children who are exposed to violence. Therefore, an additional dimension is introduced to the one that emerged "clean" from the study findings. The reference list appears at the very end of the chapter in order not to disrupt the continuity of the text.[1]

4.1 Study 1. The perception of daily reality among children exposed to their father's violence against their mother: An intense bipolar experience

4.1.1 Introduction

This study was designed to examine the complexity of the experience of children exposed to their father's violence against their mother, in regard to the escalation stages of the interparental conflict.

The body of knowledge in the field to date has dealt mainly with the outcomes of children's exposure to interparental violence and has therefore advanced the perception of a population at risk in need of assistance and support. Nevertheless, this body of knowledge has scarcely examined the way in which these risks were expressed in practice and thus provides limited information about how to cope with the phenomenon.

4.1.2 Literature review

The literature review on the influence of interparental violence on children shows that living in a violent environment has a negative impact on their physical, cognitive, emotional, social, and behavioral development (e.g., Fong et al., 2019; Graham-Bermann & Edleson, 2001; Holt et al., 2008; MacMillan et al., 2013). It was found, for example, that compared to children from normative families, children living with violence suffer from emotional distress, anxiety, depression, mood swings, posttraumatic reactions, and suicidal thoughts (e.g., Evans et al., 2008; Sonego et al., 2018). They demonstrate lower academic and social capability (e.g., Carlson et al., 2019; Jouriles et al., 2001) and show more frequent use of drugs and alcohol, as well as more frequent displays of aggressiveness and other anti-social behaviors (e.g., Fong et al., 2017; Foy et al., 2011).

A limited number of studies—mainly qualitative and clinical—focused on how children experience the violent incidents. The overall data that emerged from these studies provide a degree of depth of understanding of the complex, multidimensional experience of children who are exposed to violence (Ericksen & Henderson, 1992; Humphreys, 1991; Peled, 1993). Peled (1997) suggested four characteristic types that represent this experience: 1) Living with the Secret, in which the child denies the existence of the violence and acts as if it does not exist; 2) Living with Conflicts of Loyalty, in which the child is aware of the violence but cannot take sides; 3) Living in Terror and Fear, in which the child is completely aware of the violence and identifies with the victim, and 4) Adopting the Violent Model, in which the child is aware of the violence but identifies with the aggressor. Based on these types, the cognitive processes that lead to their appearance were examined, providing an understanding of how these processes influence the child's meaning-making system (Eisikovits et al., 1998).

Later, the aforementioned theoretical conceptualization was expanded to a general theoretical model, which includes three components: The child's construction of the reality, parental expectations, and influences from outside the home (Eisikovits & Winstok, 2001). According to this model, the child's construction of the reality will largely be a result of parental expectations, which define the awareness of violence on a continuum ranging from denial to exaggeration. A normative construction of the reality is likely to be a result of essential influences from outside the home (e.g., Anderson, 2012; Gewirtz & Edleson, 2007; Cameranesi et al., 2022).

To understand the children's overall experience, it is important to examine their perceptions, involvement, and the meaning they attribute to the escalation of the interparental conflicts to all-out violence.

In the literature dealing with escalation in intimate violence systems, several studies have examined the way in which interparental conflicts led to all-out verbal aggressiveness and physical violence. These studies represented the masculine (Winstok et al., 2002) and feminine viewpoints (Eisikovits et al., 2002) on the process, as well as an integrative viewpoint (Winstok, 2007).

In this context, it was found that men perceive their actions during the conflicts as reactivity to their partner's behavior. They tend to focus on the partner's actions, which they perceive as undermining the interpersonal balance and threatening their existential reality. In contrast, the women see the transition from a nonviolent to a violent reality as a process. They evaluate the change as marked by distinct junctures, which each hold the possibility of escalation to violence or of an escape from it. The attempt to unify the two viewpoints while refining the points of similarity and difference between men and women led to a general view. According to this view, both the man and the woman involved have the inner potential to see themselves both as aggressors and as victims. Therefore, individuals perceive the situation as an ongoing problem, in which they are the victim, and the instigator of the problem is the aggressor (Winstok, 2007, 2013).

4.1.3 The research questions

As can be seen, in all the studies on the topic of interparental conflicts escalating to all-out violence, the children's viewpoint has not received attention. This is despite the fact that these studies were based on the assumption that the children are not only influenced but also have an influence on the way the conflicts arise, develop, and escalate. In other words, and in this context, the child is an active agent. In light of this, the central research questions were as follows: 1) How do the children see their father, their mother, themselves, and their siblings throughout the escalating interparental conflict? 2) How are the children involved in all the stages of the escalation process? (What are they doing? What is their role?)

4.1.4 Study method

The aim of a phenomenological research is to understand the meaning of the human experience through descriptive means: What do people experience and how do they interpret the world in which they live (Moustakas, 1994)? The present article was based on a study in Israel that explored the phenomenology of children's exposure to violence in families in which the father was violent toward the mother (Carmel, 2010). Since the focus of this research was on the experience of violence regarding the escalation of the interparental conflict, namely, learning about the experience in relation to the process and the development of the theoretical conceptualization in this context, the methodological guiding principles of the present qualitative study were the phenomenological tradition and the grounded theory approach (Creswell, 1998).

4.1.5 Sample and participants

Data collection for the study lasted approximately a year and a half, from August 2006 till December 2007. Location and recruitment of study participants included several stages: Receiving approval from the university ethics committee; receiving approval from the Ministry of Social Affairs and Social Services to conduct the research among their clients; establishing a multidisciplinary team within a large center for the prevention of violence in central Israel in order to consolidate ways of approaching violent men and women victims of violence (to obtain their consent to interview their children); and locating the children based on the study criteria. The final sample was based on 27 children, 13 boys, and 14 girls between 7 and 12 years. They were sampled from a population of children growing up in families in which the father was violent toward the mother, according to reports by social workers treating families and children in centers for the treatment and prevention of violence around the country. The children were from secular, traditional, and religious Jewish families of Iraqi, North African, and Eastern European origin.

Theoretical sampling was chosen for the study (Patton, 2002) and participants were selected based on their ability to contribute to the emerging theory (Patton, 2002). Thus, the children were located according to the following criteria: 1) Gender, boys and girls; 2) received treatment, children who had participated in at least 8 (out of 12) group treatment sessions alongside children who had not received treatment in the context of the violence in their families; 3) characteristics of the harm, children who were exposed to their father's violence toward their mother alongside children who, in addition to this exposure, had also personally experienced the father's violence. It was also decided that violence would be defined as one or more physical reactions within the 18 months preceding the interview, so that the memory would be fresh in the child's mind. The study population was sampled based on a sampling table, allowing a fitting representation of each criterion, with even distribution of the children's ages, enabling appropriate representation of the various aspects of the phenomenon.

4.1.5.1 Procedure for recruiting interviewees for the study

The interviewees were located and recruited in several stages:

1. After receiving approval from the Ministry of Welfare and Social Affairs to conduct the study with their clients, a multidisciplinary thinking team was set up within the framework of a large center for the prevention and treatment of family violence in central Israel. This was necessary to decide which client (the father or the mother) should be approached first by the team to receive their consent to interview the child. A decision also had to be made regarding the best way to approach the client (how to present the study) and guidelines as to how to approach the child. Within this forum, we chose to perform a pilot study in which women treated at the center would be approached for their consent to interview their children (working on the assumption that they would then try to persuade their partners to give their consent as well). This would be compared with initially approaching men being treated at the center, who would then try to persuade their female partners either in person or via an official application by therapists at the center. Based on the pilot study comparing an initial application to six men in therapy and six women in therapy, there was **no chance** that the men would give their consent if they were not being treated at the center and, specifically, if they had not had 8 consecutive therapeutic sessions. In contrast, the women's consent was found **not to be dependent** on whether they were in therapy.

Regarding **the way to approach the male clients**, the best way to obtain their consent to interview their children was for their therapists to explain to them, individually, that the overall aim of the study was to develop a more effective way of working with the children to help them cope with their exposure to the conflicts and arguments at home. This strategy allowed me to enter the next stage of the conversation with the man and to present the aims of the study in more detail while relating to his own painful position as a childhood victim of exposure to violence who had not received any attention and/or treatment. It is important to note that this was the point at which the men broke down, began to cry, and shared their difficult childhood experiences. Following this episode, all the men, without exception, consented to their son's or daughter's participation in the study. Through meeting with me, they seemed to reach the understanding that there was a genuine, honest desire to help the children, without judging them as parents who had harmed their children. I believe that emphasizing the fact that they had been victims of difficult circumstances themselves was what opened their minds to the idea of allowing the children to talk.

I then conducted a pilot study to explore **the best way to approach the children** (after receiving their parents' consent) to receive their consent to participate in the study. The results showed that the easiest way would be for the mother, first, to ask them herself, and I would then present the study to them, while emphasizing my occupation and the fact that I regularly meet with other children who are undergoing the same kind of difficult experiences. However, when the children were approached by their therapists at the center (whether the child was being treated there, or not), they demonstrated some form of resistance. This made it difficult for me to contact them directly, afterwards, and in some cases, an additional meeting was necessary to establish trust between us.

2. Based on those understandings, I sent all the directors of family violence prevention and treatment centers, all over the country, a short description of the study aim, the study questions, and the research method; details of the suitable criteria and procedures for recruiting children for the study; and a copy of the approval by the Ministry of Welfare and Social Affairs and accompanying documents (the researcher's declaration of confidentiality vis-à-vis the Ministry). At a later stage, meetings were arranged with staff in the centers whose directors reported having found candidates who adhered to the research criteria. Out of all the family violence prevention and treatment centers that I contacted, candidates were located in nine centers: Four in central Israel, two in the south, two in the north, and one in the east.

3. After receiving the approval of the various center directors to be assisted by practitioners who were treating families living with violence (perpetrated

by the father against the mother), I contacted these practitioners personally. After their initial application to the parents of the potential candidates, I first met the father in person and then the mother. This initial acquaintance ensured that both parents trusted me as a researcher and proved itself helpful in assisting the parents to convey to the children the importance of their participation in the study. More importantly, the children understood that they had their parents' permission to talk about what was happening at home. During these meetings, I signed a confidentiality declaration form as a researcher, and the parents signed an informed consent form authorizing their children's participation in the study.
4. After receiving the consent of all sides, I met the children individually. I introduced myself as a therapist for children who are experiencing family violence, alongside being a researcher. I emphasized that we would have one or two sessions to give them the opportunity to tell their life stories as they wished while, at the same time, contributing to the knowledge about other children in similar family situations. Finally, if the children expressed willingness to participate in the study, we arranged to meet at a time and place of their choice. Some of the children chose to be interviewed at the violence prevention center, and others, mainly those who were not being treated at the center, asked me to come to their homes either in the morning or the afternoon, when their mother was at home.
5. I called the next meeting with the child a "getting to know you" meeting, in which we told each other what we like to do, talked about our hobbies, and played two or three board games chosen by the child after I presented several possibilities. Our cooperation surrounding these games enabled us to form a direct rapport and to undergo a transition from the status of "researcher" to the status of "friend." This is a helpful means of balancing the power relations between the adult and the child and ensures that reliable information will be obtained (e.g., Eder & Fingerston, 2002; Fine & Sandstrom, 1988).

4.1.6 Research instrument

Data for the broad study were collected via in-depth semi-structured interviews according to an interview guide based on theoretical and empirical literature. The interview guide included five content categories: 1) The family's everyday life, e.g., "Tell me what it is like at home. What do you do there? What do you talk about?" 2) the initiation, development, and conclusion of interparental conflicts that do not escalate into violence, e.g., "Tell me about an argument that got worse but did not reach the hitting stage. What do you think influences the ending of the argument at this stage?" 3) the initiation, development, and conclusion of interparental conflicts that escalated to violence, e.g., "Tell me about the worst argument that you remember. Did someone get hit?" "How does it happen that an argument turns into a violent quarrel?" 4) the children's experiences of the conflicts (both violent and nonviolent) and the way they understood and interpreted what they witnessed, e.g., "What do you feel when the argument gets more serious?" "What do you think about in those situations?" and 5) children's involvement in the interparental conflicts (both violent and nonviolent) and their perceptions and attributed meanings to this involvement, e.g., "Where are you when the argument between your parents begins? What do you do? What effect do you think your behavior has on your parents?" The present study was based on analysis of the data pertaining to the children's everyday lives and to the analysis of the data concerning the children's involvement in the escalation as well as their experience in relation to this involvement.

4.1.7 Data collection

Like the process of locating participants for the study, the data collection adhered to the accepted ethical principles for studying sensitive populations (Peled, 2001). The children received explanations about the study and were asked to sign a participant consent form. They were assured of confidentiality, with the clarification that if they disclosed a situation that threatened either them or their family members, confidentiality would be waived, and the appropriate authorities would become involved. The recordings of the interviews were marked only with numbers, with no identifying details, and the children were told that they were entitled to stop the interview at any stage.

The interviews took place in one to three sessions and were audio recorded and transcribed verbatim. The child set the pace, so that each session lasted between 60 and 90 minutes. All interviews were conducted by the author, who had 15 years of experience in clinical consultation work with children exposed to violence in their families. The interview was preceded by a practice stage to reduce tension and create a balancing effect between the interviewer and interviewee.

Regarding the end of the interview, it was agreed with the staff that the children who were treated in the violence prevention center would meet with their therapists two weeks after the interview. This was to follow up on their emotional state and to see if any new material arose in relation to the home dynamics that required attention. Regarding the children who had been contacted initially by me (i.e., those whom I had reached through the men being treated at the center), it was agreed that I would contact them the day after the interview and one week later to get an impression of their emotional state. It was also agreed that the center would continue to be in direct contact with the mother to enable follow-up of the family relationship balance. It is important to note that one of the secondary benefits of this study was the fathers' reaction to the interview. I was surprised to hear that some of them asked (via their therapists) to contact me so that they could thank me personally for allowing them to see themselves as someone who is helping their children. In addition, several fathers remarked to their therapists that their children returned from the interview in a calm state of mind and that they would be happy if the children could continue to meet me on a permanent basis. In these cases, treatment for the children was offered through the center. In my view, the nonjudgmental approach from a stance that enabled the men to experience themselves as contributing to change and to be perceived by society not only as abusers helped put them less on the defensive.

During the interviews, several of the children said that they could not answer one question or another because their fathers had asked them not to answer if they were asked about that subject. I respected their wishes, of course, and even stressed the importance of exercising this consideration to protect themselves within the family relationships at home. I added that, if they felt in the future that sharing the information was the right thing to do, they could turn to a school counselor for assistance. In these cases, I recommended that the violence prevention and treatment center perform a broader examination, through informing the welfare services of the need to follow up the child's reactions and emotional, social, and scholastic functioning at school, as well as through attempting to learn more about the home family dynamics via the mother.

4.1.8 Data analysis

After transcribing the interviews, content analysis was conducted in four stages: The interviews were divided into units of meaning and coded; by comparing interviews, the content categories were phenomenologically reduced; the categories were collected into central themes, which were then conceptually linked (Denzin, 1989; 1997). In addition, the data were examined, conceptualized, and recompiled while relating to situations, contexts, interactions, action strategies, and outcomes and were finally linked to a general theoretical wording (Corbin & Strauss, 2008).

4.1.9 Findings

The analysis of the interviews with the children reveals that their life's reality is composed of two simultaneously contradictory yet complementary experiences: An experience of extreme nothingness and an experience of extreme fullness, derived from the violent interparental conflicts. Each of these experiences will be examined, and the unique dynamics between them will be analyzed.

4.1.9.1 The experience of nothingness

The experience of nothingness is the basis of nihilist ideology, the knowledge that everything is meaningless and worthless. People live in a world of vague wandering, a world of goalless paths. The emptiness that prevails in the world is total. No fullness contradicts the emptiness. Nevertheless, the emotions that are more alive are those of desolate emptiness, sickness of mind and body. Any involvement in the world is perceived as half-truth, half-falsehood, and unimportant, and thus the wish to act and to believe collapses (Nietzsche, 1968).

An analysis of the interviews with the children reveals existence in an empty and worthless world, incorporating a mixture of emotions: Boredom, emptiness, helplessness, confusion, lack of control, loneliness, and a lack of intimacy. A compound of these negative emotions is what defines the experience of nothingness of children exposed to their father's violence toward their mother and is at the basis of their everyday existence.

The children's descriptions show that the shaping of this complex, varied, and multidimensional experience in their consciousness is an outcome of the encounter with several elements: Communication between family members at home, on all its verbal and behavioral levels; the set of cultural values according to which the children examine their daily reality; and the parents' mode of involvement in daily interactions with them. In the following paragraphs, I will examine each of these components and the way in which they contribute to shaping the experience.

4.1.9.1.1 INTERNAL HOME COMMUNICATION

The children's descriptions of the family's daily life expose minimal interpersonal interaction, devoid of real content (neutral, impersonal) and of reciprocity. It is the encounter with these communicative components that leads them to recognize that the communication is meaningless. The following quotes will illustrate the children's perception of communication in their homes:

> We go to the mall together and we go in the car together and just talk. The truth is that I usually talk to each one separately. But sometimes, I listen to their conversations. (Ayelet)
>
> We didn't use to do anything together. They used to say to me: "Why are you hitting? Why do you do things that Mom and Dad don't allow?" On Fridays, Dad used to come home with the groceries and I arranged them in the fridge and then I helped Mom again. (Hodaya)
>
> Dad sometimes plants flowers in the garden with me. That's how he spends the time with me until Mom comes home. (Gal)

Conspicuous in all the quotes is the children's use of time and space to express the way in which they perceive the nature of the internal home communication. It is limited to a defined geographical location, takes place at specific times, and is characterized by the interlocutors' location in one space without genuine attunement between them. The definition or presentation of the verbal content as vague intensifies the minimal nature of the communication. Thus, it is through this limited content that the monotonous interaction between the parents and children, which occurs only occasionally and in a specific place, is emptied of meaning.

4.1.9.1.2 INTERNALIZED CULTURAL VALUES

The second component, in light of which the experience is shaped, is the encounter with a set of cultural values (that the children have internalized as part of the socialization process), according to which the children examine their everyday reality. In the shadow of this comparison, they experience the reality at home as different and distant from existing according to the necessary order. Thus, the value of "family," which the children perceive as representing norms of "togetherness" and of interest in everyday life, dissolves in their consciousness vis-à-vis the discovery that it is nonexistent in their home. The value of "parenting," which the children perceive as representing educational norms, dissolves in their consciousness vis-à-vis the discovery that it exists only in definitional terms. The following quote illustrates a comparison regarding the cultural value of "family."

> At my house, erm ... nothing much. Most of the time, Mom cleans and cooks and sometimes we go out to all sorts of places and most of the time they get mad at my two dogs who dirty up the house and that makes me mad because they threaten to give them away .... (David)

The boy begins by describing the atmosphere at home as nothing special and then elaborates on what has led him to this conclusion. Through the use of expressions pertaining to frequency, "most of the time" and "sometimes," he places their home "togetherness" as marginal to the family reality and therefore worthless. Following on from this, he elaborates on the essence of the togetherness by emphasizing its absence: The parents are engaged in cleaning or in arguments about the cleaning, and the children are busy among themselves. In this context, the "island of togetherness," the family outings, are swallowed up and blurred. The boy chooses to describe the reality at home in relation to the perception of the family's cultural value. In the child's perception, family represents a source of togetherness, intimacy, and reciprocity between parents and children. The absence of this as well as the "minimal existence" show what the family togetherness represents for him.

The gap between the current situation (his life's reality) and the ideal situation (the cultural value that is rooted in his consciousness) is what leads to the shattering of the family value, which cannot provide the necessary meaning to life. The boy is left with a sense of deep emptiness, which he expressed in his description of the atmosphere at home as "nothing much." The following quote illustrates shaping the experience of nothingness in light of the encounter with the cultural value that defines "parenting."

> If we argue, my Mom says: "I'm tired. I'm fed up, I can't control you anymore. I'm too tired to manage you." And then she helps and starts to be like a real mom. (Li'el)

The good score that the girl gives her mother for parenting at the intervention stage is based on some external benchmark defined as "real parenting." The use of the word "real" implies the existence of some external value that is a source of comparison. The same external value, which defines parental involvement as "real parenting," also defines the lack of intervention and the inability to exert parental authority as deficient parenting. The result of comparing the current situation with the ideal is the sense of weakness and helplessness described by the girl in relation to the home reality with a lack of parental occupancy. The conclusion regarding the parental behavior at home is of half-truth and half-falsehood, which creates a sense of confusion and lack of control.

4.1.9.1.3 PARENTING STYLES

The children's encounter with parents' types of intervention in daily interactions with them creates an additional dimension of the experience of nothingness: Living in chaos in a reality where there is no-one to educate, teach, distinguish between good and bad, between permitted and forbidden, and between one type of good (e.g., mediocrity) and another (e.g., excellence). In this context, an overall analysis reveals a common essence in the parenting types described by the children: The absence of parental direction regarding appropriate behavior and the attempt to bring about behavioral change by a means that the child perceives as ineffective. On the mother–child relationship level, the children describe parenting styles that are characterized by the absence of meaningful parental authority for the child. On the father–child relationship level, the children describe the use of aggressive or violent reaction patterns.

4.1.9.1.3.1 Mother–child relationship

> We talk about everything; everything. About the family, friends, arranging things, like how to do up the house. About responsibility, about caring for my little brother. And once my sister drank from some bottle and I was really scared because I thought she was drinking some kids' medicine. And what if she had died? (Adi)

> Mom used to say to me: "Dan, go to your room till I tell you to come out." After I'd been there a few minutes, she'd say: "Dan, come here a

minute," and that was the end of the punishment. It wasn't a punishment at all because I just played on my computer. That behavior of hers is funny. (Dan)

4.1.9.1.3.2 Father–child relationship

Let's say we're arguing ... about my little brother who did something. And then he says to me: "You can take care of him!" And I tell him that I can't. "Yes you can!" And I say I can't. So I say to him, "Let's say, but Dad, only if we say such and such," I say to him. "Only if" and then he says that it can't happen. (Yael)

Everything used to make him angry and when he started to get angry, I would be quiet. He used to try and hit me. (Yossi)

4.1.9.2 Escalation

Analysis of the interviews shows that in a situation of meaninglessness, the way in which children do find meaning is through the escalation of the interparental conflicts to all-out verbal and/or physical violence. The escalation provides the children with a sense of fullness in the following ways: They observe the drama; "something" has now replaced the "nothingness." Suddenly the screen lights up; there are actors, a plot, and something is happening, action. Suddenly the darkness is illuminated with a dazzling, shining light, giving great vitality. Boredom is replaced by interest, action, the event, and the tension.

To learn about the fullness that the escalation introduces into the children's lives, we will observe the following quotes:

Interviewer: Can you tell me about the last argument that you remember between your parents?

It was about money: "You don't earn a lot of money."

"That's not right. I earn more than you do;" "No you don't, you don't work much! You hardly work!"

"I'll throw you out of the house!" "You have no right to do that!"

"I do!" "OK, throw me out!" That's it. (Uriah)

Interviewer: Can you tell me about the last argument that you remember between your parents?

Where are we eating on Saturday, at my mom's mom's or my dad's mom's? I get up on Saturday morning. We were invited for the meal, and suddenly Mom sees Dad getting the car ready and she says: "We need to go eat by my mom." And then he says: "What? No way! We're eating by my mom." And then the fight started. (Shir)

Both quotes reveal a conspicuous recurring pattern of how the interparental argument is presented: Immediately after opening the subject of the interparental conflict, the children move on to quoting the parents. This style of presentation as a dialogue between the protagonists, reminiscent of a literary play, gives the reader the sense of being in the drama itself. The subject of the argument presented at the beginning serves as a kind of title or name for the scene that will be acted out. The protagonists in the dramas presented to us here as readers are the parents themselves, and the exchanges between them represent a conflict of interests, which construct the plot being formed.

The description of how the arguments started as parts of a play watched by the children teaches us about the interest, activity, tension, and drama that are introduced into their world through watching the interparental conflicts as they unravel before their eyes. The nothingness is suddenly replaced by "something" of great volume. Just as a play adds interest and enrichment to the audience's world, so the interparental interactions that are played out before the children add variety and interest to their lives.

Nonetheless, the meaning that the escalation injects into the children's lives is not only an outcome of the interest and tension, derived from their position as spectators of the drama, but also is an outcome of the children's role as partners in constructing the reality. An analysis of the findings shows that the children's "choice" of escalation as a way to fill the vast space, the vacuum in which they live, dictates to them a very specific action script. Even though the parents create boundaries for them regarding their means of involvement, with the message that "as long as the argument is developing, just watch and stay out of it," but afterward, in the dramatic stages, they expect them to become involved, which conveys the message to the children that they are expected to take part in constructing the outcome of the violence. Defining the boundary that the parents have set between watching and participating as penetrable (as mentioned, the children penetrate it when the dramatic activity begins) gives the children meaning, not only by being spectators of the drama but also by being partners in constructing the reality.

The children identify the different stages of the conflict's escalation, as follows: Initiation of the conflict, the development of the conflict, the stage of verbal aggression, an intense conflict expressed through threats and initial physical contact, and the violence stage expressed through actual physical aggression. An analysis of the children's movements in the internal home space and/or the space outside the home throughout all these stages of escalation and an analysis of the findings regarding the children's action patterns in the different stages of the escalation show that the children's roles throughout the process can be divided into three main functions: 1) Allowing the escalation norms to be expressed unhindered; 2) preparation for active involvement in the conflict; and 3) taking an active part in helping to end the conflict.

In the next section, I will examine the children's mode of involvement regarding the developing stages of the conflict.

4.1.9.2.1 ALLOWING EXPRESSION OF THE ESCALATION NORMS AND PREPARING FOR ACTIVE INVOLVEMENT

4.1.9.2.1.1 Initial stage of the conflict

> When the argument starts, I am in the kitchen. Sometimes in my room. In my room, at the computer. If I'm in the kitchen, I go to my room. If I'm in my room, I stay there, playing on the computer. (Jacob)

> When an argument starts, I go to my room with my brother. They argue and argue. We hear things all mixed up. I don't get involved and neither does he. (Lilach)

> When my parents start arguing, I try to cheer my sisters up. I take them to my room and explain things to them. So that way, I have something to do besides just getting stressed. (Amos)

> Listen, I'll tell you briefly. They argue, right? We argue between ourselves. And then when it gets a bit worse, I go to my room. Don't want to hear, don't want to be involved. I am in my room. (Gil)

An analysis of the children's quotes shows that they behave according to a predetermined action pattern. This is apparent from the generalized wording, which refers to fixed actions that do not change (when an argument starts … I …). They always distance themselves from the scene, specifically in their rooms. The first quote provides a special emphasis regarding the place where the children are expected to be. The child emphasizes his choice to remain within a spatial arrangement that is away from the scene itself. Being far from the scene as well as the use of distraction tactics, such as playing and keeping up the spirits of the younger siblings, might shed light on the defined role that is shaped for the children: Not to hinder the development of the interparental conflict. The last quote strengthens this thesis when the child describes his behavior pattern, according to which the children themselves are those who provide the components for intensifying the argument that began between the parents. When the required conditions for the development of the argument are achieved, the children leave to their rooms, where they behave as if they are not interested in what is happening. The use of the verb "hear" rather than "listen" regarding the developing interparental conflict might also indicate the adoption of a passive role, since, at this stage, the children are clearly expected not to be involved in the argument.

4.1.9.2.1.2 Development stage of the conflict

> When I was in my room and the argument had already turned into a quarrel, I tried to listen to what was happening. I wanted to see who was right: If Dad was lying, I would tell him afterwards that he is a liar. I am like a judge: "I

know what you did; I know I can catch you out because I heard what you said, and now you're cheating." (Hodaya)

When the quarrel gets bad and Dad and Mom are yelling, then I say to my brother: "Avi, soon, when the cursing starts, go and stop them!" My brothers and I stay in the room upstairs and he goes down to try and separate them. (Naomi)

The first quote starts with the girl's reference to the familiar scenario. When the argument develops into a fight, the girl is supposed to remain in the spatial arrangement in which she was when the argument began (in her room), from where she begins to gather information about what is happening. The use of the verbs "to listen" and "to see" emphasizes that, at this stage, the girl becomes an active participant in the developing interparental conflict. She is not listening simply to find out what is being said but is engaged in active, goal-directed listening to become a party to the fight. The continuation of the description reveals the nature of involvement expected of the girl: To be a "juicy" witness who gathers incriminating information against her father for the purpose of becoming involved in constructing the outcomes of the conflict later on. The girl's comparison of herself to a "judge" expresses the gap between the way in which she is supposed to perceive her role in the escalation (an external audience to the developing interparental drama) and the role that she plays in practice.

In the second descriptive section, the girl discloses the required coordination and cooperation between her and her siblings so that the older brother will succeed in his attempt to intervene at the verbal aggression stage (when the parents are cursing at each other). The girl describes the role division between the siblings. She and several brothers sit and listen to the developing argument, and at the right moment, when they identify the turning point to the next stage, the eldest brother is called to prepare for active intervention. The role division described here shows that the siblings are positioned on two fronts: At the "rear" and on the "forward line," when the role of the rear is to identify the most appropriate time for the forward line's active intervention. This will achieve two goals: First, a division of attention when each front can focus best on its designated task, and second, cooperation with the pseudo-normative situation, according to which the younger siblings are not involved in the parents' fight. Only one of them gets involved out of necessity at a specific point. The pathos with which the girl describes her role in sending her brother to attempt the task of separation indicates her full participation as an actress in the drama (behind the scenes and not on the stage itself, but as a participant nevertheless).

4.1.9.2.1.3 The intense fighting stage

When the argument gets really, really bad, worse than the usual shouting and cursing, I check to see if the coast is clear, to make sure they can't see me, and then I cross over to their room. There, behind the door, there's this rail with clothes hanging on it. So, I hide behind that, and peep through the keyhole. Because after that, I can come out to protect my mom. (Dana)

When the really bad cursing starts, I go and call Hila and then, when the hitting starts, we separate them. (Nitai)

So it's like that, they get really angry at each other, and then start cursing each other. And most times, my sister answers me and we get ready to separate them. (Michael)

These three quotes emphasize the existence of an additional, more serious stage of escalation than the verbal aggression stage (shouting and cursing). This stage is characterized by even more aggressive communication ("worse than the usual shouting and cursing") and an intensifying emotional component ("get really angry at each other"). Regarding this stage also, the children describe their behavior according to a fixed, predetermined action script: Movement within the home space and toward the spatial arrangement that is close to the scene of the event. In this context, two variations in location are described: 1) In a room close to the scene itself, from where the child can observe what is happening, and 2) in the open space close to the scene of the event. Either way, the aim of this mobility is to gather information and cooperation between the siblings to separate the parents physically when necessary (when the fight escalates to a violent outburst). Emphasizing the girl's need to hide behind the clothes rail, despite being inside a closed room while the other children wait in preparation for the start of the physical violence, accentuates the tension between the parents' expectations. On the one hand, they expect the children to be active participants in the escalating drama, and on the other hand, they expect that they will not interfere in the interparental drama before it has reached its "boiling point."

Analysis of the findings regarding the children's roles in the escalation shows that at the developmental stages of the conflict, namely when the argument is initiated, intensifies, and turns into a serious fight that almost reaches a violent eruption, the children play two major roles: 1) Enabling the norms of escalation to develop and 2) gathering information in preparation for involvement in the critical stages of escalation. The nature of these roles changes according to the conflict's development. At the initiation stage, the central role is to enable escalation of the argument to an angry quarrel and gathering information is limited to passive listening ("We hear things all mixed up"—the initial stage of the conflict, quote no. 2). At the two stages at which the quarrel develops and then intensifies into a serious fight, the emphasis from the children's point of view is on collecting information, despite being physically located in a spatial arrangement outside the scene of the event.

Nonetheless, the children's location outside the scene of the event at the stages at which they are mentally and emotionally involved in the conflict might indicate the importance of the additional role that is shaped for them in these stages: Not to hinder the realization of the escalation norms.

The tension between the spatial arrangements in which the children are positioned during the developmental stages of the conflict and the active action strategies demanded of them might emphasize the importance of the two aforementioned roles: 1) To be a fixed audience that gives validity and structure to the play being acted between the parents, thus allowing the escalation norms to be expressed unhindered and 2) to be actors participating in the drama itself, even if not at the front of the stage, and therefore to be involved in how it is shaped. These roles shape additional meanings for the children within the framework of the escalation: Turning time into a goal-oriented concept, which is a kind of solution to the boredom described as characterizing their daily routine and being in a close, intimate relationship with their parents and siblings. These two additional layers create stratification for the children's sense of fullness during the escalation and therefore constitute a suitable response to the intense and multidimensional emptiness that the children mentioned in their descriptions of their family's everyday life.

4.1.9.2.2 TAKING AN ACTIVE PART IN HELPING TO END THE CONFLICTS: THE CHILDREN'S MODE OF INVOLVEMENT IN THE DRAMATIC STAGES

4.1.9.2.2.1 *The verbal aggression stage*

> When the argument gets serious, with curses and shouting, then I separate them ... when I try to separate them, then my sister helps me. We take charge so that they won't come near each other, one to the living room and one to the bedroom ... at least for half an hour or so, or an hour, sometimes they calm down. (Shlomi)

> When they get to the shouting stage, it is tedious and boring but mainly annoying, and after that, my sisters cry and the volume goes down a bit. And then I would enter the picture. I would go out of the room and say: "Stop it now! Stop arguing! You see what you're doing to them?" ... And sometimes they stop arguing. (Ronen)

> When he is shouting really loudly, I go out of the room. I say to him: "Enough, Dad, take a drink of water, let's go downstairs, come and sit with me" ... sometimes he listens to me. (Itzik)

4.1.9.2.2.2 *The violence stage*

> When the hitting starts, we separate them. Hila shouts, "Stop! Stop!" and I go in with my body. Sometimes, I push him and then he moves sideways and that's it. (Nitai)

When the fight gets serious, pushing, hitting, we would cry and scream. We don't separate them because we would also get hit. Sometimes, they stopped because of that. (Anat)

An analysis of the children's descriptions regarding their behavior and its outcomes in the stages of verbal aggression and violence shows the special nature of these stages, as distinct from the other stages of escalation. Both these stages have the potential to either end or escalate the fighting and thus are critical junctures in the conflict. The children's active participation in these stages of the conflict gives them meaning, not only by virtue of being actors in the drama but mainly by being partners to constructing the family reality as violent or nonviolent.

A comparison of the children's action patterns regarding each of the stages reveals similar action strategies: Physical and verbal attempts to separate the parents; attempts to divert the parents' attention away from the fight to the children; and attempts to calm the father or both the parents. Nevertheless, an observation of how the tactics themselves are built shows that at the verbal aggression stage, the tactics are divided up into several layers (the child makes use of several action strategies), where each layer reinforces the previous one, and in the verbal aggression stage, the children make intensive use of one tactic. This difference might show that at the verbal aggression stage, the parties still have control over their anger, and a de-escalation script remains a real possibility. At the violence stage, however, either one or both of the sides lose control, which requires one intensive act. Either way, the complex activity required of the children on the cognitive, emotional, and physical levels in these stages might show that they are players who participate in the drama and whose role influences the sequence of events. The tension, action, and interest, which were a product of a conflict of interests between the protagonists (the parents themselves), have now been taken up by the attempts at separation by those currently at the front of the stage—the children.

Through the children's direct involvement in the escalating interparental conflict, they are in actual contact with them, whether physically separating them, attempting to divert their attention, or by being close to them to calm them down. All these variations enable intimate contact between the parents and children, as is the case with the sibling interaction. The direct involvement in the escalating interparental conflict requires cooperation, coordination, and being together for prolonged periods, which are fundamental elements for creating reciprocity.

4.1.10 Discussion

An analysis of the children's perceptions of the relationship with their parents and with their siblings and of the interparental relationship exposes an experience of existing within a void, within a meaningless, directionless reality, combining internal emptiness, boredom, and immeasurable loneliness, as well as feelings of uncertainty and lack of control.

The existential experience that emerges from the children's descriptions and exposes acknowledgment of a reality that lacks any kind of essence is, in fact, the experience of nothingness, the experience at the foundations of the nihilist ideology (Nietzsche, 1968). Nietzsche, however, sees the experience of nothingness to be the product of a conscious process that individuals undergo in relation to the cultural values according to which they live and in relation to their own inevitable end within an infinite world (Nietzsche, 1968). The experience of the children in this study, however, is a product of an encounter with specific components: Certain characteristics (such as scarce or meaningless communication), the cultural values on which their daily routine is based, and the parental models to which they are exposed. Thus, while the experience of nothingness to which Nietzsche refers is total in the conscious sense, recognizing that the world is absolute non-existence, the experience of nothingness as shaped among children exposed to violence shows its totality in terms of sensation. Still, the experience of nothingness among children exposed to violence is shaped in a conscious context, but because it is structured vis-à-vis specific components and not on the general metaphysical and cultural level, it leads to the recognition of the existence of emptiness that prevails in everything in the individual's close environment. This is what makes the experience mainly an emotional one regarding the sense of internal emptiness. The intensity of the experience and its totality are derived, in this context, from its being stratified and related to many different aspects.

In the shadow of the crumbling set of cultural values that was assimilated in their awareness (values of parenting and family), the children's enlistment in the escalation process can be seen as the awareness of a need for change and a need to adopt a new set of concepts, which will enable the construction of the reality as coherent and therefore meaningful (Nietzsche, 1968).

The children's involvement in the escalation process shows that they acquire meaning during the process in three ways: 1) Through the interest that is injected into their lives, an interest that gradually increases with the development of the drama taking place between the parents and reaches a climax with the children's participation in the drama itself; 2) through making time goal-oriented: the children are partners in the entire escalation process, both in enabling the unhindered expression of the escalation norms or in helping create them as well as assisting in bringing the conflicts to a close; and 3) through interaction with their parents and siblings, which is made possible through the escalation process. Furthermore, the severity of the tension experienced by the children and the variety of roles they are required to play give their involvement in the escalation a powerful dimension, which is a type of adequate "response," a genuine "counter-experience" versus the immeasurable void, the vacuum that they experience in their everyday lives. However, a deep analysis of this meaning that is achieved shows it, apparently, to be a pseudo-meaning, for the following reasons: 1) Despite the children's potential ability to predict the nature of the process—either escalation or de-escalation—the children describe uncertainty regarding the way in which the conflict will develop at each stage. This situation leads to a sense of the loss of the ability for control in the close environment in particular and in life in general. 2) Even though the children's involvement in the escalation allows them to be in direct or indirect contact with their parents and siblings, because the parents are so immersed in the argument itself and the siblings are goal-oriented, this type of interaction, once the escalation has ended, might leave the children with a sense of deep isolation. Even so, this set of values can serve as a practical means of temporarily breaking the unfathomable nothingness in which the children live.

Thus, the two extreme situations that exist side by side in the children's lives create mutually strengthening relations of tension and fulfillment. The deeper the sense of emptiness, the greater the need to fill the vacuum with the powerful "something"; at the end of the escalation process, that powerful "something" (the child's experience of the escalation) is shattered even more powerfully in comparison to the cultural values assimilated in the children's consciousness. This increases the sense of the vacuum and strengthens their motivation to replenish the powerful "something." The sense of total fullness and of total emptiness is an outcome of the comparison to the same benchmark: Those cultural values that dictate the desired social order (Ben-Ze'ev, 2000, 2010).

An analysis of the findings regarding the children's action patterns at the different stages of escalation shows the existence of two central modes of behavior: Indirect participation in the conflict through the use of diversion tactics and active listening for the purpose of gathering information at advanced stages of the conflict and direct participation in the conflict through active intervention to separate the parents. These modes of behavior are dependent on the specific stage of the conflict. That is to say, in the developmental stages, the children choose the indirect mode of behavior, whereas in the dramatic stages, in which they can potentially have an impact either to bring about the end of the conflict or its escalation, the children choose the direct mode of behavior. The children's description of a fixed behavioral pattern and their mention of clearly defined stages of the conflict reveal the existence of a predetermined script regarding their involvement in all the different escalation stages.

The findings of the study regarding the children's behavior in the escalation according to a predetermined script provide insight into their acting within a set of familiar social scripts, which delineate the boundaries of the entire process (Gergen, 1999). Therefore, the children's actions are neither random nor personality- or situation-dependent but adhere to scripts dictated to them by the parents. In this context, both types of expectations were characterized as being used by the parents in most of their parenting actions: The first type was named "framing expectations" and the second type was named "scripting expectations"

(Eisikovits & Winstok, 2001). While the first group of expectations discusses the range of possibilities offered to the child for constructing his/her reality, the second group determines the specific ways in which the child will react to the world within the boundaries of the experience (Eisikovits & Winstok, 2001).

The tension between the spatial arrangements and the active tactics adopted by the children in the different stages of the conflict, even if indirect, as well as actually being at the scene of the event itself only at the critical stages (scripting expectation), might indicate the parents' intention to shape a pseudo-normative reality for the children. Within this reality, the children are not party to disputes and their components that are not related to them and participate "only" by providing assistance to end the conflict. Thus, the violence is limited and minimized as an option in conflict situations, in the way that if it poses a danger to the children, they make sure that they are protected by changing the predetermined action tactic to end the conflict (framing expectations).

The messages conveyed to the children via the aforementioned types of expectations are directed toward blurred awareness of the violence so that the children do not deny its existence because they are involved in the stage at which the conflict becomes violent but see the possibility of ending it when the two sides cannot reach an agreement. Therefore, the children are actually guided to relate to violence as part of a normative conflictual reality in which the sides are equally responsible for the initiation, development, and ending of the conflict.

Therefore, unlike the theoretical conceptualization regarding the children's construction of the interparental violence based on parental expectations, which define awareness of violence on a continuum ranging from denial at one end to exaggeration at the other (Eisikovits & Winstok, 2001), this study suggests that the children's construction of the interparental violence is dependent on parental expectations that are directed toward blurring the violence and understanding of the reality, as well as constructing the interparental conflicts as normative. The inconsistency between the theoretical and empirical findings can be explained by the fact that the theoretical conceptualization was constructed according to findings of studies among pre-adolescents (Peled, 1997; Katz, 2022) and adolescents (Goldblatt, 2003; Katz, 2016; Miranda, 2022) and not among children. According to these studies, the adolescents are active participants who maneuver the situation in the individual and family contexts alike. They adopt roles either on their own or their parents' initiative and, in certain cases, avoid taking on these roles, even when compelled to do so. These findings might suggest that, over the years, the parents' expectations change, and they redefine the range of possibilities offered to the children for constructing their reality through active involvement in the same violent reality. At the same time, the adolescents are influenced by the peer group, whereby they are exposed to other behavioral norms and codes, which are in line with normative reality. This influences them to act in accordance with these codes, even if they differ from their parents' expectations.

4.2 Study 2. The perception of escalation of interparental conflicts among children exposed to their father's violence against their mother: Characteristics of the exposure to violence and its connection to child sexual abuse

4.2.1 Introduction

This study focuses on the question of the children's perception of the interparental escalation process throughout all its stages, in an attempt to understand what, in the children's conception, creates such complexity of psychological and physical abuse.

4.2.2 Literature review

Since 1980, research in the field of children exposed to violence has increased dramatically while documenting the relationship between exposure to violence and a wide range of behavioral, emotional, and cognitive problems (e.g., Kitzmann et al., 2003; Vu et al., 2016). Additionally, the research in the field of exposure to violence provides decisive evidence of a direct correlation between living in a violent reality and direct child abuse. This is true with different samples and with different methodologies that were used, which makes systematic comparison difficult (e.g., Hester et al., 2007; Macvean et al., 2018). Specifically, many studies that examined the correlation between exposure to violence and child physical abuse reported overlapping rates between 32% and 55% (e.g., Downes et al., 2019; Edleson, 1995). Other studies that examined the correlation between exposure to violence and other types of child abuse found a correlation with sexual abuse ranging between 40% and 70% (e.g., Saunders, 2003; Bancroft et al., 2012; Sitney & Kaufman, 2021). Despite the high rates of abuse that were revealed, there has been a dearth of theoretical models that can provide insights into the mechanisms behind the victimization process. In the context of sexual abuse, the proposed explanation relates to extending the control to a weaker person as part of the need to create coercive intimacy (Bancroft et al., 2012). Another proposed explanation is the man's exposure to a family violence model in childhood (Sitney & Kaufman, 2021).

To understand the children's overall experience, one must examine their perceptions, attributed meanings, and mode of involvement in the escalation process of interparental conflicts to all-out violence. The present study focused on the children's perception of the escalation process.

A broad consensus in the literature holds that escalation is an emotional process that involves intense feelings such as anxiety, anger, helplessness, humiliation, shame, guilt, envy, hostility, low self-esteem, and a sense of failure (e.g., Gergen, 1994). The presence of such emotions leads to imbalance, resulting in an experience of a lack of control and a loss of the ability to predict, plan, and navigate the course of life. In conditions such as these, the violence becomes a tool that is perceived by those undergoing this process as a means of acquiring power and control (e.g., Scheff & Retzinger, 1991).

Later studies since the 2000s, which dealt with escalation in the context of intimate violence (Eisikovits et al., 2002; Winstok et al., 2002; Winstok, 2007), attempted to develop a theoretical model that exposed the structure and the dynamics of the violence in intimate relationships from the point of view of the aggressor, the victim, and the dyadic perspective.

Specifically, the findings show that men perceive themselves as entitled and obligated to protect their existential dyadic relationship while recognizing the costs and benefits involved in the use of violence to achieve this goal. They create rules, act as judges of when these rules are violated, and then take steps to enforce them. These men's assessment of the amount of control they have over their actions and over the advantages and disadvantages of these activities have a great influence on their attempts to reestablish the balance that was lost in their couple relationships.

In contrast, women see the transition from a nonviolent to a violent reality as a process. Control of the situation is a key variable in managing the process, which may or may not lead to violence, and can explain why they stay in the relationship despite the violence (Eisikovits et al., 2002).

The attempt to unify the two viewpoints has led to the general view that both the man and the woman involved have the inner potential to see themselves both as aggressors and as victims (Winstok, 2007). When the focus moves from a specific to a wider problem, which threatens the overall couple relationship, the use of violence might be perceived as an action worth taking, even though, at this point, a new problem is created, which might cause the conflict to spiral out of control (Winstok, 2013).

As is apparent from the review, none of the studies dealing with escalation in intimate relationships have placed central focus on the children's perspective. In light of this, the question at the core of the present research is: What is the process that leads from a nonviolent reality to a violent reality from the children's perspective?

4.2.3 Study method

This was a qualitative study based on the grounded theory approach (Glaser & Strauss, 1967; Corbin & Strauss, 2008). The rationale behind research based on these methodological principles is anchored in the lack of a suitable theory and in the need to expose the meaning of the experience for the individuals involved in the process (Creswell, 1998). Indeed, the aim of the present study was the development of a theoretical model that explains how children exposed to their father's violence against their mother interpret the transition from a nonviolent to a violent reality. As mentioned in the introduction to this chapter, the sample and participants, research tool, data collection, and data analysis were the same for both studies presented here. Therefore, to avoid repetition, details of the study method can be found in Section 1. Specifically, the present study was based on the analysis of content categories relating to the children's understanding of all stages of the escalation.

4.2.4 Findings

The analysis of the findings regarding the children's understanding of the different stages in the development of the escalating interparental conflicts shows that the children see the process in a normative context. They understand the initiation of the conflict as symmetrical, sometimes initiated by the father and sometimes by the mother. They perceive the development of the conflict as an argument around a trivial, everyday subject and the partner violence as an outcome of the argument reaching an impasse when the sides fail to convince each other to reach a general agreement. This is despite their descriptions of an argument that develops based on the man's interpretation of the woman's words as a violation of the desired balance in the partner relationship and despite describing clearly that the man initiates the escalation as well as deciding when to end the confrontation.

The children's understanding of the process will be addressed in relation to the following themes: The circumstances of the violence; the signs of the conflict escalating to a violent quarrel; the variables that influence the escalation of the conflict to a violent quarrel; the dynamics of the components that create the escalation; the management of the process by the two sides; and the results of using the strategies taken.

4.2.4.1 The circumstances of the violence

The children perceive that the conflicts arise as a result of the parents' arguments around different subjects relating to everyday life: Work, money, children, and extended family. Even though they describe the internal home reality as essentially conflictual and the escalation against the background of the man's understanding that the woman's words violate the desirable partner balance, the children's perception shows that they understand the context of the conflict to be trivial, in other words, as a normative argument between the partners, which arises around routine daily issues. In this context, the children's quotes expose two types of understanding: The first sees the responsibility for initiating the conflict, as well as its input, as mutual. The second sees the responsibility for initiating the conflict to be the father's, because he starts the argument, but considers the responsibility for developing the conflict as resting with both the father and the mother, who make a joint contribution to its formation. The following quotes will be presented to learn about the different types of understanding:

> *Interviewer*: What makes your parents start arguing?
>
> Let's say, my dad goes shopping and my mom wrote a certain thing on the list and he forgot and didn't buy it, something like that ... and ... err ... say ... my dad said something to my mom and my mom didn't hear him. Then they start arguing about whether he said it or not, and things like that. Or, say ... my mom asks my dad to do the cleaning, or the other way round. I said my mom but it could also be my dad. I'll give you an example. My dad asked my mom something in the morning. She was in the bathroom and didn't hear him, and then I said something to her and she did hear me. And then she came out and she didn't answer him, so he asked her what he had asked her before: Who is taking us to school? He wasn't supposed to take us, and then she said to him: "OK, you take us," because she didn't have a car, and then he said: "You didn't ask and yes you did ask," and the mess continued from there. (Shira)

The girl begins her description by listing the factors that arouse confrontations between her parents, with a brief reference to each. Her careful comparison between her parents is conspicuous. Her mode of description presents the mother and the father as initiating conflicts in equal measure, in addition to her explicit emphasis that both sides can be the reason for the argument ("I said my mom but it could also be my dad"). This might indicate that the child perceives the parents' mutual criticism as the context in which the conflict arises; in one instance, the mother criticizes the father, and in another case, the father criticizes the mother's behavior. Furthermore, the girl does not use a dramatic tone, creating the impression of a normative interparental conflict ("My dad asked my mom something ... and then he came out and she didn't answer him ... what he had asked her ... and then she said to him ... and then he said ...").

Nevertheless, bringing an example of the way in which the interparental conflict arose exposes a different reality. The girl says that, when the mother was in the bathroom and did not hear her father's question, the father interpreted the mother's apparent disregard of him as an attempt to belittle his words. In support of his view, he refers to the fact that the mother did answer the girl when she spoke to her. The father initiates the escalation because he assumes that if he is not answered, he is being ignored. The girl's example was supposed to support the thesis that the interparental conflict was an outcome of trivial everyday matters. However, it exposes a different reality in which the father interprets the mother's remarks as contempt, which creates a sense of loss of respect and personal insult, to which he reacts through escalation.

The gap between the girl's construction of the context as the development of conflicts as a daily routine and the description of the context as the father's interpretation of the mother's derisive behavior toward him shows that the violence has become a taken-for-granted presence in the home. Hence the perception of the father's remarks as having equal value to those of the mother, despite the different context in which they are spoken.

The next quote illustrates another type of understanding of circumstances that evoke those same violent arguments:

Interviewer: What kinds of things make your parents start arguing?

For instance, when Mom doesn't make the food tasty. When Mom is tired and she can't do the cleaning and when she can, then I think Dad forced her to do the cleaning and to throw out the garbage. They argued about children's crap ... Mom made one little mistake, and then Dad would already be yelling. Because, for example, if Mom didn't add salt, he could get up himself and take some without starting. (Saul)

In contrast to the previous quote, in which the girl emphasized both parents' responsibility for starting the argument, in the present quote, the boy describes a reality in which the father initiates the conflict. According to his description, every act by the mother is judged as intact or faulty according to the dimensions determined by the father regarding the accepted way to run a home. The rest of the description completes the picture concerning the circumstances in which the conflicts arise: If the father judges the mother's behavior as faulty, she is punished. The example of the salt, in which the boy perceives the father's reaction as extreme ("if Mom didn't add salt, he could get up himself and take some without starting") just emphasizes: 1) The father's constant comparison between the mother's behavior in the present and the standards that he determined as proper; 2) the link between the result of the judgment and the punishment; and 3) the immediacy of the reaction after deciding to administer the punishment.

Despite the comprehensive description that exposes a violent reality, the boy presents his perception of the circumstances that give rise to the arguments: "They argued about children's crap." Through the use of the word "crap" to define the topic of the conflicts and the comparison to the children's world, the boy brings the circumstances down to a trivial level. Thus, the father's remarks become marginal and what remains is the child's attitude toward those conflicts as foolish disputes. Through this "game," which transfers the father's criticism of the mother from the center to the margins, the responsibility for initiating the argument is still placed with him. However, the responsibility for its development is placed on both sides, as making an equal contribution to its formation. The use of the plural provides additional support for this thesis.

An analysis of all the findings regarding the circumstances that arouse the father's escalation against the mother shows that the same mechanism stands at the basis of the two types of understanding: The perception of the violence at home as taken for granted. This perception, which is an outcome of living in a reality rife with violent conflicts, directly impacts the view of violence as an option within a conflict. It gives a normative dimension to the circumstances in

142   Experience of interparental violence

which the conflict arises, which are viewed as part of the trivial routine, namely an argument between the partners on various issues.

4.2.4.2 Signs of conflict escalation to a violent quarrel

This theme relates to the signs through which the children can predict the escalation of the conflict to an all-out violent quarrel. In this context, an analysis of the children's descriptions indicates the existence of two components, which they perceive to be involved in the dynamics of the escalation: A communicative component and an emotional component. Although the communicative component relates to the changing character of the argument, which moves away and oversteps the boundaries of the relevant topic to personal matters or to those that touch on the partners' past scripts, the emotional component relates to the intensity of the anger rising on both sides to a loss of control and, in this context, the children relate to a variety of signs, such as tone of voice, facial expressions, volume of the shouting, and an increased level of annoyance.

In the context of the signs of the quarrel described by the children, they present two types of understanding of the development of the process. In the first type, the escalating conflict, namely the developing communicative component and the effect of the cumulative anger on both sides, is mutually nourishing, so that each side's input to the conflict increases the other side's anger. This in turn nourishes the conflict and elevates the other side's anger. In the second type of understanding, the mother's behavior is what nourishes the father's cumulative anger, and thus the dynamics of the escalation depends on the mother's continuous input to the conflict and the subsequent rise in the father's anger level. That is to say, in the second type of understanding, the escalation components were split, in that the children perceived the mother as responsible for the communicative component and the father for the emotional component. Nevertheless, in both types of understanding, it is obvious that the father is the initiator of the escalation. The following quotes illustrate each type of understanding:

4.2.4.2.1 FIRST UNDERSTANDING PATTERN

> *Interviewer*: What are the signs that tell you that an argument that began normally will become more serious?
>
> Sometimes, they raise their voices. They get angry with each other. Dad starts shouting a bit and then Mom starts shouting a bit and they are yelling. And there are the things they say. For example: Dad says to Mom: "You're not good at anything." And then she answers him: "I'm better than you, fatso. They start insulting each other." For me, the sign that the argument will soon start to get violent is their threats. When he says to Mom: "Be careful!" And when Mom says to him: "Of what?" And he says to her: "You

already know. Don't you know?" "No, I don't know." And then it starts ... like, touching in not a nice way. (Yoav)

4.2.4.2.2 SECOND UNDERSTANDING PATTERN

The stage at which I understand that the argument will end up with yelling and cursing is when Mom gets angry. She answers him back and argues with him, and then Dad starts yelling. After that, when he is really yelling, the cursing starts ... the sign for me that the argument will get violent is when I see that my mom isn't doing anything, and that irritates my dad. He tries to pull her into an argument, but she keeps quiet. And after that, I know the hitting will start. (Or'el)

In the context of the escalation dynamics, the two types of identified understandings reveal a conception of the violent conflict from a normative viewpoint. In the first type of understanding, the mutual anger is the outcome of the other's behavior, and in the second type, the father's anger is the outcome of the mother's behavior. In both cases, the anger is understood as part of an emotional script according to which the anger is a natural reaction to the other's annoying or hurtful words or behavior, which are perceived differently by the other side. This understanding places overall responsibility for the intensification of the conflict on both sides, even when the mother, in the second understanding pattern, is perceived as leading the escalation.

4.2.4.3 Variables that impact the escalation of the conflict to a violent quarrel

In the children's descriptions, they refer also to variables that they believe to be the cause of intensifying the interparental conflict. An analysis of the findings reveals three types of understanding in this context: 1) The parents' motivation, or lack of it, to continue the quarrel; 2) the parents' ability or inability to control their rising anger, and 3) the mother's behavior as a motive for the father's escalation. Each of these types of understanding and their implications for the escalation dynamics will be examined.

4.2.4.3.1 FIRST UNDERSTANDING PATTERN: THE PARENTS' MOTIVATION OR LACK OF MOTIVATION TO CONTINUE THE QUARREL

Interviewer: What do you think will influence the quarrel and make it more serious? What will cause the argument to get even worse?

If neither of them want to listen, nothing. If it doesn't bother them, or anything, then it will start to develop and the argument will get a bit bigger and a bit bigger, until it starts ... if they get fed up, it can stop growing, and if not, it can get to the point at which it explodes. Even if they're about to explode, they can think better of it if they get fed up. If they can't be bothered anymore, they will suddenly think of some idea. (David)

4.2.4.3.2 SECOND UNDERSTANDING PATTERN: THE PARENTS' ABILITY OR INABILITY TO CONTROL THEIR RISING ANGER

Interviewer: What do you think makes arguments get more serious, with shouting and cursing, and even coming to blows?

When they get really angry. Like … when an argument starts, they build two walls right away; the wall of anger and the wall of calm. The wall of calm tries to turn off the anger. But sometimes, the anger gets bigger and bigger, and then the calm gets bigger, but it isn't strong enough, so sometimes the anger wins. Sometimes the calm wins and then there won't be violence between them. And sometimes the anger and the calm are equal. (Guy)

4.2.4.3.3 THIRD UNDERSTANDING PATTERN: THE MOTHER'S BEHAVIOR AS A MOTIVE FOR THE FATHER'S ESCALATION

Interviewer: What turns the argument into a violent quarrel?

When Mom annoys Dad. She causes it. She tells Dad what to do and then he gets even more annoyed with her. If she doesn't make him angry, then he can stop. (Inbar)

Interviewer: Explain to me how she makes this happen.

Because at first, they had an argument. And then he said to her, don't make anything, I don't want to eat in the evening. Mom made the cauliflower in her own way and then he got even more annoyed that she didn't make it the way he likes it, and then he came and threw out the cauliflower and then it got really bad. (Inbar)

An analysis of the children's types of understanding in relation to the variables that impact the argument's escalation to a violent quarrel shows that all the children understand that the process is composed of two alternative options: To escalate further or to end the argument. Therefore, the key variable that is perceived as responsible for channeling the process includes an impact in one of these two directions. Moreover, in some cases (again, regarding each of the understanding types), the children describe the creation of an option for the process to start over again, even after it had apparently come to a close. This was influenced by the variable that they perceived to trigger the escalation ("And sometimes the anger and the calm are equal"; "And then he said to her, don't make anything, I don't want to eat in the evening. Mom made the cauliflower in her own way and then he got even more annoyed"). This shows that an additional option exists in some of the escalation scripts, which is a type of static situation of tension "on standby for explosion," which can be defined only in retrospect as the point at which the argument ended or as the turning point to escalation.

It can be understood from the above that 1) the children perceive the escalation process as including at least one escape option, which shows it to be controllable by the sides that are involved, at least on a partial level ("if they get fed up, it can stop growing ... Even if they're about to explode, they can think better of it if they get fed up."—first quote). 2) The identification of two options for the development of the conflict shows the possibility of predicting two scripts: One, in the direction of exacerbating the quarrel and second, in the direction of bringing it to a close. Nevertheless, situations such as multiple junctures throughout the process or renewal of the quarrel after it has stopped because of a reenactment of the key variable might impair the predictive capability. This is because they are required constantly to be on the alert and to reevaluate the script at any given moment. 3) The perception of the process as including an option to end it and control it directs the children to perceive the home reality as conflictual in essence but not as necessarily violent, which assists in constructing a pseudo-normative reality at home, in which the conflicts are perceived as arguments between the sides, with violence as only one of the options for bringing them to a close. The creation of pseudo-normativity might also explain the fact that only some of the children perceive the motivational variable as influencing the development of the arguments, whereas others identify such a variable but do not see it as a key variable, since it is not inherent to the argument and is not connected to the communication developing between the sides.

4.2.4.4 The escalation dynamics

This theme refers to components identified by the children as leading the escalation process and to the interaction that takes place between these components. The children's descriptions expose three components that construct the intensification of the quarrel to the stage of all-out violence: The escalating conflict; the degree of rising anger; and the extent of control of the abating anger.

Understanding the forming dynamics as developing thanks to a communicative component that takes part in it indicates understanding of the process in the context of a normative conflict, when the parents wish to completely exhaust the subject of the argument.

Regarding the process itself, the children's descriptions indicate their understanding of a spiraling process, in which the interplay between the different components creates the dramatic effect. Thus, the level of aggression reached during the process is an inherent part of the escalating conflict (the communicative component). The following quotes illustrate the understanding patterns of the process:

> What happens there is that if they are both as determined as each other not to agree, then it can reach a point where they're hitting each other. The argument can't stop and then they start to get very angry with each other; my dad with my mom and my mom with my dad. Like, one yells why this and why that, and the other doesn't even listen and says the same thing. And afterwards they kind of start threatening, that this one won't give and that one won't give. If my dad gets really angry and my mom less so because she still hasn't reached that level of anger, then he starts, say, threatening her a bit or pushing her a bit and suddenly something happens that, like, it's impossible. They explode and then there is hitting. But my dad hits really hard. (Shahar)

> When they are, like, arguing, they annoy each other until a kind of friction is created, when they start to get to the climax of their anger and then they really go up a level. Then they start, and that's it, totally fighting with each other. Sometimes, my dad is really agitated. (Harel)

> They argue. Mom annoys Dad and then he gets angry at her, and then he starts yelling. And then Mom says to him: "Be quiet, you're waking Shlomit." Then he really yells at her and says: "There'll be no quiet, no quiet!" And then Mom says to him: "Why, what will you do to me?" And then there are screams. He doesn't control himself and starts hitting – Dad. (Shlomit)

As can be seen, while the first two quotes expose an understanding, according to which the mutual argument will lead to mutual emotional escalation and to both sides losing control, with the man having a physical advantage, the third quote exposes an understanding, according to which the father's rising anger leads to his loss of control. The first quote exposes also the existence of "internal" motivation for the escalating conflict, namely the wish to totally exhaust the issue under dispute between the sides. In the children's perception, when the sides do not reach an understanding but a situation in which each side is entrenched in his/her own stance ("What happens there is that if they are both as determined as each other not to agree, then it can reach a point where they're hitting each other"), they will aspire to end the conflict by violently imposing their opinion on the other side. In other words, as long as the sides believe that they can convince each other, they will do so by verbal means, but when they reach an impasse, they resort to the physical option. The violent option is legitimized by virtue of its perception in the context of conceptual exhaustion of the argument. This view is valid also when the loss of control is attributed specifically to the man.

4.2.4.5 The sides' management of the escalation process

In the children's descriptions, they refer also to their parents' action strategies for regulating the escalation dynamics and bringing the process to a temporary close (which creates an option to end the conflict) or to a final conclusion. Analysis of the findings reveals that the different modes of action are linked to the understanding patterns that were identified in relation to the variables that influence the escalation of the conflict to a violent quarrel.

4.2.4.5.1 FIRST UNDERSTANDING PATTERN: THE PARENTS' MOTIVATION, OR LACK OF MOTIVATION, TO CONTINUE TO ARGUE

The children's descriptions show that when the parents lack the motivation to continue to argue, they will adopt one of the following action strategies: 1) One side will convince the other that his/her opinions, intentions, or words are right; 2) enlisting an option that is external to the dispute to reach a compromise between the sides; and 3) one of the sides surrenders. The following quotes illustrate the separate action strategies, and their unique characteristics will be examined:

> *Interviewer*: Can you describe to me how the argument ended?
>
> They started arguing with each other. And then they didn't have the strength to argue anymore, so like when my Dad forgot to buy something at the supermarket, he said to her that he must have missed it out, and then, in the end, they started talking more calmly. (Limor)

I know what makes it [the argument] almost stop, when they're fed up of arguing, and then my sisters are crying. Because then, when they cry, the argument gets a bit worse and then it finishes … because then Mom says to Dad: "Look what you've done, now the girls are crying." And then he answers her: "I did that? You're the one who always starts an argument with me!" And then Mom says: "OK, we're both at fault, we both argue." (Gal)

> When they've both had enough of arguing, then one of them proves to the other that he is right, or one kind of gives in. Like, the one who gives in doesn't say that the other one is right. He doesn't change his view but stops arguing. (Ran)

The first quote illustrates how the key variable in the escalation (as perceived by the girl)—motivation—elicits an action strategy of mutual persuasion between the sides for the purpose of ending the conflict. In this context, it is noteworthy that the girl mentions the existence of a process. The willingness to listen enables the persuasive action strategy to take place leading to contention between the sides. She describes a process in which the sides gradually reach a compromise, which reduces the intensity of the mutual anger. The use of time-related vocabulary throughout the description emphasizes this point. From the perspective of the escalation dynamics, this might show that the de-escalation and escalation scripts are similar in character. They both involve a spiraling process in which the dynamics between the escalation components creates a weakening or strengthening of the dramatic effect.

The following descriptive quotes by Gal and Ran also illustrate the use of strategies that are essentially communicative and are perceived as related to the argument between the sides. Even though Gal describes enlisting the option to end the argument, which is external to the dispute itself—the effect of the escalating conflict on the children—this is still a topic that is related to the argument in its broad context and therefore might be perceived as inherent to it. Even though Ran's description refers to a strategy in which one side surrenders to the other, the context is still the subject under dispute.

4.2.4.5.2 SECOND UNDERSTANDING PATTERN: THE PARENTS' ABILITY OR INABILITY TO CONTROL THEIR ANGER

The children's descriptions show that when the parents' anger increases with the intensification of the argument, they will sometimes utilize anger management strategies. At the point of action, they will make use of one or more of the following strategies: 1) Creation of physical distance between the sides; 2) changing the spatial arrangement either inside or outside the house; and 3) using self-calming techniques.

> When they get angry, then they don't hear anymore. The only thing that interests them is to get away from each other and cool off. To go downstairs to calm themselves down. But sometimes, they don't manage to do that, and then it [the violence] happens. (Roy)

This quote illustrates how the elevated level of anger ("When they get angry") reduces their level of control ("then they don't hear anymore"). In such a situation, when both sides implement action strategies channeled toward gaining control over their anger, the process will be aborted, and escalation of the conflict will cease. The fact that they make use of three tactics to gain control over their anger, as well as turning to various calming strategies, both internal and external, is indicative of the emotional intensity involved in the escalation process. Great effort is required to reduce the dramatic effect that is created during the escalation. Hence, it can be assumed that even though the use of one action strategy might bring immediate calm, the anger will be so intense that the tension will remain in the air and any little thing can reignite the conflict.

4.2.4.5.3 THIRD UNDERSTANDING PATTERN: THE MOTHER'S BEHAVIOR AS A MOTIVE FOR THE FATHER'S ESCALATION

The children's descriptions show that at the point at which the father becomes angry in the escalating conflict with the mother, she will sometimes implement a strategy to manage the father's anger. The following quote demonstrates the nature of this action strategy:

> *Interviewer*: How does it happen that the shouts and curses in the argument will end in a situation of calm and not of violence?
>
> When they will stop the argument and will start afresh. The one who stops it is Mom. There are things that she says that make Dad stop being angry.

The girl implies the existence of two options: The parents either bringing the conflict to a close or not. Even though she describes the mother as the one who can stop the argument, in her overall view, she presents both parents as responsible for ending it ("When they will stop the argument and will start afresh"). This reveals an understanding of the conflict on two levels: The internal development level, in which the mother is perceived as leading the process and as responsible for bringing it to a conclusion, and the general level, in which both sides are perceived as responsible for the argument's development, positioning the context of the dispute as part of the trivial daily routine.

The girl describes the essence of the strategy as words that will calm the father's anger. Emphasizing the essence in a general and not a unique manner shows that, in practice, only the mother knows how to calm him down. The calming words cannot be judged in normative terms as soothing or enraging but are judged from the father's unique perspective.

An analysis of the findings regarding the action strategies used by the parents to regulate the escalation dynamics shows that all the children understand that a motivational component is involved in the process. The children are divided in their understanding of this component's place in forming the conflict escalation. While in the first understanding pattern, the use of the action strategy depends on the creation of conditions in which the partners lack the motivation to continue to argue; in the second and third understanding patterns, the motivational component is perceived as an action strategy in itself. (In the second understanding pattern, when the parents become angry, they can choose a strategy of motivation to argue or a strategy to manage or regulate their anger. In the third understanding pattern, when the father becomes angry, the mother can choose a strategy of managing the father's anger or of continuing to argue with him.) Either way, even if the motivation is perceived as a key variable in the process (first understanding pattern) and even if it is perceived as an action strategy (second and third understanding patterns), the understanding that motivation is a component of the process shows that the children identify a motive for the development of the argument and perceive it in two different ways: As "external" to the conflict or as "internal" and linked to the subject around which the argument broke out. The understanding of the concluding script of the argument as involving either communicative or anger management strategies shows the understanding of the process in a normative context and the understanding of the conflict's dynamics as related to the "internal" motive linked to the argument itself. Nevertheless, the existence of another type of understanding indicates the identification of an external motive that is not related to the dispute itself.

4.2.4.6 Results

The children's descriptions reveal the existence of three options for developing the process: The first in the absence of an action strategy and the second and third as outcomes of enacting such strategies. The possible results of the way in which the parents behave in confrontations that arise between them are as follows: 1) Escalation—intensification of the dispute on a time continuum to all-out violence; 2) de-escalation—making the cumulative effect of the dispute continually less dramatic until the conflict is brought to a close; and 3) a static situation of a possible explosion—maintaining the cumulative effect of the argument at a level of tension that enables temporary calm, even though anything can reignite the "flame of the dispute." Each of the aforementioned options was illustrated and analyzed in the previous sections.

4.2.5 Discussion

Analysis of the findings regarding the construction of the escalation process from the children's perspective reveals the existence of a predetermined script according to which the parents act. The following list of observations is evidence of the construction of a conflict escalation process between the parents to all-out violence as a relationship script in which the individuals are involved: The children's description of the context in which the conflict is formed as a general pattern of occurrence (rather than as an example of specific conflicts); the children's ability to present the conflicts on a developmental curve; reporting the order of events in the conflict as interrelated in a way that gives meaning to what has gone before and prepares the ground for the next stage; and describing the development of the process as a drama in which the tension is built up, thanks to the "acting" of the two protagonists, the parents.

These findings are consistent with Gergen's (1994, 1999) proposed conceptual framework of social construction for understanding the development of emotional occurrences. In his opinion, the development of such occurrences is not intra-psychic or situation-dependent but is part of a set of social "scripts" that are derived from fixed expectations (Gergen, 1994, 1999). In these terms, we can see emotional expressions as components of specific cultural scripts, detailed here below, which receive meaning only by virtue of their position in a relationship script.

Constructing the context for the development of arguments as daily trivial issues; perceiving the escalation process structure as symmetrical, i.e., both sides are perceived as equally responsible for escalation throughout all stages of the process; seeing the escalating conflict, i.e., the developing communicative component as a central component in escalation; understanding the escalation dynamics as driven by the motivation to exhaust the subject of the argument, to the stage of an impasse, and then physical aggression is used to bring the conflict to a close; and the use of normative strategies (communicative and emotional) to end the argument—all of these provide an insight into the emotional escalation as being a part of a cultural script, in which each side expresses its dissatisfaction with what the other has said, in order to bring about a change in the sides' adjustment to the relationship (change in perception or attitude).

In contrast, the descriptive level exposes a reality in which the father escalates the conflict by interpreting the mother's words and behavior as undermining his honor or his authority as decision-maker and head of the family. Furthermore, the children describe an escalation process with an asymmetric structure, according to which the father initiates the escalation and the mother either aligns herself with him (in the first and second understanding patterns) or scarcely reacts (in the third understanding pattern). The children describe the escalation dynamics in its advanced stages as driven by a motivational component, which implies the existence of an external reason for the appearance of the violence, which is not connected to the subject of the argument itself. All of this indicates that the emotional escalation is part of a cultural script within which the father causes the escalation in order to restore what he perceives to be the balance in the partner relationship: With him as the determining authority whom the mother has to obey.

Those gaps between the children's level of understanding and their descriptions indicate the existence of various hints in reality, which might direct the individuals to construct those same scripts in one way rather than another.

Two processes that were exposed in the analysis of the children's descriptions might explain the source of the gap: The first relates to living in a reality replete with violent conflicts, which directly influences the perception of the violence as taken for granted and is therefore understood to be one of the options in the conflict. The second relates to the construction of a pseudo-normative reality in the framework of which the escalation abounds with the adoption of accepted behaviors. Examples of such behaviors are making use of communicative and anger management strategies to bring the escalating conflict to a close. Even though scrutiny of those behavioral norms exposes external rather than inherent use of them (the communicative strategies that were used were elicited artificially for the purpose of ending the conflict and were not connected to an inherent solution to the conflict), the actual use of them is a concrete hint to the children of the existence of a normative reality. Within this reality, the conflicts reflect an event script in which both sides wish to bring about some kind of change in adjustment to their relationship, when the conflict sometimes deteriorates to violence when the sides do not reach an agreement and one side tries to force his/her opinion on the other.

Besides the fact that the two aforementioned processes shape a context of a distorted construction of reality in which the abusive and dangerous are perceived as trivial and routine, the children's assimilation of such a perception may mean that they seek hints that obscure the abuse, disregard dangerous signals, and adhere to those explanations in a normative reality that may fit the abusive reality in which they live. Their learning and assimilation of these latent processes might explain the gradually increasing gap, over the years, between developing a normal reading of reality and internalizing accepted social norms and the children's perception of the reality, which draws on approaches that justify use of violence, expressed through difficulty in understanding social situations. In addition, this learning might explain the inclusion of the learned cognitive strategies in the field of direct abuse, especially sexual abuse. The fact that both parents construct a normative reality and create a consensus that everything at home is running as it should only reinforces the perceptual distortion among the children.

Sexual abuse, either in the family or by an external abuser, in many cases, develops over a long period of time (Berliner & Conte, 1990). The multistage process frequently negates the sexual nature of the abuse, whether by characterizing it as "not sexual," by instilling an element of unique love into the relationship or by positioning the child as a full partner in the relationship (Conte et al., 1989). In such cases, the context of violence against women may provide perfect conditions for child sexual abuse, as the children learn to seek hints of normativity in their everyday reality. Within the framework of sexual education, they will have social explanations at their disposal related to preparing for intact adult couple relationships; specifically, they may find support in concepts such as love or mutuality in the broad social sense (concern for others and giving to others). The parental consensus regarding the existence of a normative life routine at home provides an additional condition for the existence of sexual abuse. In this context, the fact that the mother is a victim of violence herself, as well as of sexual abuse, which was found in high percentages among women victims of violence (e.g., Gilbert et al., 2009; Hébert et al., 2021), might prevent her from being alert to signs of abuse in her son or daughter (Lev-Wiesel, 2015).

The study findings complement the theory that deals with escalation of interparental conflicts to all-out violence. While the studies by Eisikovits et al. (2002) and Winstok et al. (2002) exposed the structure and dynamics of violence in intimate relationships from the perspective of the aggressor and the victim, the present study exposes the children's perspective on the process. The findings show that children, similar to women, see the transition from a nonviolent reality to a violent reality as a process marked by junctures, which each hold the possibility for either escalation or escape. However, unlike the woman's view, which sees her ability to control the situation as a key variable in managing the process, the children see the escalation dynamics as dependent on the variable of both parents' motivation to exhaust the subject of the argument. While the mother's viewpoint can be explained against the background of her use of a survival mechanism (Eisikovits et al., 2002), the children's perspective is derived from the parents presenting a picture of a normative context for the internal home reality. Following on from this, the present study suggests viewing children as distinct victims of the domestic violence dynamics rather than as co-victims of the abusive domestic reality created by the male perpetrator, as suggested recently by Katz (2022).

The study findings contribute to the literature on violence against an intimate partner. In this context, exposing the gap between the children's understanding of the relationship script and the latent script as it emerges in the children's descriptions serves as a basis for the school that sees violence as an expression of power and control that men impose on women (DeKeseredy & MacLeod, 1997) and explains the risk in blurring the context. The need of both parents to shape such a reality serves as a distorted filter for how the children view the reality and gives them to understand that violent conflicts are legitimate within couple and interpersonal relationships. Nevertheless, these findings constitute a possibility of in-depth understanding of how a violent-free context allows the assembly of a completely different puzzle, still based on reality.

The immediate implications of the study findings for the type of treatment required for the population of children exposed to violence are that it must include a cognitive element focused on an intact social view. This focus might be important, especially because of the fact that the blurring of the violent reality might explain not only the difficulty of understanding the social situation and legitimizing the violence but also the high percentages of children who are directly harmed by the father's violence. Trivialization of the harm is made possible by the children's perception of the violent reality at home as normative. Since learning over many years, which includes considering a distorted reality as normal, is deeply ingrained, the position of authorities from outside the home needs to be increased significantly in the children's lives. This demands of the community rethinking and reorganization, as well as enlisting the education system to treat these children. In any case, it is important that the treatment of children will be distinct from the treatment of the mother and will be recognized as the treatment of child abuse victims. This is based on the study findings, which clearly reveal the children's perception of both parents being responsible for the violence.

Nevertheless, it must be taken into consideration that such work might distance the children from their families (as part of the clearer understanding that they are living in a world of falsehood) and might cause them to relinquish their survival mechanisms that they need for optimal functioning within the escalation scripts of the violent confrontations. The solution might be to work with the children on creating alternative spaces through the various types of art (Carmel et al., 2014), where they will experience components of the normative world but outside their routine, everyday context. Such an experience might be a bridge to the normative world, not from a place that contradicts their internal home reality but from a place that might provide them with an alternative option for the future. The next stage in the therapeutic process will be direct confrontational cognitive work. In cases in which there is a reasonable suspicion of physical and/or sexual abuse of the children within the framework of their exposure to violence, the intervention will need to take a different direction to stop the abuse immediately, understanding that the home environment is not a safe and protected place. This notwithstanding, acquaintance with components of the normative world through creating alternative spaces might be a key variable in acquiring a new language, which is different from the one imprinted on them in the home space.

Note

1 These sections are closely based on studies published by me (Carmel, 2015, 2016). Please see the reference list.

References

Anderson, K. M. (2012). Fostering resilience in daughters of battered women. In D. Becvar (Ed.), *Handbook of family resilience* (pp. 495–514). Springer.

Bancroft, L., Silverman, J. G., & Ritchie, D. (2012). *The batterer as parent: Addressing the impacts of domestic violence on family dynamics* (2nd ed.). Sage.

Ben-Ze'ev, A. (2000). *The subtlety of emotions*. MIT Press.

Ben-Ze'ev, A. (2010). The thing called emotion. In P. Goldie (Ed.), *The Oxford handbook of philosophy of emotion* (pp. 41–62). Oxford University Press.

Berliner, L., & Conte, J. (1990). The process of victimization: The victim's perspective. *Child Abuse and Neglect, 14*(1), 29–40. https://doi.org/10.1016/0145-2134(90)90078-8

Cameranesi, M., Shooshtari, S., & Piotrowski, C. C. (2022). Investigating adjustment profiles in children exposed to intimate partner violence using a biopsychosocial resilience framework: A Canadian population-based study. *Child Abuse and Neglect, 125*, 105453.

Carlson, J., Voith, L., Brown, J. C., & Holmes, M. (2019). Viewing children's exposure to intimate partner violence through a developmental, social-ecological, and survivor lens: The current state of the field, challenges, and future directions. *Violence Against Women, 25*(1), 6–28. https://doi.org/10.1177/1077801218816187

Carmel, Y. (2010). *Escalation of interparental conflicts from the children's perspective* (Unpublished doctoral dissertation). University of Haifa, Israel (Hebrew).

Carmel, Y. (2015). The perception of daily reality among children exposed to their father's violence against their mother: An intense bi-polar experience. *Academic Journal of Creative Art Therapies, 5*(2), 326–345. http://ajcat.haifa.ac.il/images/dec_2015/ifat_eng.pdf

Carmel, Y. (2016). Children exposed to their father's violence against their mother: The link between the children's perception of the escalation and their experience of complex psychological, physical and sexual abuse. *Academic Journal of Creative Art Therapies, 6*(1), 355–377.

Carmel, Y., Sigad, L., Lev-Wiesel, R., & Eisikovits, Z. (2014). Pathways to resilience among Israeli child victims of abuse and neglect. *Child Indicators Research, 8*(3), 551–570. https://doi.org/10.1007/s12187-014-9255-5

Conte, J. R., Wolfe, S., & Smith, T. (1989). What sexual offenders tell us about prevention strategies. *Child Abuse and Neglect, 13*(2), 293–302.

Corbin, J., & Strauss, A. (2008). *Basics of qualitative research: Techniques and procedures for developing grounded theory* (3rd ed.). Sage.

Creswell, J. W. (1998). *Qualitative inquiry and research design: Choosing among five traditions.* Sage.

DeKeseredy, W. S., & MacLeod, L. (1997). *Women abuse: A sociological story.* Harcourt Brace.

Denzin, N. K. (1989). *Interpretive interactionism.* Sage.

Denzin, N. K. (1997). *Interpretive ethnography: Ethnographic practices for the 21st century.* Sage.

Downes, J., Kelly, L., & Westmarland, N. (2019) 'It's a work in progress': Men's accounts of gender and change in their use of coercive control. *Journal of Gender-Based Violence, 3*(3). https://doi.org/10.1332/239868019X15627570242850

Eder, D., & Fingerson, L. (2002). Interviewing children and adolescents. In J. F. Gubrium & J. A. Holstein (Eds.), *Handbook of interview research: Context and methods* (pp. 181–201). Sage.

Edleson, J. I. (1995). Mothers and children: Understanding the links between woman battering and child abuse. Paper presented at the Strategic Planning Workshop on Violence against Woman, 31 March, Washington, DC. National Institute of Justice.

Eisikovits, Z., & Winstok, Z. (2001). Researching children's experience of interparental violence: Towards a multidimensional conceptualization. In J. L. Edleson & S. A. Graham-Bermann (Eds.), *Domestic violence in the lives of children* (pp. 203–218). American Psychological Association.

Eisikovits, Z., Winstok, Z., & Enosh, G. (1998). Children's experience of interparental violence: A heuristic model. *Children and Youth Services Review, 20*(6), 547–568. https://doi.org/10.1016/S0190-7409(98)00025-5

Eisikovits, Z., Winstok, Z., & Gelles, R. (2002). Structure and dynamics of escalation from the victim's perspective. *Families in Society, 83*(2), 142–152. https://doi.org/10.1606/1044-3894.29

Ericksen, J. R., & Henderson, A. D. (1992). Witnessing family violence: The children's experience. *Journal of Advanced Nursing, 17*(10), 1200–1209. https://doi.org/10.1111/j.1365-2648.1992.tb01836.x

Evans, S. E., Davies, C., & DiLillo, P. (2008). Exposure to domestic violence: A meta-analysis of child and adolescent outcomes. *Aggression and Violent Behavior, 13*(2), 131–140. https://doi.org/10.1016/j.avb.2008.02.005

Fine, G. A., & Sandstrom, K. L. (1988). *Knowing children (Qualitative Research Methods Series No. 15).* Sage.

Fong, V. C., Hawes, D., & Allen, J. A. (2017). A systematic review of risk and protective factors for externalizing problems in children exposed to intimate partner violence. *Trauma, Violence, and Abuse*, 1–19. https://doi.org/10.1177/1524838017692383

Fong, V. C., Hawes, D., & Allen, J. L. (2019). A systematic review of risk and protective factors for externalizing problems in children exposed to intimate partner violence. *Trauma, Violence, and Abuse*, *20*(2), 149–167. https://doi.org/10.1177/1524838017692383

Foy, D. W., Furrow, J., & McManus, S. (2011). Exposure to violence, post-traumatic symptomatology, and criminal behaviors. In V. Ardino (Ed.), *Post-traumatic syndromes in childhood and adolescence: A Handbook of research and practice* (pp. 199–210). Wiley-Blackwell.

Gergen, K. J. (1994). *Realities and relationships*. Harvard University Press.

Gergen, K. J. (1999). *Invitation to social construction*. Sage.

Gewirtz, A. H., & Edleson, J. L. (2007). Young children's exposure to intimate partner violence: Towards a developmental risk and resilience framework for research and intervention. *Journal of Family Violence*, *22*(3), 151–163. https://doi.org/10.1007/s10896-007-9065-3

Gilbert, R., Widom, C. S., Browne, K., Fergusson, D., Webb, E., & Janson, S. (2009). Burden and consequences of child maltreatment in high-income countries. *Lancet*, *373*(9657), 68–81. https://doi.org/10.1016/S0140-6736(08)61706-7

Glaser, B., & Strauss, A. (1967). *The discovery of grounded theory*. Aldin.

Goldblatt, H. (2003). Strategies of coping among adolescents experiencing interparental violence. *Journal of Interpersonal Violence*, *18*(5), 532–552. https://doi.org/10.1177/0886260503251071

Graham-Bermann, S. A., & Edleson, J. L. (Eds.). (2001). *Domestic violence in the lives of children: The future of research, intervention, and social policy*. American Psychological Association.

Hébert, M., Lapierre, A., MacIntosh, H. B., & Ménard, A. D. (2021). A review of mediators in the association between child sexual abuse and revictimization in romantic relationships. *Journal of Child Sexual Abuse*, *30*(4), 385–406. https://doi.org/10.1080/10538712.2020.1801936

Hester, M., Pearson, C., & Harwin, N. (2007). *Making an Impact*. Jessica Kingsley.

Holt, S., Buckley, H., & Whelan, S. (2008). The impact of exposure to domestic violence on children and young people: A review of the literature. *Child Abuse and Neglect*, *32*(8), 797–810. https://doi.org/10.1016/j.chiabu.2008.02.004

Humphreys, J. (1991). Children of battered women: Worries about their mothers. *Pediatric Nursing*, *17*(4), 342–345.

Jouriles, E. N., Norwood, W. D., McDonald, R., & Peters, B. (2001). Domestic violence and child adjustment. In J. H. Grych & F. D. Fincham (Eds.), *Interpersonal conflict and child development: Theory, research, and applications* (pp. 315–336). Cambridge University Press.

Katz, E. (2016). Beyond the physical incident model: How children living with domestic violence are harmed by and resist regimes of coercive control. *Child Abuse Review*, *25*(1), 46–59. https://doi.org/10.1002/car.2422

Katz, E. (2022). *Coercive control in children's and mothers' lives*. Oxford University Press.

Kitzmann, K. M., Gaylord, N. K., Holt, A. R., & Kenny, E. D. (2003). Child whitnesses to domestic violence: A meta-analytic review. *Journal of Consulting and Clinical Psychology, 71*(2), 339–352. https://doi.org/10.1037/0022-006X.71.2.339

Lev-Wiesel, R. (2015). Intergenerational transmission of sexual abuse? Motherhood in the shadow of incest. In R. Lev-Wiesel, J. Cwikel, & N. Barak (Eds.), *Guard your soul Mental health among women in Israel*. The Ben Gurion University of the Negev Center for Women's Health Studies and Promotion and Myers-JDC-Brookdale Institute. The Smokler Center for Health Policy and Research (Hebrew).

MacMillan, H. L., Wathen, C. N., & Varcoe, C. M. (2013). Intimate partner violence in the family: Considerations for children's safety. *Child Abuse and Neglect, 37*(12), 1186–1191. https://doi.org/10.1016/j.chiabu.2013.05.005

Macvean, M. L., Humphreys, C., & Healey, L. (2018). Facilitating the collaborative interface between child protection and specialist domestic violence services: A scope review. *Australian Social Work, 71*(2), 148–161. https://doi.org/10.1080/0312407X.2017.1415365

Miranda, J. K., Olivares, N., & Crockett, M. A. (2022). Growing up with intimate partner violence at home: Adolescents' narratives on their coping strategies. *Journal of Family Violence*. https://doi.org/10.1007/s10896-021-00345-7

Moustakas, C. E. (1994). *Phenomenological research methods*. Sage.

Nietzsche, F. W. (1968). *The will to power; a new translation by Walter Kaufman and R. J. Hollingdale, edited with commentary by Walter Kaufman*. Vintage Books.

Patton, M. Q. (2002). *Qualitative evaluation and research methods* (3rd ed.). Sage.

Peled, E. (1993). *The experience of living with violence for preadolescent witnesses of women abuse* (Unpublished doctoral dissertation). University of Minnesota.

Peled, E. (1997). Intervention with children of battered women: A review of the current literature. *Children and Youth Services Review, 19*(4), 277–299. https://doi.org/10.1016/S0190-7409(97)00018-2

Peled, E. (2001). Ethically sound research on children's exposure to domestic violence: A proposal. In J. L. Edleson & S. A. Graham-Bermann (Eds.), *Domestic violence in the lives of children* (pp. 111–132). American Psychological Association.

Saunders, B. E. (2003). Understanding children exposed to violence: Toward an integration of overlapping fields. *Journal of Interpersonal Violence, 18*(4), 356–376. 76. https://doi.org/10.1177/ 0886260502250840

Scheff, T. J., & Retzinger, S. M. (1991). *Emotions and violence: Shame and rage in destructive conflicts*. Free Press.

Sitney, M. H., & Kaufman, K. L. (2021). A chip of the old block: The impact of fathers on sexual offending behavior. *Trauma, Violence, and Abuse, 22*(4), 961–975. https://doi.org/10.1177/1524838019898463

Sonego, M., Pichiuli, M., Gandarillas, A., Polo, C., & Ordobas, M. (2018). Mental health in girls and boys exposed to intimate partner violence. *Public Health, 164*, 26–29. https://doi.org/10.1016/j.puhe.2018.07.003

Vu, N. L., Jouriles, E. N., McDonald, R., & Rosenfield, D. (2016). Children's exposure to intimate partner violence: A meta-analysis of longitudinal associations with child adjustment problems. *Clinical Psychology Review, 46*, 25–33. https://doi.org/10.1016/j.cpr.2016.04.003

Winstok, Z. (2007). Toward an interactional perspective on intimate partner violence. *Aggression and Violent Behavior*, *12*(3), 348–363. https://doi.org/10.1016/j.avb.2006.12.001

Winstok, Z. (2013). *Partner violence: A new paradigm of for understanding conflict escalation*. Springer.

Winstok, Z., Eisikovits, Z., & Gelles, R. (2002). Structure and dynamics of escalation from the battered perspective. *Families in Society*, *83*(2), 129–141. https://doi.org/10.1606/1044-3894.37

Chapter 5

Intervention with children exposed to interparental violence

Change in trends and the implications of this

5.1 The experience of children exposed to interparental violence—new dimensions for understanding

The findings of research dealing with phenomenology of the experience of exposure to violence from the perspective of its underlying processes—escalation of interparental conflicts to all-out violence and the children's involvement in these conflicts (Carmel, 2010)—show that the children's reality is composed of two fundamental experiences: Violence and everyday family life. As opposed to the feelings of emptiness, boredom, isolation, and absence of intimacy, which are typical of the children's everyday family life and create a sense of suffocation, the violence that breaks into the daily routine injects vitality, interest, action, excitement, tension, and meaning. Unlike in a normative situation in which the everyday reality creates wholeness and meaning, in the violent reality, it is crisis and the breaking up of the whole that creates a whole and meaningful experience. This reversed situation may explain why children living in a violent reality are drawn into the violent experience. The strength of this experience, and its emotional and cognitive intensity compensate for the deficiency, vacuum, and existential boredom created by the reality of everyday life. Breaking up the whole, unraveling the everyday fabric of family life, is what introduces an exciting, intense experience comparable to spiritual uplifting, a powerful sensory experience involving complex mental processes.

Constructing the whole and restoring the overall functioning of everyday family life demands fusion of fractures. The children are given a guideline as to how to go about restoring the routine through the parents' portrayal of a normative everyday family life context. They do so by seeming to adhere to parental behavioral rules, such as preventing inappropriate communication from reaching the children's ears, as well as by presenting escalation of violence as only one of many options to end the conflict. Thus, they bestow a normative dimension on the circumstances of the conflict's development and resolution. The nature of this guideline not only enables fusion of fractures to restore the whole but gives an impression of a well-constructed whole with components that create an experience of completeness. Nevertheless, the experience of wholeness is shattered when put to the test by the children against their everyday reality. The parts of the whole are reassembled discordantly vis-à-vis the external normative reality, the world outside the home, creating an unharmonious whole and a complex emotional experience. The internal domestic wholeness becomes half true and half untrue and, later, leads to a split emotional experience, lacking a unifying internal thread.

Although the use of components of the normative reality to mend the family system's broken pieces creates an illusion of wholeness, making daily functioning in a discordant system somewhat easier, it simultaneously creates and deepens distortions in the perception of what is normative and how normative components actually create a whole. This situation makes it even more difficult for the children to understand which of the external everyday reality components have the potential to create a whole and, if they choose these components, how they can be connected to create a whole. Therefore, the external normative option offered by therapists might not be attractive to the children. If the normative external reality is not understood, the parts are not an option for creating a full, meaningful whole. Since meaning is a product of perfect integration of parts, the world outside the home does not constitute such an option. The alternative option constitutes violent incidents which, beyond the experience of arousal, tension, and interest, give meaning to time, to the sense of partnership toward a meaningful goal (either stopping the violence or enabling it to continue in accordance with the developing script), and to interaction between family members (siblings and parents)—all those elements that, in the socialization process outside the home, the children have learned to view as essential for creating meaning. The violent existence, the fragmentation created by the violent incident, is what becomes, for the children, paradoxically and contrary to expectations, an attractive context for constructing meaning. If that is the case, even though the fusion of fractures following the violent incident enables a temporary return to routine, the violent incident itself enables a huge release of tension following cumulative frustration, as well as providing temporary relief from a boring routine to construct meaning. The violence serves as a **means** of reducing tension and venting frustration, as well as a **goal**, through attaining meaning and a sense of tremendous sensory and cognitive vitality; hence, its strength.

The meaning of the situation described is that two deep processes are required in order to depart from the violent reality: 1) Replacing a powerful, vibrant, negative experience with a positive one; and 2) reconstructing a normative context and recognizing its components. This type of response may be provided by art therapy, which, with a unique variation that integrates several modes of intervention, will facilitate work on the processes mentioned above. In this chapter, I will suggest a new intervention direction for the population of children exposed to violence. Its innovation lies in the content that I attune to the children and in the way I combine the various possibilities offered by art therapy with art education.

5.2 What is the connection between art and living in a domestic violent reality?

As illustrated above, living in a violent reality involves processes of breaking and rebuilding. In the framework of the violent reality, returning to the routine demands fusion or sticking together of parts. In this context, the children learn how the whole (the everyday reality) may be reassembled via the broken parts, like a jigsaw, when the picture to be formed is known in advance, if we practice putting it together, again and again.

Nevertheless, as well as this putting-together process, which is similar to copying or imitation, they learn an additional assembly process, which enables the use of broken parts to create a whole containing vitality and meaning—the violent reality. Even though this putting-together process is part of the breakage and hence, an outside observer would not perceive it as the building of a whole, an internal recognition of the process reveals a compositional masterpiece, as illustrated in the previous chapter. We are talking about situations of uncertainty, which demand continuous improvisation and attempts to find solutions in accordance with the changing reality (see Chapter 4, Section 4.2). There is a fundamental script, dictated by the parents, regarding the conduct expected in the various possible situations, but the dynamic reality demands continuous rereading of the map, reevaluation of the situation in relation to how to behave, and to assemble the puzzle as developments occur. All this leads to tension and arousal as well as to a sense of meaning when the whole is put together in accordance with what is defined as "constructing a violent reality."

The second process, which shows the children how to create a "complete whole," involves cognitive characteristics such as spontaneity, interplay of components, imagination, motivation, originality, thinking out of the box, and intuition. These cognitive skills underlie creativity or creative thinking.

Although creativity is not restricted to art, creative thinking is characteristic of art. Art is a process involving exploration, change, creation of images, working with individual imagination, and sometimes tackling the unknown. Individuals connect to their own creative source, where there are no role models or examples to copy (Malchiodi, 2007). Successfully copying a drawing of a jug or precise reproduction of a particular statue may give individuals a sense of satisfaction, but they will not lead them along a creative process in which they will either discover or develop their own personal, authentic imagination.

It can be seen, therefore, that living in a violent reality involves the use of cognitive processes that are similar to those underlying art: Finding solutions, experimenting with new ideas, and improvising in a broken context—of violence. It is actually in the context of the whole, the context of constructing the family's everyday reality, that the opposite process, the uncreative imitation process, is learned. Therefore, use of art therapy as an intervention that enables a process of breaking an existing system and building another system may help to create something new and unique **in an everyday family life context**—a whole that contains something else, something good. Both the engagement in the process and the creative act itself will make the process meaningful and worthwhile. From this perspective, art therapy may serve as a process that is simultaneously **parallel but in contradiction to what was learned in the violent reality**: Creating an aesthetic whole as a counter response to a whole that arouses painful, unpleasant emotions, as a counter response to a "living" whole, but which creates a picture of ugliness (the violent being). The fact that the children possess the cognitive skills to break up and reassemble creatively, as part of the violent reality in which they live, may help them to internalize the nature of the craft of putting together in the context of doing art.

5.3 Art therapy—use of nonverbal language to gain insights, reconstruction of self, and change

Art therapy is based on the integration of two disciplines: Art and psychology. Aspects of visual art, the creative process, human development, behavior, personality, and mental health are important components in defining this field. Nonetheless, art therapists' work with different populations and a lack of consensus about the definition among the practitioners themselves create complexity that is an obstacle to distinguishing it from other therapeutic disciplines (Malchiodi, 2007).

Although art therapists have come up with numerous specific definitions of art therapy, most of them fall into two main categories: Art as therapy and art psychotherapy (Malchiodi, 2007). The first category, art as therapy, includes belief that the creative process of doing art has the power to bring about internal healing. Doing art is perceived as an opportunity to express one's imagination, authenticity, spontaneity—an experience that, with time, can lead to personal fullness, emotional repair, and change (Kramer, 1993; Malchiodi, 2007). This perception sees the actual process of creating art as therapeutic (Malchiodi, 2007). The second category, art psychotherapy, is based on the idea that art is a tool of symbolic communication. It follows, then, that the products—drawings, pictures, and other artistic expressions—are perceived as helpful for communicating personal issues, emotions, and conflicts. Psychotherapy is essential for this approach, and the artistic images become important for evoking verbal communication between the individual and the therapist to achieve understanding.

In fact, most therapists practicing art therapy combine both approaches, art as therapy and art psychotherapy, to different degrees. That is to say, the idea that doing art is a therapeutic process in itself and the idea that the products of art are relevant for therapy are both perceived as important. The emphasis placed on either one of these approaches in therapy depends on the goal of the therapy itself, the personal needs of the patient, or the philosophy with which the art therapist comes to therapy (Malchiodi, 2007, 2020).

5.3.1 The process of creating art as therapy

Creativity is often defined as the ability to bring something new into existence, unifying opposites, impressions, ideas, and concepts that appeared initially unconnected, or "giving life" to a new idea. In a creative moment, individuals begin to identify the limits of their thinking and the way they observe the world and leave behind prior beliefs and perceptions. In this sense, creativity involves courage (Cohen, 2000; Gardner, 1993). In recent decades, creativity has become defined as human potential, an ability that we can develop ourselves if we so wish (Cohen, 2000).

Since the creative process in visual art is an experience that engages both the brain and the senses, it is considered to involve additional unique creative aspects to those mentioned earlier (Malchiodi, 2007, 2020). Lusebrink (2007), an art therapist, talked about the fact that artistic creativity incorporates a number of experiences: 1) On the kinetic-sensory level, the encounter with artistic materials creates a physical experience; 2) on the perceptual-emotional level, the individual creates a connection between the artistic materials and his/her ideas and emotions; and 3) on the cognitive-symbolic level, the individual makes use of the artistic materials to create a personal symbol that will express emotions and thoughts or portray events. In art, the courage to create something new and something unique can provide satisfaction and involvement that make the creative act meaningful and worthwhile (Malchiodi, 2007, 2020).

Since, like therapy, the creative process incorporates finding new solutions to old ways of being; the creative process offers opportunities to be exposed to and experiment with new ideas and new ways of being; and since, in addition to that, both processes involve improvisation, change, and transformation, the experience of doing art has healing and rejuvenating potential (Malchiodi, 2007, 2020). The experience of vitality may be especially powerful in the context of creating art because the encounter with the "I" is shaped through artistic materials that create an intense sensory experience. In this context, Czikszentmihalyi (1990) spoke about being captivated in a mental and emotional state that he called flow. This is a state of elation, of full immersion in the current activity, while feeling positive and fully energized. Everything round about is forgotten, except the task in hand and awareness and action become one. Elliot Eisner (2002) talked about attaining this state not only in the context of the creative process itself but also through the completed work, the state of the product. Observation of the product while exploring the complete harmony of its components may also create such a sense of elation.

5.3.2 Images of art as helping to evoke verbal communication surrounding personal issues, emotions, and conflicts (art psychotherapy)

Some art therapists focus more on talking about images than on creating them. Among other things, this focus derives from the perception of art as a way to express feelings and perceptions in relation to complex, conflictual, and traumatic situations that would not have arisen via the verbal channel (Malchiodi, 2015). The theoretical orientation used by art therapists for talking about the content of the image created by the individual, and the attitudes and emotions it evokes (according to the individual's own interpretation) are part of the therapeutic relationship. Art therapists make use of different philosophies and techniques appropriate to them (Malchiodi, 2007).

5.4 Art education—the arts as important tools for developing complex and refined forms of thinking

Even though the art education field is considered as a knowledge discipline in itself, as distinct from art therapy, as such, I found it to be especially relevant for intervention with children exposed to violence. Therefore, in this section, I will refer to a thesis underlying art education as presented by Elliot Eisner (2002, 2008), a founder of the discipline, as well as to the nature of the work as outlined by him.

Eisner's central claim is that the arts are critical tools for developing complex and refined forms of thinking. Moreover, he claims that these forms of thinking are very relevant for coping with the ambiguity and uncertainty of everyday life created by postmodern culture (Eisner, 2002, 2008). Another of Eisner's claims is that complex forms of thinking require pedagogical attention, i.e., *mediation* is an important condition to advance thinking. Learning how to think artistically requires *guidance and learning* and will not develop in and of itself, merely through observation. According to Eisner (2002), art education has the following aims: 1) To teach the students to think artistically, namely to develop their sensitivities, nurture their imagination, and enhance their technical skills in order to work better with materials; (2) to develop the students' ability to recognize the qualities that are the components of art; (3) to help students understand the historical and cultural context in which art is created and therefore reflects (content and form reflect social norms); and (4) to explore and discover the value of art: aesthetics—the school of beauty—and to talk about the place of beauty and how important it is in a work of art. Successful teaching of art can thus be considered an art in itself.

Eisner explains artistry as a form of practice accomplished through the imagination, involving a technique of clarifying and organizing expressive qualities to achieve aesthetically pleasurable results. Artistry is refined through receiving others' criticism of the work and learning needs to include guidance toward a certain idea (Eisner, 2002). Such is the case with the teaching of art. He does not talk about instructions given according to a particular guideline but about creating conditions for learning, situations providing tasks and materials, engaging the students in meaningful learning, and connecting them to other aspects of the world. In practice, art teachers will teach the students how to stimulate the imagination; technical knowledge, reading the products (the quality) of the work; problem-solving (e.g., the size of the figure, its position on the paper, and its movement in order to create harmony among the parts); developing a personal viewpoint; and connecting earlier works with current works and present works with the external world.

Ultimately, in Eisner's view, the following types of thinking (intelligence) will develop through learning the arts (Eisner, 2008): 1) Attention to relationships, with the goal of creating relationships between the parts that lead to ultimate pleasure. A perfect composition is achieved when there is harmony among the parts, referring to a process involving visual analysis and synthesis. The nuances among the parts influence the whole. 2) Improvising intelligence, meaning the ability to change direction, even to redefine goals, when new, better options arise. (3) Use of materials as a medium. (4) Shaping form for conveying expressive content. (5) Exercising the imagination. (6) Shaping the world from an aesthetic perspective, meaning seeing the world in a new way. (7) Creating life, a sense of vitality. When a person knows how to read art, the form, it is experienced as emotional fullness, full of life, of joy.

5.5 Art therapy groups

While doing art individually can be fulfilling, therapeutic, and healing, doing art in a group has unique advantages (Malchiodi, 2007, 2020), such as 1) infusing hope, as part of the individual's belonging to a support group. This experience of group support and partnership usually nurtures hope. 2) Interaction, in that groups provide an opportunity for social interaction. 3) Universality, in that groups show participants that others have similar problems. 4) Catharsis, in that group therapy, like individual therapy, may also help the expression of painful emotions or experiences. (5) Altruism, in that therapeutic groups emphasize mutual help (Yalom, 1995, Malchiodi, 2020). Doing art in a group connects members of the group through shared projects and/or sharing art that was done during the therapeutic session (Malchiodi, 2007, 2020).

5.5.1 Art psychotherapy groups

In art psychotherapy groups, therapists often take an active part in determining the themes and planning artistic group actions with particular goals that are not exposed to clients (Malchiodi, 2007). Most groups are limited to several sessions and follow a fixed format of open discussion, some kind of experimental process, and subsequent discussion. In groups where a guided theme is lacking, participants may tend to work on ongoing projects.

5.5.2 Open studio groups or art studio groups

Open studio or art studio groups provide a different type of experience from art psychotherapy groups. Since art is the main activity, the therapeutic space is designed as an art studio or an art classroom, and the clients may be perceived as artists or as people engaged in art, who have come to benefit from doing art as a process of self-expression, exploration, and healing (Malchiodi, 2007). While acquiring insights is at the center of this type of art therapy (exactly like in the art psychotherapy groups), the therapy sessions in an art studio group may focus on experiences of creating art. **The materials and equipment are accessible, and clients are encouraged to make independent choices** to choose the media through which they wish to work and the direction to take. **Art skills are also learned and thus, whoever wishes to improve creative expression can do so**. Other therapeutic sessions may focus on expressive experiences of art. The participants share feelings about their artistic experiences and give feedback on each other's work.

5.6 Intervention with children exposed to interparental violence—principles

As I noted at the beginning of the chapter (Sections 5.1 and 5.2), the findings of the study that examined the phenomenology of the experience of children exposed to violence (Carmel, 2010) show that the children's everyday family life is characterized by an experience of emptiness, desolation, and absence. This reality, as shown by the study findings, is a product of destruction, abuse of the other, breaking of intimacy, betrayal of the ideal representation of social norms, and lack of parental emotional availability, which introduced violence into the children's lives. Nevertheless, paradoxically, it was actually the violence that was shown to provide a powerful counter-experience for the children, an experience full of vitality. Even though the results of the violence spread destruction and the mending of these fractures form a whole that lacks essence, the violence itself constitutes a genuine, albeit temporary, means of release from the desolation, from that whole that is lacking in essence, created by the violence itself.

To use a metaphorical description, in the children's being, it is as if the foreground and background of the picture have changed places. The daily routine, the fundamental being, has made room for the background, i.e., the violent events that break the routine by their colorfulness and fullness of content, thus constructing meaning. This existential reversal, which is a genuine survival need since people are unable to tolerate long-term existential emptiness (absence calls to fill the vacuum), is at the center of the children's lives.

Two complementary processes are involved in this existential reversal: The first is the script that parents teach children about how to mend the fractures and return to a pseudo-routine; and the second is the violent script, in which the parents teach the children how to behave in the violent reality and to participate in its construction. The first script creates a whole on the level of a model, but the essence, the content of the model, is empty. The second script creates fragmentation on the level of the model, but the essence, the content of the model, is full. These two complementary yet opposite processes are responsible not only for the existential reversal and the children's choice of the violent existence but also for the distortion and undermining of the perception of what is normative. This is because constructing the whole, which relies on gluing together the fragments containing normative elements, does not create the same whole to which the parental script appears to be directed. Therefore, the home reality is constructed as half true and half false, whereas the broken reality succeeds in creating a whole with harmoniously linked components. Specifically, in the broken reality of family interaction, through cooperating around a shared goal and implementing action strategies, they join together into a unified whole. The violent context facilitates a logical connection of components, which, in a normative context, were shown to be irrelevant.

Breaking up and putting back together are, therefore, a central theme in the everyday lives of children exposed to violence, since the violence necessitates gathering and mending of the fragments for routine daily functioning. However, the putting together that is learned in the children's daily routine context does not succeed in creating a sense of a tolerable existence and demands new solutions to create a new form of being. The challenge, in this context, is a dual one: first, because of the intensity of the violent experience, which genuinely competes with the sensory dimension that it offers. Second, because of the fact that normative elements also lie within the components of the violent context, which blurs the violent reality and gives the illusion of living a normal routine.

The process of creating art that involves finding new solutions for old ways of being, as well as exposure and experimentation with new ideas and new ways of being, may be a real alternative to the script of violence and the powerful experience it creates. This is 1) because of the emotional intensity within the creative artistic process. The experience of vitality may be especially powerful in the context of artistic creativity since the encounter with the artistic materials creates a powerful sensory experience; 2) because of the aesthetic value of art: The beauty provides a positive context for those feelings of vitality created by doing art, which turns the sense of emotional fullness to a feeling of elation and ultimate pleasure; 3) because of the power of art to connect "intrinsic" with "extrinsic" in two senses: In the sense that the form and content of artistic creativity reflect social norms and in the sense that just as art imitates life, the reality, over time, can be shaped from an aesthetic perspective (namely, life can imitate art).

From what is written above, it can be concluded that the motivation for change, i.e., adopting a new or different solution from those to which the children are accustomed (turning to violence as a way of breaking the boredom and the empty routine), may be created in the presence of two conditions: First, if the children can bring themselves to an elated sense of ultimate pleasure, intense joy revolving around doing art as well as around reading the art (the form); second, if the children successfully acquire the ability to shape the reality external to the home from an aesthetic perspective. Acquiring a sense of elation can increase the children's desire to work with art (Eisner, 2008) and to read art (Eisner, 2008), motivation that will be able to color their routine home life in shades of meaning and happiness, which are an outcome of the sense of achievement and success surrounding completion of the work of art. Achieving the ability to shape the reality external to the home from an aesthetic perspective, that is to say, to create an experience of wholeness as a type of imitation of art may help the children to understand the normative world and its latent potential to create an experience of wholeness. This in turn creates motivation to see the normative, outside world as a genuine solution, through wanting to adopt it as their life's reality (that differs from the reality offered by the violence).

To create the two aforementioned conditions, it is essential to have not only a process of creating art as therapy but also to integrate art education principles into this therapeutic process, as well as to use art psychotherapy to deepen the therapy, encourage the children to express thoughts, motivate them to act, practice behaviors, and help them choose options. Below, I will detail the principles of the proposed intervention program.

5.6.1 Integrating the principles of art education in a process of creating art

As I described in detail in Section 5.4, one of Elliot Eisner's main claims (Eisner, 2002, 2008) was that mediation is an important condition to advance thinking. According to Eisner, the form of artistic thinking demands guidance and learning and will not develop in and of itself, merely through observation.

As a solution to their boring everyday reality, children exposed to violence "choose" construction of the violent script as its powerful sensory fullness affords, an experience that can be defined as "emotionally extreme." Furthermore, the components of the violent context incorporate normative elements, which create among the children an illusion of living in a pseudo-normative reality. These components are strengthened further by the "seeds" of normativity that fill the children's routine, planted by their parents in everyday family life. In my view, therefore, an emotional and cognitive process is required that not only enables the children to touch a process of artistic creativity but that will also deepen their technical, emotional, and cognitive capabilities regarding the way in which they will be able to achieve the most aesthetically pleasing results. As mentioned, the experience of violence is powerful and provides sensory and cognitive fullness. Thus, an experience of parallel intensity is needed for the purpose of creating motivation in the children to replace the violent experience with another experience, as well as to gain a deep understanding of what normativity is to adopt it as a way of life.

Only the opportunity to practice art can facilitate such a process, an exercise that will include the following components (Eisner, 2008): Stimulation of the imagination; developing technical skills to work better with materials; problem-solving for organizing expressive qualities (a process that is empowered through other people's criticism of their own work) to achieve the most aesthetically pleasing results; developing a personal point of view and connecting between earlier and current work as well as between current work and the outside world. Such a comprehensive exercise will enable development, referred to by Eisner (2002) as "artistic intelligence," based on several forms of thinking. Of these, the following are relevant specifically for intervention with children exposed to violence: 1) Attention to relationships that create a complete, aesthetic composition among parts (a perspective underlying creation of life and a sense of vitality). When individuals know how to read art, they experience it as emotional fullness, as replete with positive, joyful vitality; 2) improvisation, thinking that enables the ability to change direction with the emergence of new, better options; 3) shaping the world from an aesthetic perspective, meaning a new worldview in a historical and cultural context.

5.6.2 Integrating art psychotherapy through a process of creating art

Since the children have a distorted understanding of normativity, they need to undergo a profound relearning process, which may be problematic for two reasons: 1) They have thoroughly learned how to select the seeds of the intrinsic home normativity and to arrange them in a way that fits the normative reality as conceptualized in the cultural socialization processes. A perception such as this is very difficult to change. It is acquired as part of the everyday reality and violent events script, constructed by both parents as part of the captor–captive existence. (The man is interested in establishing such an existence in order to blur/negate the violent reality, and the woman is interested in it as a defense mechanism enabling her to split between life and the violent reality to explain why she remains in a position of captivity). 2) Through the psycho-educational work, the children's confrontation with the absence of a normative reality inside the home may worsen their situation, regarding their place in the escalation script (their change of places as actors) as well as their ability to connect to the two central figures with whom they continue to live in the difficult or escalating everyday reality and regarding the double message conveyed to them by the society responsible for their mental health: "Your internal home reality is flawed to the extent that it is a danger to your mental health and your human existence, but we expect you to continue to function within it nonetheless." Therefore, the use of a creative art process that constructs a bridge to understand the fundamentals of the normative world may serve, on the one hand, as a genuine way to reconstruct normative scripts, and on the other hand, as a way to offer an alternative option for the everyday reality, in a manner that is neither confrontational nor direct. In other words, doing art may serve not only as an alternative to a powerful negative experience but also as a means of acquiring a language through which the children will understand which components are the foundation of normativity and the way in which to organize them to create normativity in a cultural context shaped by the society that is responsible for the well-being of its members. The fact that such a language is anchored in a powerful emotional experience will help them develop the motivation required to deal with learning and testing the language. Furthermore, as one who proposes an alternative option, a type of solution situated external to rather than inside the home may be a realistic, silent, and non-threatening "competitor" for the children and their parents. Since acquiring an aesthetic perspective does not profess to change internal home behavior, but turns to the outside, it does not endanger the children, does not deal with a change in the domestic rules of the game, but engages with seeking options that are external to the home (namely, integration in community life, school, and neighborhood). Nonetheless, the creative art process, as well as the children practicing developing various competencies, might not be enough to create the motivation required for change—as mentioned, because of the intensity of the experience of the violence, the learning process ingrained throughout the years, and the parents being central figures in the child's life. Therefore, an additional element is needed, which will serve as a means to help create the change. This additional element that I would like to suggest, which may assist in the process of change and healing, is a combination of art psychotherapy in a creative art process. This will be done by introducing the breakage theme as a theme around which the artistic activities will be planned. This theme will serve also as a means of developing a discussion about how a whole can be created from the breakage, about which options the children identify to construct a whole (mending/imitation versus creating a new "picture" from the parts through turning to external sources), as well as a means of developing a discussion about the place of breakage inside the home and how it influences the reality outside the home.

5.6.3 Therapy in small groups

Although doing art in a group may have a special significance also because of the need to acquire deep, optimal understanding of the organization of expressive qualities (comparison between members of the group is required to develop a critical viewpoint and to deepen understanding of harmony among the elements), also for the purpose of creating an effect of competition among the group members (something that may create motivation for change), as well as the need to experiment with the effect of surprise, as well as to develop a personal viewpoint, the place of the violent experience and the potential of vitality that it evokes among the children may jeopardize their ability to work in a group. This is because the deeper the sense of boredom and emptiness around mending the whole, the more they will resort to violence. Therefore, in my view, work is required in groups of a maximum of three children with three facilitators, for in-depth individual work to achieve the sense of wholeness and joy in a positive aesthetic context, which should create motivation for change.

5.7 Context-focused intervention: Children exposed to interparental violence

As I explained thoroughly in the previous section, the intervention proposed below will be based on art therapy in its broad context and will unify the art as therapy approach with the art psychotherapy approach. Additionally, I will propose integration of the principles of art education in a therapeutic context. The innovation of the proposed intervention is as follows: 1) In the new content toward which it is directed, existential content that I found, empirically, to be an important, if not central, layer in the experience of exposure to violence. 2) In turning to a different type of intervention than has been implemented to date with children exposed to violence. The choice of this specific type of therapy—art therapy—was based on content that emerged from the findings of the phenomenological study of the experience of exposure to violence. That is to say, it is the content that steered the choice of the type of therapy presented below. 3) In the combination of the therapy components: Introducing principles of art education as well as of art psychotherapy into the creative art process. Specifically, in art as therapy, the consulting approach to solving problems will be included, an approach that uses artistic images to find new solutions for existence. Even though art therapists sometimes work with both approaches—art as therapy and art psychotherapy—they tend to connect them rather than integrate them. The perception of art education in a therapeutic context is unique to the intervention presented below.

The proposed intervention design is for 24 sessions, meaning that the basic recommendation is weekly sessions for children over a 6-month period. These will be group sessions, with three children of the same gender in each group. Three therapists will be present at each session (either art therapists or therapists with expertise in integrating art or art techniques in their work). This will enable individual work parallel to group work, which will enhance the children's ability to achieve an experience of positive wholeness as well as insights that are important for accomplishing change and healing. Each session will last between 1.5 and 2 hours, since the nature of the sessions demands time for work, and physical and metaphorical space. The target age group is 6–18 years, with an appropriate age range for each group, i.e., no more than 2 years difference between children in the same group (6–8, 8–10, 10–12, etc.). The gender of the therapist will depend on the children's age. For younger children, in the 6–10 age group, I recommend female therapists (because a masculine presence may trigger difficult reactions in the shadow of the nature of the domestic abuse), whereas for older children, in the 10–18 group, I recommend mixed groups of male and female therapists (in view of more complex cognitive processes involved in processing the trauma). At a later stage, the therapy will be individual to deepen the experience and insights and to facilitate change and healing. In certain circumstances, which I will address further on, and only if such conditions are possible, I will propose the integration of an additional intervention introducing more components.

The sessions will have a unified structure and will include the following components:

1. Dismantling the whole by breaking, cutting, separating, and dividing into segments. The whole can be an object, a picture, a film, music, a poem/song, or a story. The whole will be related to violence in some way, for example, 1) the music chosen for the sessions will include sounds of breakage, shouting, crying, cursing, and discordant notes and 2) a family photo. In this context, the children can be asked to bring a picture of their nuclear family to the sessions or a picture that they have taken themselves with their smartphone; 3) objects, such as a jug, a bowl, a cup. Objects familiar from home that may be deliberately broken during violent events; 4) a poem/song or story in which the content or storyline includes violence or violent events; and 5) a film about violence or with violent content. The soundtrack should include music that conveys suspense, discordant sounds, heavy breathing, etc.
2. An attempt to mend the fragments/parts to form an original whole (using photography or another way of documenting the original).
3. Taking an additional whole as an example of the original (an object as an example of the original object that was broken; a picture, as an example of the original picture that was cut up) and breaking it again. This time, however, the guideline will be to choose to build something completely new from the broken parts. In other words, to put together a whole that has new meaning. If the child cannot think what to choose and asks to stick the parts together to restore the original model, s/he will be allowed to do so. This is also one of the possibilities and must not be ruled out.
4. At the end of each session, the children will be asked to give their attention to:
a. The initial mending
    - How they feel about the whole that was put together based on the original model: Are they more or less comfortable than with the original? If less comfortable, what creates the feeling of discomfort?

- What would they like to do with the "mended whole?" Would they like to break it again and then try to make it more whole? Would they like to create something else? What do they think will happen if they break it and stick it together again?
- How can something else be created?
- Does the process remind them of something? At home? Outside the home? In what way?

b. To build the whole (second building)
- What do they think of the "new whole?" How do they feel about it? What creates this feeling?
- Does their feeling toward the new whole differ from how they felt toward the mended whole that they "stuck together" according to the original model? In what way? What do they think creates the difference?
- What did they feel while working on the "new whole?" In what way, if at all, is this feeling different from the feeling that was aroused by sticking together the parts according to the original model?
- What do they think of the "other" wholes, which were created by the rest of the group? Is it surprising that others in the group produced a different result? Yes/no and explain why.
- Which act of putting together did they enjoy more? The mending/sticking or the creation of a new whole with different meaning? Why?

The children's narratives will be constructed individually in relation to each stage of the session. The questions will be asked by the group facilitators. Each therapist will ask the child whom s/he works with individually, without sharing with the rest of the group. Only once the children's personal narratives have been written will the content be discussed in the group.

Three sessions can be devoted to each "artistic whole," i.e., three sessions surrounding each distinct area of art (visual art, music, singing, movement, and drama), to increase the range of the experience of happiness, to illustrate a variety of possibilities that may lead to a sense of flow (Czikszentmihalyi, 1990), and to enable comprehensive practice of the technical, emotional, and cognitive principles which, in the end, can lead to change and healing. In addition, the repeated experience in that field of art of taking apart and putting back together will demonstrate that any additional break distances the possibility of creating genuine fusion and restoring the parts into an overall, integrated whole.

As the sessions progress, toward the middle of the process, it is important to engage with the children/adolescents in comparing earlier work with current work. This is to evoke criticism to develop the skills acquired to improve compatibility among the various parts that build the whole, to achieve an "aesthetic whole." The comparison will be made also on the individual level, by the therapist and the specific child, as well as with the rest of the group. The discussion in the group context will revolve around the question of whether, in the children's opinion, there are things in everyday life external to the home, which, when they are occupied with them, create similar feelings that they described in relation to building a whole with new meaning. What, for example? This type of discussion may deepen the children's understanding of social norms' latent potential to create existential wholeness and how the aesthetic context helps them do this.

As I mentioned in the previous section that dealt with the principles of the intervention program (Section 5.6), the nature of the proposed work creates an external alternative to home and therefore 1) it does not endanger the children. The search for a solution is outside rather than inside the home and, therefore, in no way attempts to change the "rules of the game"—those parental scripts on which their everyday family life is based, including the violent events. 2) It does not convey a confusing and contradictory message to the children. From the policy shapers' perspective, the state, as the authority attempting to protect the children from abuse, does not tell children that violence is dangerous, on the one hand, while expecting them to acquire home self-protection strategies and, thus, take responsibility for protecting themselves, on the other. Instead, the state will refer them to options outside the home (as part of the search for shaping a meaningful whole that has cultural legitimization, e.g., in the school system as part of social and community initiatives). Inclusion in such options may also provide physical protection for the children because it instantly reduces the time that the children choose to spend at home and, existentially, creates alternative options for ways of being as a solution for the future. Nonetheless, to validate the social message conveyed through such an intervention, the state will be obliged to allow the children to spend a prolonged beneficial period of time outside the home. This can be achieved through providing funding for social initiatives and community projects for the children, such as helping older people, renovating buildings, cleaning up the environment; groundbreaking research projects in a variety of disciplines according to the child's areas of interest; activity related to enhancing the role of the theater in the children's and adolescents' leisure time; and projects related to improving the quality of life of people with disabilities—and all on a daily basis. Thus, for example, the children will be able to spend extended periods outside the home, but not in a place that threatens the victim (the mother) with removal of her children, but in a place that respects and recognizes the fact that she is a captive in impossible circumstances that require a creative solution to be found. In such a context, the mothers will be able to provide embracive support to their children, in accordance with the specific strengths and changing circumstances of the captivity.

At this point, it is important to emphasize that the proposed policy is relevant both for situations in which the parents are living with intimate partner violence as well as for situations in which the woman is in the process of separating from her violent partner or is even completing the legal separation. This is because today, when courts make decisions surrounding visitation rights in situations of violence, in a way that almost totally disregards the history of the woman's abuse, or alternatively, gives equal weight to abuse and to the need to uphold the parental rights of the man (e.g., Birchall & Choudhry, 2022; Casas Vila, 2020; Coy et al., 2015; Feresin, 2020; Halperin-Kaddari & Zafran, 2022; Henry, 2017; Meier, 2020; Neilson, 2018; Perrin, 2017; Silberg & Dallam, 2019; Webb et al., 2021). The children's potential of being violently abused or exposed to violence does not change. On the contrary, during separation, the rules of the game are changed, with the man in a position of lack and increasing his obsessive attempts to regain control of the woman as well as his attempts to make use of the children.

An alternative solution for cases in which the woman is trying to separate from her violent partner may be enlisting the court system in favor of changing child visitation rights specifically in contexts of violence against women. In these contexts, I will propose an intermediate alternative solution to the one proposed by policy and legislation researchers in the field of exposure to violence (Coy et al., 2015; Perrin, 2017). Instead of overall supervision of child-contact arrangements (e.g., Coy et al., 2015) or alternatively, contact arrangements that, despite not allowing joint custody, do allow contact arrangements suitable to a normative life (e.g., Perrin, 2017). I suggest the possibility of limited child-contact arrangements, once a week, in order to reduce the possibility of friction and the violent men's use of the children against the woman. Such contact arrangements may be an opening for a better relationship with both the man and the woman due to the reduced friction and the children's ability to function better in their daily routine. An option such as this may also provide an opening for a new narrative in the field, placing emphasis on creating the possibility for the children to develop a new, better relationship with their father, focused on their own needs rather than on their father's distorted relationship with their mother.

5.8 Deepening the therapy in the field of children exposed to interpersonal violence

It will be possible to introduce an additional component to the intervention only after creating conditions for the children to be outside the home for prolonged periods on a daily basis and after assessing the children's stage in the process of gaining insights regarding alternative solutions to the violent reality and motivation to act to achieve change. This component will enable direct confrontation with the violent script and with the script of mending the fragments after the violence; both scripts are dictated by the parents and are responsible for constructing the perception of the violent home reality as normative. Introduction of this additional component to therapy may sharpen and deepen the children's understanding of the normative components and thus help them choose components suitable for creating a meaningful and full existence in a cultural context directed toward normative socialization.

The aforementioned suggestions are relevant, to the same extent, for situations in which the woman is attempting to separate from her partner. Since, as noted earlier, until the court system recognizes the need to create alternative conditions to those of the internal domestic captivity, the children will continue to remain captive, even if the parents are separated. The intervention program that I will propose below can be defined as a clinical consulting intervention. I shaped the program during my years of professional work as a child therapist in a shelter for abused women and in a violence prevention center. There, I was also the head of treatment of children exposed to violence, allowing me to draft directions for work around child visitation arrangements, contact with therapeutic authorities in the community, and outlining the nature of the child's support in the school system. This overall view helped me to deepen my understanding of the field and to shape a context-focused individual intervention program.

This program involves components of cognitive behavioral psychology and of resilience theories, especially certain components of the self-control model (Ronen, 1994, 2021). It is based on findings of studies that examined the correlation between living in a violent reality and the development of negative symptoms among children (e.g., McTavish et al., 2016; Black et al., 2020), as well as on findings of studies that conceptualized the experience of exposure to violence (e.g., Eisikovits & Winstok, 2001; Goldblatt, 2001; Peled, 1998).

5.8.1 Stage 2 of the intervention: Assessing the type of experience that characterizes the child's reality and drafting the appropriate intervention

In this context, four case studies will be presented (cases that I treated during my clinical consulting work in the shelter), where each case presents a different type of experience in accordance with the types identified in the professional literature dealing with exposure to violence: Living with the Secret, Living with Conflicts of Loyalty, Living in Terror and Fear, and Adopting the Violent Model. The case studies will serve as a basis for analyzing the kind of work and for presenting the intervention principles.

First case study—Yossi

The mother arrived at the shelter with her two sons, aged 12 years (seventh grade) and 10 years (fifth grade), following the father's severe physical violence against the mother (as reported by the mother). She gave the impression of being intelligent and warm, very cooperative, and with great awareness of her children's state and their problems.

In my conversations with the mother, she told me that Yossi, her elder son, was verbally and physically violent toward her and toward other children at the shelter. She complained that the boy stalked her incessantly and eavesdropped on her conversations with other women. At night, he placed objects by the door to make sure that she kept her promise not to leave the room, even after he had fallen asleep, preventing her from participating in the various activities at the shelter. He also dictated when she could go out, with whom, and where to, including the type of clothes she was to wear.

In the sessions with me, Yossi showed extreme impatience and restlessness. He moved constantly from game to game, gave up easily, and stated every few minutes that he was "fed up" and "bored" and wanted "just to lie on his back and do nothing" because "in any case" he was "stupid and worthless." In another session, he told me that he was "not interested in anything." Toward the end of that session, he curled up into a fetal position and asked me to hug him "because no one in the world loves him." His use of the reactions of anger, fear, and despair simultaneously during the sessions expressed his distress in three parallel circles both during and outside of the sessions.

As the therapeutic process progressed, Yossi began to tell me that he missed his father terribly and would very much like to meet with him, and in general, if given the chance, he would escape from the shelter and return to his father. Yossi told me that he did not love his mother and was prepared, at any moment, to telephone the neighbors and reveal her whereabouts to his father. He said that he did not like his mother to hug him because he was angry and unwilling to have a female mentor, only a male. In one of the sessions, Yossi asked me how babies come into the world and said that he "is waiting to have babies so he can hit them like his father hits him."

Second case study—Avi

Avi is Yossi's younger brother. The reports of 10-year-old Avi in the shelter showed that he behaved nicely toward the other children, listened and tried very hard to please the house mother (a central figure in the shelter who serves as a support and role model for the women in organization and housekeeping), helped when assistance was needed, organized the children for their afternoon snack, came on time to the afternoon club, did his homework. The mother reported that Avi listened to her and tried very hard to help, and whether with organizing the room, listening to the rules, or even offering to help her with her duties at the shelter. The only conflicts in which the boy was involved were with his brother, where he was verbally abusive and even violent.

In one of my earlier sessions with Avi, I asked him to "draw a boy or a girl." Avi first drew a girl and then a boy and told the following story about them:

> Once upon a time, there was a girl called Sivan. Sivan went to the Luna Park, bought a balloon, and was playing with it. She bumped into a man and fell over. At first, she cried, but after that, she began to be his friend. The man was called Yossi and he had a yellow balloon. They went home and they live together until this very day.

In another session with Avi, we talked about school. Avi told me that it was hard for him to understand what was permitted and not permitted in school. When I asked what he meant, Avi replied: "I like to make problems. Sometimes I behave like my dad. Behaving like a king. As if I'm allowed to do everything. So everyone knows that they can't mess with me."

In the following session, among other things, I asked Avi about school: "How is it going at school? What happened this week?" He replied:

> It's OK. I started behaving like how I really am because I already feel better. When people annoy me, it gets dangerous. Everyone has to include me, because otherwise, they know what will happen to them. I'm like my dad. I behave like a king. They are scared of me. Everyone was scared of my dad. For instance, if he was walking along at the market, he could take an apple without paying, because if they didn't let him, he would punch them.

In another session, I asked Avi to lie down in the middle of a large piece of card, and I drew around his body. He was asked to mark three places on different parts of his body and to relate each of them to one of his parents and to himself. In the part relating to his father, he noted the following: "My dad hit my mom, pulled her hair and all the neighbors saw." When I asked: "What else can you say about your dad, maybe about things you used to do together?" Avi replied: "I can't tell you anything about him. I have nothing good in connection with Dad. Only bad things. He hurt my mom, she used to cry because of him, and [hurt] us sometimes." In the part relating to his mother, he noted the following: "I have lots of good things related to Mom. She takes care of me and does things, but I am also angry with her. She often lets Yossi hit her and behave not nicely toward her, like she used to let Dad, at home." In the part relating to himself, he wrote nothing, choosing to leave it empty of content.

Third case study—Miri

The mother arrived at the shelter with her two daughters after the father held a knife to her throat, threatening to kill her and to commit suicide. The threats were made in the presence of their two young daughters, aged 2.5 and 6.5 years. The woman reported very severe physical violence against her, which had escalated since she had announced that she was moving in the direction of wanting a separation. She reported being forced to have sex whenever it suited her partner without considering either her wishes or the circumstances, for example, whether the girls were awake or not (in the afternoon). He would simply lock himself in the bathroom with her. She began to distance herself from him in this aspect, as well, which was also a reason for the escalation. The mother said that, recently, she had felt an extreme change in both her daughters' behavior: A tendency to be irritable, aggressive, and extremely restless, which is what, she said, finally spurred her on to leave the relationship.

In one of my early sessions with Miri, she referred to several violent acts that she said her father had perpetrated against her. "Dad squashed my mouth," "shut me in the shower and the toilet," "hit me," "bit me," "said he would kill me, he threatened me with a knife." The words were spoken with blunted affect; the little girl told me about very serious actions without expressing anxiety. In a conversation with the mother in which I checked these facts, she completely denied that Miri had been exposed to physical abuse. She said that the father never stayed alone in the house with the children because he did not know what to do with them. However, she recognized her husband's abuse of her in the child's narrative. (He had indeed bitten her, locked her in the toilet, and done other things stated by Miri.)

In the subsequent session, Miri drew a lion, and said: "The lion is the wisest and strongest animal. That is why I like that animal the best. It can easily beat any other animal and can say: 'Go away from here! I am a mighty king!'" Later in the session, Miri told me about a monster that comes out of the closet and a father who hates people so much, hates his wife and her children, that he behaves violently toward his wife. He threw her and cut up her baby.

In another session, Miri wrote a letter to her classmates at her previous school. (She had attended first grade near her home for the first half of the school year). Among other things, she wrote:

> I am hiding in a safe place because Dad said he would kill me, and we were scared and decided to leave.
>
> They gave me candy, there is a big playroom here, there are Barbie dolls and all kinds of animals. I like playing with the animals in the forest. And in the forest, there are all types of bad creatures and also kind animals. While I was playing, I saw the lion biting the lioness, and the lioness devouring a million birds. I also saw a gorilla that hit a wart hog and a rhinoceros killing a lioness and a giant camel throwing an elephant. And I make wishes from this goldfish. I want to be a princess with a golden crown.
>
> I miss you but I need to be in a safe place with high walls. Because my dad hits my mom and wants to kill her. He is very strong, this dad. He can break my bones. So, I decided to leave.

About six months after arriving at the shelter, Miri was told that she could start meeting her father. (The subject of visits had not arisen beforehand because the father had refused to see his daughters.) The girl's initial reaction was: "Great, what fun." After a few seconds, however, she said: "Actually, I don't want to go to meet Dad. I am scared of Dad because he is dangerous. He is like a wild animal." During the next few days, the mother reported an extreme regression in the girl's behavior, fear to sleep in bed alone, crying for no apparent reason, outbursts of rage, and violent behavior toward her mother. The school also reported a severe change: Lack of concentration and extreme restlessness. The child calmed down only once she was told that the issue of visits was being abandoned. After that, we worked with guided imagery and I coaxed Miri into a state in which she could see herself sitting with another social worker in the room and with her father. The possibility of Miri having been either physically or sexually abused directly was raised and investigated again, based on her anxiety both before and during the meetings but was ruled out.

In additional sessions, Miri said:

1. "I'm a coward. That is what everyone says about me. I have bad dreams because I'm scared. I am scared of my dad and even of my little sister, Hodaya."
2. "One day, some children annoyed little Kuki. Kuki got annoyed and called out: I am bigger than everyone. I will call my big strong dad and he will cut you up into bits because my dad is a giant."
3. "Once upon a time there was Thumbelina. She was small and lonely. She was so scared that she hid in her nest so they wouldn't eat her in the forest. And then Tom Thumb came and saved her."

Fourth case study—Yuval

The mother arrived at the shelter, after a referral by the police and the welfare services, with three children: two boys, the elder aged 8 and the younger aged 6 and a girl aged 3.5. The previous year, another daughter, the eldest child in the family and from the mother's previous partner, had been moved to an out-of-home placement facility because of her deteriorating mental state. The woman described life at home as "Sodom and Gomorrah." The situation was so bad that the father had begun breaking things at home. The mother told me that the main reasons for their quarrels were his severe methods of punishing the children and his isolation of her from her family and girlfriends. The situation finally came to a head when he threatened to kill her in front of the children and within earshot of the contact-center security guard.

The child in the case presented below is 6-year-old Yuval. The mother told me that he had been in school exactly one week when the psychologist was brought in because he was unable to sit in the classroom. This incident had happened while staying in their third shelter (before arriving at our shelter). In a meeting attended by the school psychologist, social worker, consultant, and principal, it was immediately recommended that the child go back to preschool. The mother described the child as constantly restless. If someone annoyed him or displeased him, he would fly into a rage and would calm down only if he got his own way. He was unable to sit still for a moment. Everything irritated him, and he would have outbursts of anger. If he decided something, no one was allowed to say no.

In one of the sessions with me, when he was asked to draw a boy or a girl, Yuval chose to draw a "monster." He drew a monster with two arms, two legs, one eye, and a mouth full of teeth (a symbol of aggression). After that, he added two hands and a hammer. I asked: "What does the monster do with its hands?" At first, Yuval answered: "Not telling." After a minute's silence, he added: "It's to do with being bad, but I'm not saying how."

Yuval arrived at the next session angry. There had been an incident at preschool that day (after his first week). He had arrived at preschool with his mother, and when she tried to leave, he began to cry. The mother tried to force him to stay, and the child became distressed and started throwing things. The preschool teacher's attempts to calm him failed. In the end, Yuval and his mother returned to the shelter, where she was cross with him and, as a punishment, would not speak to him. I received this information before the session. When Yuval entered the room, I told him that I knew what had happened. I suggested that we look inside ourselves to see what is happening there and making us feel like we do. I said: "So, let's open a window and try to peep at what is happening inside you—at why you sometimes feel that you have to get angry."

Yuval's reaction: I have a lot of secrets, lots and lots of secrets, but I don't tell them to anyone. Never, I will never tell.
I said: That is your choice whether to tell or not. Only you decide if you want to talk about the secrets and when. But meanwhile, let's decide between us that we are not talking about the secrets, not trying to check what they are. Just knowing that they are there, trying to give them some shape and then trying to change their shape, to change them from being very troublesome to less troublesome. Do you agree?
[Yuval nods his head in agreement.]
I continued: Try to draw what was inside you today when you got out of bed [placing a piece of paper and crayons in front of Yuval].
Yuval: There was nothing.
I said: You know that, when I get angry, I feel as though I have a big mess inside. I feel as though bits of paper are starting to turn round and round inside me, all mixed up. I will draw it for you.
Yuval: [And then Yuval took the crayons and began to color very hard] I feel like this.
I said: Excellent! [I encouraged him] Here. You are looking through the window. This looks like a serious mess to me. A kind of "mega mess."
Yuval: [Smiles and asks for another piece of paper to keep on drawing]
I asked him: Is that what you felt like today?
Yuval: Even worse. Come here and I'll show you. [And Yuval drew a mess again]
I then asked him: What do you think? [I transferred the thinking task to him] When there is a mega mess, what can you do with it? To me, it looks so big that if we leave it like that, it will just get bigger than us.

Yuval: Don't know.

Then I said: I have an idea! Let's take this big mess and try to put it into a frame. [I brought pieces of paper and scissors, and drew a frame on a piece of paper]

Yuval: [Yuval cut a smaller piece of the paper and stuck it inside the frame] I want to do that again! [Yuval repeated the action several times. Then he began to cut up the small parts and to put them together like a jigsaw puzzle]

I asked: What needs to be done to put the mess inside the frame?

Yuval: Make it smaller.

I said: Quite right. So, each time a mess starts to form, you can try to think how to shrink it so that it won't grow bigger, or if it does grow, make it smaller and put it inside a frame. And then, when it is in the frame, it will be in one place and won't be a disturbance inside your whole body.

In the next session, I played a game with Yuval: "Hand on the Heart:" A game with cards that present emotions or thoughts, and the child has to respond in some way. Let's see what we can learn from the things that he said.

I asked: What can you tell me about Dad?.

Yuval: That it's lots of fun to be with him. But I don't remember anything. I don't know how to tell what was fun with him.

I said: Yuvali, all the children and mothers in this home have come here because something not good happened between their Mom and Dad. Can you tell me why you came here?

Yuval: Because Mom wanted us to come. I don't know why we came.

Yuval: My wish: If I had a lot of money, I would buy a house and my brother and I would live there alone. It would be fun to live by ourselves because they don't tell you what to do.

I asked: What was the saddest day of your life?

Yuval: Nothing

Yuval: Another wish: I would like to turn into a creature from outer space. Because then, if someone would bother me or scare me, I would threaten him.

I asked: When you argue with someone, how do you argue with him?

Yuval: By hitting. As if I am shooting an arrow at the enemy.

I asked: At your house, when Mom and Dad argued, what happened?

Yuval: I don't know.

I asked: Can you tell me what happened when you were at the child-contact center?

Yuval: Nothing happened at the contact center with Dad. We came here because Mom felt like it. She doesn't know what a crazy life is.

5.8.1.1 Diagnosing the types of experience and presenting ways to treat them

I diagnosed the type of experience that characterizes each specific child with reference to two dimensions: First, the child's worldview in the family context and in the broad existential context; and second, perceptions and values that the child presents toward the use of violence and conflict resolution. As I will prove in the following paragraphs, the attitudes to the use of violence and conflict resolution are identical for all the experience types—that is to say, all the children, regardless of which type they belong to, have attitudes that justify violence. However, the experiential stance of each experience type is different. That being the case, the tension between the visibility level (existential being, worldview) and the essential level (the attitudes justifying violence) is what dictates the nature of the different intervention for each type of experience. The point of departure and the nature of the work are different, but the goal is to reach that same inflexible nucleus at the basis of a distorted perception of reality.

I diagnosed the child's worldview (Dimension A) by referring to the gathering of information based on the therapeutic sessions, the family dynamics as reflected in conversations with the mother (and in this context, I relate to the internal domestic dynamics in the home, described by the mother, as well as those that she described in the shelter or the center), the child's behavior at school, and reports of the child's behavior at the shelter. It is important to emphasize that the children will often choose to "split" their behaviors: to behave in one way at the shelter and in another way at school; to express a certain way of thinking in the presence of certain figures and another way of thinking in the presence of others; and another variation that I encountered was a particular type of behavior that continued for several months, followed by a stark change in behavior, as though it was not the same child. Therefore, it is important to gather information from as broad a range of spaces as possible in which the child takes part, besides the therapeutic space, because he will frequently bring only part of his worldview. Only gathering a broad range of information will lead to a correct diagnosis of the experience of violence.

Thus, **Yossi** is a clear case of **Adopting the Violent Model** (the type of experience is "living in an aggressive context"). Yossi talks about missing his father and wanting to stay with him. He is angry with his mother, restricts her actions to the extent of total control of her behavior, and expresses the wish to harm those weaker than himself. The **case of Avi**, however, may confuse us into thinking that his worldview is "adopting the stance of the victim." Indeed, Avi splits his eager-to-please behavior, in the shelter, with aggressive, violent behavior in school. If we, as therapists, either will not collect information about what happens in school and work only with the emotional-personal level or if we will not find out if the child's behavior in school is consistent with what happens in other frameworks (such as the scouts or other afternoon clubs), we may miss an entire side of the child's worldview. In such a case, we would fail to diagnose Avi as acting out of **loyalty conflicts** (experience type: "living with conflicts of loyalty").

Similarly, **diagnosing Miri's worldview** may be confusing, but in a different way, since, on the one hand, she expresses her fear while creating a type of cohesion between her fear and anxiety that her father will harm her mother. On the other hand, she apparently admires powerful figures and, in cases of distress, summons a violent and abusive figure to help her ("I will call my big strong Dad and he will cut you up into bits"). If we will not know how to make a separation and distinguish between Miri's worldview, where the world is interpreted as a dangerous place in which people need to live in constant fear, and her perception of violence as legitimate and the attitude that violence is a means of conflict resolution (when someone gets annoyed, it is permitted to enlist the help of someone who will harm the "abuser" in return), we may mistakenly diagnose her worldview as "loyalty conflicts" and not as **adopting the victim model** (experience type of "living in terror and fear").

In this case, it may be helpful to observe Miri's behavioral pattern in different spaces and to examine whether the splitting that we identify is between different behaviors: wishing to please and victimhood versus aggression and violence, or between behavior (fear, avoidance) versus thinking (justification of the violence). In Miri's case, her avoidant/frightened behavior is clearly consistent in all spaces. Legitimizing violence is a belief/perception underlying her existence, but it has no behavioral expression.

The case of Yuval might also be confusing, since even though elements of denial of the violence can be clearly identified in his words, to the extent that it becomes a secret with himself and the others, his behavior includes elements of violence and aggression. Again, diagnosing his explosive behavior as "adopting the violent model" would be erroneous because it will be attributed to an existential stance and not to belief/perception regarding violence. **The nature of Yuval's behavior** in all spaces is characterized by denial and an absence of coping (experience type of "living with the secret"). His behavior is uniform; there is no splitting. He legitimizes the violence through things that **he voices and outbursts of rage** as being part of seeing violence as a necessary strategy to relieve tension (which explains his outbursts of rage) and as part of a perception that abusive behavior and threats are effective means of exerting power and control over others (a perception that he voices when verbalizing wishes, for example).

Following on from the above, for children diagnosed as **Adopting the Violent Model**, the treatment aims are as follows:

1. Connect with the child from a place that rules out abuse of the other but simultaneously enables connection to physical strength as a mode of behavior in the world. This goal will be accomplished by connecting the child to

contexts that have cultural legitimization in society and in which physical strength is used, such as different branches of the martial arts. If the connection is actually created by the therapist, it may provide a common denominator for communication between the therapist and the child and serve as an opening to discuss what makes the use of strength legitimate in one context and illegitimate in another.
2. Include the non-abusive parent (the mother) in shaping the legitimate context for the child to use strength. This is to create a basis for communication with the person whom the child perceives as worthless and weak. For example, the mother will also join a martial arts class or will somehow share the cost of the child's martial arts club.
3. Reduce anxiety, since adoption of the violent model is often due to intense fear of the abuser, his strength, and his potential to cause harm.
4. Impart anger management skills.
5. Create awareness of the world of legally binding rules and social norms through understanding the rationale behind them (social order; protection of citizens from harm).
6. Experience behaviors defined as socially legitimate.

For children who are diagnosed as being in an **ambivalent state** ("loyalty conflicts"), the main treatment objective is: To make the child aware of the contradictory and split parts in order to try to redefine the situation and enable integration of the parts. The work is cognitive and emotional. Use of a picture of an emotions wheel, for example, may assist in locating hidden emotions, such as sadness and anger. For example, if I mentioned that when my mom got hit, I felt deep sadness, how can I behave in a way that hurts other people?

Adopting the Victim Model will dictate the following therapeutic goals:

1. Reducing the perception of evil as monstrous, reducing its dimensions to a reasonable containable and controllable size. The goal: Creating a sense of control in the world. There is evil in the world but it can be channeled and managed; it is not overwhelming evil.
2. Acquiring self-control skills as a way to conduct oneself in the world (as an alternative to the use of strength). When the child has self-control skills, it will be possible to show him that the choice of strength and violence is exactly what he wished to avoid.

On the operative level, the therapist will make use of:

1. Guided imagery and desensitization to reduce anxiety. This is in addition to strengthening the sense of competence, for example, through playing inside a room, participating in valued projects.
2. Broadening the range of reactions in situations of stress.

3. Developing self-control skills to increase the sense of strength and control in the world.
4. Attempting to reexamine the relationship with the father in order to connect the good and the bad parts to form an integrative personality.

The therapeutic goal with children whose experience is diagnosed as **Living with the Secret** are:

1. Increasing the general sense of strength through working on enhancing the counter-strength to fear—courage.
2. Learning about the different emotions and how to conceptualize them.
3. Starting to observe these emotions.

The direction for treating the experience of denying the violence is, first of all, to make the child aware. To coax the child to talk about the existence of difficult things that he has learned not to talk about or that talking about them might cause danger or harm to the family. Therefore, the first stage is too early to talk to the child about what happened. Just acknowledge that it happened. An additional point: Since the issues are so difficult and complex, it is not a good idea to start by talking about the violence, about what happened at home. It would be better to begin with other difficulties. Nonetheless, the subject of difficulties must be broached, initially, in a very indirect way because, in these children's homes, denial is a learned strategy for general coping with stress situations. The aim in this context is to develop some preliminary inner observation, something within the child that will allow him or her to touch a minute fragment of what is happening inside and, subsequently, to develop resourcefulness skills. There is a problem; let us see how we can solve it.

5.9 Exposure to interparental violence: Implications of the nature of the abuse for working in the school context

The insights from the previous section may have very important implications for the nature of the reaction required of the educational figure, such as the teacher and school principal, and of the educational-therapeutic figure, such as the school's educational consultant. If children exposed to interparental violence, when behaving either violently or aggressively, are treated only from a judgmental stance, which negates violence completely, without conveying the additional message that individuals reflect their innate environment (by showing empathy with what motivates the child to behave aggressively or violently, such as a learning pattern or way of thinking), the children will resist and reject the educational figure and render them unable to listen to that figure. In cases of victimhood behavior and identification with violent figures through adopting aggressive behavior in certain contexts, the child must be approached from a position that examines which needs the connection to violence comes to fulfill. Beyond the aforementioned methods, the work with all the children exposed to violence needs to include imparting communication skills, strategies to distinguish between assertive behavior and aggression, and conflict resolution skills.

In the context under discussion, the unique role of the educational consultant as leading therapeutic and systemwide processes in school (Dollarhide, 2003; Blachar et al., 2009) will be expressed in several areas:

1. In providing teachers with knowledge and accessibility to the field of children exposed to violence, with the aim of helping them locate children who might belong to this category. The teachers, in daily contact with the children, observe their interactions both inside and outside the classroom and hear how the children speak. In view of this, they may have important data for analyzing the nature of the children's thinking and for locating problems related to social interaction. The teachers' important role is not only in assisting the location of students who may be suffering from family violence but also in forming strategies of how to behave vis-à-vis these children in the classroom based on a deep understanding of their core problems and needs. Appropriate behavior may be of great assistance in shaping the most beneficial classroom climate for all the students. Of course, the educational consultant will assist and support the teachers in all these processes and will consider creating a multidisciplinary team.

In discerning those children who express symptoms that might be consistent with exposure to interparental violence. For this purpose, the educational consultant will meet the children individually. Locating these children is necessary on the community level as well, with highest on the agenda being to reach the risk population, especially due to the large scope of the phenomenon and the severity of the child abuse. It is necessary also in school, which is interested in creating a beneficial educational climate (Shadmi & Zimmerman, 2008). From the aforementioned, it can be understood that treating children who are exposed to interparental violence in the same way as children who behave violently under different circumstances may intensify their reaction, resulting in harm to these children and to their environment. On this level, the educational consultant will serve as a facilitator, a coordinator, and leader of the entire educational-therapeutic team's conduct.

In cases of locating and exposing interparental violence, the educational consultant will mediate with the community and will formulate a program to support the child in the school system, alongside intervention of the welfare services. Such a program is crucial, since it is supposed to provide a response for these children at a time when all those supporting and treating them are instructed not to speak to them about the difficult subject that they have exposed in order not to confound the investigation. The type of support may focus on empowering the children by including them in various social and scholastic assignments in the classroom and making them a part of a leading team. Another option is to choose a subject for discussion in the area of life skills, such as how to think about a difficulty as a challenge. Dealing with this issue will help them to learn to redefine situations as a means of coping with a complex reality. Following on from this, it will be possible to teach the children why states of collapse or breakup are, actually, what lead to future growth. This is the unique role of the consultant, who can help construct a social rationale for the difficult place to which society leads children who are beginning a process of enforcement and legal authorities being introduced into the family system.

5.10 Children exposed to interparental violence—conclusions in relation to the drafting of new policy in the field

The critical survey presented in the various chapters of this book demonstrates the complexity of the field of abuse under discussion—exposure to violence. Since the child abuse is anchored in a context of violence against women, a situation of captivity within captivity is created. The complex characteristics of the women's captivity create a situation that complicates the release from captivity or, in many cases, makes it impossible. In such a situation, discussing the issue of how to treat the children becomes critical.

Since the various studies conducted in the field of children exposed to violence show, beyond all doubt, that this population is extremely vulnerable with intensely negative symptoms and high rates of direct abuse, there seems to be no choice but to clearly define this population as children at risk and to include their treatment in the child protection field. However, because of complex gender issues related to the woman's place as victim and the society's responsibility toward her, this legislative change must be anchored in an unequivocal social statement that the society does not, in any way, see the woman as a partner or as responsible for the child abuse. On the contrary, it must be emphasized that the society recognizes the captivity circumstances as severe, crippling, and neutralizing, and, therefore, the society sees fit at every stage to include the woman in the child's healing process. Following on from this, a decision in the direction of reducing the hours that the children spend at home as part of their participation in school, community, and social initiatives may be perceived by the women as a helpful step in the children's healing and recovery and not as a harmful step that points an accusing finger at the woman and punishes her by taking her children away.

The nature of my proposed work focuses on treating the children out of the recognition that treating women and men who are involved in the experience of violence is difficult and complex and can extend over many years. The children, meanwhile, will continue to be exposed to a violent reality long-term, which may change for better or for worse, over the years, in accordance with various developments. It is not my intention to belittle the importance of treating either men or women, who are entitled to receive help just like anyone suffering from some kind of problem. In my view, however, this help must be given not from a stance that creates an illusion that such treatment will help change the children's reality but from the attempt to provide them with some relief as people in complex life circumstances.

It is incumbent on us to remember that the children are our future, and we must continually see how we can give them a chance to grow up and function as healthy members of society. This social interest is of supreme importance, especially when the findings of studies and surveys in the violence field show a consistent rise in the number of people involved in the circle of violence. The data on the sharp increase in reports of domestic violence since the COVID-19 outbreak (e.g., WHO, 2020) are additional evidence of the need to find alternative solutions for action in the context discussed in this book.

References

Birchall, J., & Choudhry, S. (2022). "I was punished for telling the truth": How allegations of parental alienation are used to silence, sideline and disempower survivors of domestic abuse in family law proceedings. *Journal of Gender-Based Violence*, *1*(17). https://doi.org/10.1332/239868021X16287966471815

Blachar, E., Alter, Y., & Galon, E. (2009). *A model for analyzing the educational consultant's work*. http://cms.education.gov.il/EducationCMS/Units/Shefi/gapim/yeutz/ModelMurkav.htm

Black, T., Fallon, B., Nikolova, K., Tarshis, S., Baird, S., & Carradine, J. (2020). Exploring subtypes of children's exposure to intimate partner violence. *Children and Youth Services Review*, *118*, Article 105375. https://doi.org/10.1016/j.childyouth.2020.105375

Carmel, Y. (2010). *Escalation of interparental conflicts from the children's perspective* (Unpublished doctoral dissertation). University of Haifa, Israel (Hebrew).

Casas Vila, G. (2020). Parental alienation syndrome in Spain: Opposed by the government but accepted in courts. *Journal of Social Welfare and Family Law*, *42*(1), 45–55. https://doi.org/10.1080/09649069.2019.1701923

Cohen, G. (2000). *The creative age: Awakening human potential in the second half of life*. Harper Collins.

Coy, M., Scott, E., Tweedale, R., & Perks, K. (2015). "It's like going through the abuse again": Domestic violence and women and children's (un)safety in private law contact proceedings. *Journal of Social Welfare and Family Law*, *37*(1), 53–69. https://doi.org/10.1080/09649069.2015.1004863

Czikszentmihalyi, M. (1990). *Flow: The psychology of optimal experience*. Harper & Row.

Dollarhide, C. T. (2003). School counselors as program leaders: Applying leadership contexts to school counseling. *Professional School Counseling*, *6*(5), 304–308.

https://www.schoolcounselor.org/asca/media/asca/LeadershipSpecialist/Dollarshide.pdf

Eisikovits, Z., & Winstok, Z. (2001). Researching children's experience of interparental violence: Towards a multidimensional conceptualization. In J. L. Edleson & S. A. Graham-Bermann (Eds.), *Domestic violence in the lives of children* (pp. 203–218). American Psychological Association.

Eisner, E. (2008). What education can learn from the arts. *Learning Landscapes, 2*(1), 23–30. https://doi.org/10.36510/learnland.v2i1.271

Eisner, E. W. (2002). *The arts and the creation of mind.* Yale University Press.

Feresin, M. (2020). Parental alienation (syndrome) in child custody cases: Survivors' experiences and the logic of psychosocial and legal services in Italy. *Journal of Social Welfare and Family Law, 42*(1), 56–67. https://doi.org/10.1080/09649069.2019.1701924

Gardner, H. (1993). *Creating minds.* Basic Books.

Goldblatt, H. (2001). *The meaning of interparental violence for adolescents* (Unpublished doctoral dissertation). University of Haifa, Israel (in Hebrew).

Halperin-Kaddari, R., & Zafran, R. (2022). Bothersome alienation. *Haruv Institute, Nekudat Mifgash Journal, 22,* 50–55 (Hebrew).

Henry, C. (2017). Expanding the legal framework for child protection: Recognition of and response to child exposure to domestic violence in California law. *Social Service Review, 91*(2), 203–232. https://doi.org/10.1086/692399

Kramer, E. (1993). *Art as therapy with children* (2nd ed.). Magnolia.

Lusebrink, V. (2007). *Imagery and visual expression in therapy.* Plenum Press.

Malchiodi, C. (2007). *The art therapy sourcebook.* McGraw-Hill.

Malchiodi, C. (2015). *Creative interventions with traumatized children* (2nd ed.). Guilford Press.

Malchiodi, C. A. (2020). *Trauma and expressive arts therapy: Brain, body, and imagination in the healing process.* Guilford Press.

McTavish, J. R., MacGregor, C. D., Wathen, C. N., & MacMillan, H. L. (2016). Children's exposure to intimate violence: An overview. *International Review of Psychiatry, 28*(5), 505–518. https://doi.org/10.1080/09540261.2016.1205001

Meier, J. S. (2020). U.S. custody outcomes in cases involving parental alienation and abuse allegations: What do the data show? *Journal of Social Welfare and Family Law, 42*(1), 92–105. https://doi.org/10.1080/09649069.2020.1701941

Neilson, S. C. (2018). *Parental alienation empirical analysis: Child best interests or parental rights?* Muriel McQueen Fergusson Centre for Family Violence Research and Vancouver: The FREDA Centre for Research on Violence Against Women and Children.

Peled, E. (1998). The experience of living with violence for preadolescent children of battered women. *Youth and Society, 29*(4), 395–430. https://doi.org/10.1177/0044118X98029004001: 0.1177/0044118X98029004001

Perrin, R. L. (2017). Overcoming biased views of gender and victimhood in custody evaluations when domestic violence is alleged. *American University Journal of Gender, Social Policy and & the Law, 25*(2), 155–177. https://digitalcommons.wcl.american.edu/jgspl/vol25/iss2/2/?utm_source=digitalcommons.wcl.american.edu%2Fjgspl%2Fvol25%2Fiss2%2F2&utm_medium=PDF&utm_campaign=PDFCoverPages

Ronen, T. (1994). *The way to self-control: A guidance for children's education*. Keshet (Hebrew).

Ronen, T. (2021). The role of coping skills for developing resilience among children and adolescents. In M. L. Kern & M. L. Wehmeyer (Eds.), *The Palgrave handbook of positive education* (pp. 345–368). Palgrave Macmillan.

Shadmi, H., & Zimmerman, S. (2008). *Psychological well-being (wellness): Descriptive rationale* (Hebrew). Retrieved from http://cms.education.gov.il/EducationCMS/Units/Shefi/KishureiChaim/meytaviyut/yeda/RevachaNafshit.htm

Silberg, J., & Dallam, S. (2019). Abusers gaining custody in family courts: A case series of overturned decisions. *Journal of Child Custody*, *16*(2), 140–169. https://doi.org/10.1080/15379418.2019.1613204

Webb, N., Moloney, L. J., Smyth, B. M., & Murphy, R. L. (2021). Allegations of child sexual abuse: An empirical analysis of published judgements from the family court of Australia 2012–2019. *The Australian Journal of Social Issues*, *56*(2), 1–22. https://doi.org/10.1002/ajs4.171

World Health Organization – WHO. (2020). *COVID-19 and violence against women: What the health sector/system can do*. https://www.who.int/reproductivehealth/publications/emergencies/COVID-19-VAW-full-text.pdf

Yalom, I. (1995). *Therapy and practice of group psychotherapy*. Basic Books.

Chapter 6

Treatment modality

Treatment recommendations, planning, and intervention strategies

Based on the broad phenomenological study that centers on learning about the experience of children exposed to domestic violence throughout all stages of the escalating interparental conflict (Carmel, 2010), the main source of the damage caused to this child population is **witnessing violence**. The damage is expressed in a deep distortion of the ability to understand a normative reality and its components. As analyzed in Chapter 4, which deals with the findings of the empirical study, this fundamental damage can explain the high rate of male-perpetrated direct physical and/or sexual child abuse. A blurring of boundaries between permitted and forbidden, normative and non-normative, and between good and evil, as well as placing the responsibility on the female victim while creating total dependence and making an alternative perception impossible (for which the victim—the women and/or the child—is likely to pay a high price) create the perfect conditions for direct abuse. The victim (the child), as part of the survival need and of the need to give a normative interpretation of the situation of captivity, does not often understand the extent of the situation's abnormality.

The distorted perception of normative reality can also explain the children's problematic modes of expression in **social and cognitive** contexts. The difficulty of understanding social situations, as well as the thoughts and feelings of those involved in them, is self-evident when considering how difficult it is for these children to experience authentically and to interpret the concept of normativity correctly in a broad social context. In a similar way, the development of attitudes that justify violence is a kind of latent negative symptom of this situation.

However, the situation becomes even more complicated because those complex cognitive processes are accompanied by a feeling of intense vitality—strong turbulence of the senses resulting from an encounter that offers the opportunity to experience inquiry, challenge, strenuous thinking, and a powerful sense of togetherness that are a fitting counter-response to the existential void of daily life. The children's cognitive blindness takes shape and becomes a reality through which they gain an apparently coherent and positive feel and experience of themselves and of the world. This process explains how deep problematic layers can potentially develop until a pathology forms.

Nonetheless, in the light of empirical findings regarding the existence of mediating variables that may either reduce or increase the problem (e.g., the frequency of the violence to which the child is exposed; the mother–child relationship; existence or absence of direct abuse; the child's action strategies; and the existence or absence of abilities/skills that build resiliency—see Chapter 1), it can be assumed that context-focused work, i.e., focused on elements that are responsible specifically for creating the problem, will help the children to heal and recover.

There is another important variable to consider in the treatment of these children: The unique context of the damage caused to children living with domestic violence. The findings of my critical inquiry presented in this book expose a complex situation in which the men, as a gender group, feel threatened and, therefore, reject a specific conceptualization and context-tailored treatment for violent men. The women, as victims, also feel threatened by the social expectation that they will leave the violent partner in order to set themselves and the children free from the situation of captivity. Thus, the complex context limits the possibilities available for treating their children.

Based on the insights presented, I suggest a multistage, multidimensional intervention that will carefully unravel the children's powerful existential grain of understanding that, as indicated by my study findings, is responsible for the severity of the damage. It is a clinical consulting intervention that connects to the children's strongpoints while deeply, but carefully, touching areas where latent problems may develop.

6.1 First dimension

In my perception, the intervention needs to include art therapy that integrates three components: Art psychotherapy, art as therapy, and art education. Even though, in the world of therapy, art education is not placed in a therapeutic category, I suggest embracing, in my intervention, the approach and technique that, in my view, it offers the therapeutic field (Eisner, 2002, 2008). The complex intelligence dimensions to which this approach aspires are at the disposal of children exposed to violence only in non-aesthetic contexts. The children need this type of intelligence to create a transition from the powerful negative feeling of vitality to a powerful positive feeling of vitality in a normative context.

What will be the contribution of each of these components?

Art psychotherapy will enable us to work with the children on a theme found to be fundamental to their experience: Of dismantling and reassembling, and of brokenness and wholeness through symbolic communication. In this context, long-term group work will enable an open discussion surrounding the theme as well as giving in-depth attention to issues, emotions, sensations, and conflicts that will arise during the use of variable artistic expression as guided by the therapist. It must be noted that this theme is critically important as it can create insight into what has the potential for creating genuine meaning and where to find those components that are responsible for creating positive meaningful wholes. The out-of-home sphere, as a genuine tool for shaping the world from an aesthetic perspective, is the cognitive and emotional basis for creating motivation to perceive the normative outside world as a real solution.

The art as therapy component will allow us to shape the group therapy spaces as an art class for the children. Shaping the therapeutic space in such a way will enable therapists to include, as an inherent part of the treatment, the learning of various art skills and different mediums of expression (e.g., music, movement, and cinema). In this manner, the children will experiment with their ability to improve their creative expression and to attain complete harmony of the various components of the children's work of art, leading to a sense of wholeness. This type of exercise will encourage the children to examine and to make an independent choice of the medium to which they connect the most, creating an extremely positive feeling. In addition, this exercise will encourage the development of a personal point of view.

Including the art as therapy element as integral to the first component (art psychotherapy) will, in fact, turn art into a tool that the children will use **to solve problems around the theme of dismantling and reassembling**. In other words, the use of art will enable them to examine how dismantling and reassembling creates a whole, what type of whole, and what creates wholeness. Exploring the artwork will directly and indirectly become a deep existential exploration. Emphasis on the personal point of view, as well as allowing the children to choose the medium for their work of art, will raise their chances of experiencing the sense of elation to which a whole composition and perfect harmony of its components have the power to lead.

Adopting the art education component in the therapeutic intervention as a tool for developing complex and refined aspects of thinking (Eisner, 2002, 2008) will benefit the children in two ways: 1) Help them to deepen their perception of the therapeutic space constructed for them as an art class. 2) Help them acquire knowledge that is necessary to build an existential experience of happiness. Specifically, art education is directed at the **acquisition of technical knowledge** about materials, their different essences, and their use in ways that will change the expressive experience of art. In addition, the children will learn that art education includes **receiving others' criticism** of their work, enabling a refined understanding of how to attain completeness between the parts that are intended to create a whole (the picture or the work of art). These two learning processes mentioned above reinforce art and its creation as a focus of activity. In parallel, working art is part of a therapeutic process that is channeled toward thinking and finding new solutions of being. Stimulating the children's imagination surrounding endless opportunities for using images and metaphors that represent aesthetic wholeness, as well as acquiring cultural and historical knowledge in relation to those images and metaphors, will help the children gain meaningful, positive being.

In fact, introducing art education as an additional inherent component of art psychotherapy will create the potential for the development of a reversal process that the children need to undergo, i.e., to understand and to feel the break as something broken and not as something whole—which is how they experienced it because of the internal script that was constructed for them. This process might motivate them to seek solutions outside of the home. That is to say that they might wish to use normative reality components (e.g., in school or in the framework of initiatives and projects in which they will take part) to attain a meaningful experience, happiness, and optimal emotional well-being. In fact, they will develop the ability to see the outside reality as imitating art.

6.2 Second dimension

In the field of child abuse, there is a consensus regarding the need to create an abuse-free environment for the child by removing the abusive parent. However, in the field of witnessing domestic violence, a different line is taken. A historical review of policy shows (Jenney & Alaggia, 2012; Buckley, 2018) that the basic assumption for intervention in this specific context was changed—from stopping the abuse to harm reduction (Shlonsky et al., 2007). This change, as exposed by the analysis in Chapter 3, was derived from the need to create a solution that considers the needs of both victims of domestic captivity: The women and the children. However, it has been proven that this solution does not produce the required result. Clinicians and researchers have indicated, time and again, that this policy sends a double message and creates a conflict of interest between women and children, which often creates the circumstances of captivity (Anderson, 2017; McTavish et al., 2016). In their view, this can explain, at least partially, the difficulty of achieving meaningful effectiveness in the child intervention programs (Howarth et al., 2016; Douglas & Walsh, 2015).

In light of the analysis presented, I recommend defining a new assumption for intervention with children exposed to violence. "Child protection" is a concept that, I think, can provide a solution that will place the children's needs in the center while taking into consideration that the woman is a victim and that society's moral obligation is to take this variable into account when shaping the children's therapy. Practically, this means as follows: In cases of reports or discovery of domestic violence, immediate measures must be taken to create a situation in which the children spend as much time as possible outside the home. The intention is to prepare the community to launch social, cultural, and neighborhood projects for inclusion of children exposed to violence steered by social activism. The children actively participate in community initiatives and projects, daily, and in the afternoons and evenings.

The activities can be varied: Community theater; helping older adults with technology or including older people as counselors and guides to enrich the youngsters' knowledge on different subjects; making aesthetic improvements in the local community; engaging in environmental projects, such as solutions in the context of global warming; and many other topics that are part of building a beneficial normative lifestyle. The nature of the projects, the togetherness, the normalization, and the good feeling that will develop, the feedback, the experience of success, the activity, as well as learning how to work toward a meaningful, important shared goal while building intermediate goals, will all strengthen the meaningful, good, positive feeling aspired by the art intervention proposed in the previous section.

In other words, I see shaping the basic conditions for work as a fundamental layer of the therapy. In my view, reducing contact with the home space to a bare minimum when the captivity situation is the focus of the problem is a prerequisite for the proposed therapeutic intervention. In addition, designing the space where the children will spend time each day as ongoing contact with optimal normality (the first part of the day at school and later, inclusion in social activism projects and initiatives) should empower the process to which the art therapy is directed. The children will have a heightened sense of the good, the positive, the meaningful, and will also be exposed, in real social contexts (not only in the therapy room), to different components that can be the basis for creating a positive whole. This process will be a practical, real-life example of how components of a normative reality create an "aesthetic" whole. Little by little, this nature of work will serve as a basis for empowering their motivation to seek additional ways and additional initiatives for community-civil activism.

6.3 Third dimension

Continuing the rationale presented in the previous section, I suggest including the same working principles in the school framework as well, and this can be done on various levels. First, as introducing art education within the compulsory school curriculum. As suggested by Eisner (2002, 2008), all children can benefit from learning art as a discipline channeled toward the acquisition of complex intelligence that involves refined, delicate mental-sensory-emotional processes. In his view, this type of intelligence is an important layer for imparting the ability for optimal orientation in a post-modern, dynamic, and changing world. Naturally, this type of work will enable better assimilation of the skills needed by children exposed to domestic violence for the deep existential process that they must undergo (i.e., skills for working with different artistic materials while appreciating their different qualities, the kind of expression that the different qualities create, experimenting with different media [music, dancing, visual art, and poetry] and through them, the ability to express ideas, to train the imagination, to understand how a shape can express content, exposure to works of art, learning principles of art criticism).

An additional layer for the work at school can be psycho-educational lessons that will deal specifically with creating metaphorical spaces to be a basis for enhancing emotional well-being in daily life. In this context, a program including several sessions can be built on developing the ability to see aesthetics as a basis for aesthetically constructing reality. This theme will be an opening for the discussion regarding the following questions: How do we feel when we watch a very enjoyable play? How do we feel when we hear a harmonious concert? How do we feel when we watch an opera that provides us with a powerful, dramatic, and aesthetic musical experience in which the components are balanced with precision? How do we feel when we watch a dance in which the movement is in perfect balance with the rhythm and cultural messages? Or when it is composed of individual, contradictory elements that, when joined together, create precision and harmony? And what happens to us afterward? After the play, the concert or the poem is finished? Does everything disappear right away? Does it happen that, following powerful exposure to metaphorical spaces, we feel as though they are penetrating our daily routine and coloring it in different shades? What happened in those contexts? And then, as part of or following these discussions, the classroom can be turned into a kind of art studio where work groups create different artistic spaces: Some groups will work on putting on a play, others on writing poetry, and others may form a choir. A good idea will be to choose an expansive area, such as the school sports hall, a cultural hall, or some other large space within the school boundaries, to leave enough room for several different work groups. Again, the nature of this work will enable deeper assimilation of the way to make use of aesthetics every day. This time, however, the additional dimension will be permeation of the content. The children will learn to understand the way in which art can be used as a genuine tool, not only to create an intensely good space but also to paint daily life with its colors. The cognitive ability to use the imagination to move from the routine daily space to the metaphorical space may be a genuine tool for children exposed to domestic violence, a tool that can help them choose a means of filling the vacuum that characterizes their daily home routine. Adopting this tool as a basis for the daily experience can be a real alternative to the search for something that will break their sense of nothingness and the vacuum caused by the violence.

Another level of work in the school context can be around social activism in school. For example, schools can turn break time into a space for school community activism. Decorating the school based on different social subjects or as part of creating an aesthetic whole around a subject such as happiness, the essence of life, the quality of the environment, humanity, human contact, loneliness versus social warmth (a subject that can be very relevant for coping with the global challenge created by COVID-19), humanity as a unifying worldwide foundation, culture that creates gaps and as a means of bridging them, etc.

Following that, schools could initiate external social projects in the neighborhood or the town. In this context, projects can be on a variety of subjects, ranging from sports to science (subjects relating to the use of robots **for the benefit** of humanity, e.g., making medical improvements and **not** for purposes that are harmful to humanity) and social issues such as those already mentioned. Themes for discussion will be at the basis of this activity relating to 1) the aim of the project and 2) the direction in which to lead. What is the aim for the benefit of humanity and what is the aim that serves the individual and yet does harm to humanity as a whole? Why should one choose goals that serve the general population and how? Several work groups can be formed around this subject.

6.4 Fourth dimension

The first stage of studies in the field of children exposed to domestic violence (that began in the 1980s) indicated a clear relationship between living in violent surroundings and the development of negative symptoms in various domains (e.g., Vu et al., 2016). In the cognitive field, specifically, it was found that children who were exposed to domestic violence were likely to develop attitudes justifying the use of violence (e.g., Graham-Berman et al., 2017; MacMillan et al., 2013), such as 1) violence is an appropriate way to resolve conflicts in intimate relationships; 2) abusive and threatening behavior is an effective means of gaining power and control over others; 3) violence is an essential strategy to relieve tension; and 4) victims have brought the violence on themselves because of their behavior (e.g., Garrigan et al., 2018; Katz, 2022; Miller, 2015).

These findings are consistent with those of the phenomenological study at the center of this book. The study exposes the existence of two scripts (of violence and of mending the fragments following the violence) dictated by the parents who are responsible for constructing the "normative" perception of the violent home environment.

Therefore, introducing an additional layer to therapy that will enable direct confrontation with those violence-justifying attitudes may refine and deepen the children's understanding of the normative components, thus helping them to create an authentic, coherent, and meaningful experience. Nonetheless, I must emphasize here that the decision to use this component needs to result from an in-depth examination of the circumstances in the children's home at that point in time. That is to say, the professionals treating the family must examine 1) whether the parents are separated; 2) if separated, whether the violence toward the woman is ongoing at the point in time that the therapist wishes to move on to the second stage of the therapy (directed specifically to working with those violence-justifying attitudes); if the parents still live together, whether the treatment provided to the parents has indeed changed the home environment, i.e., initial unraveling of the state of captivity. I see this as an extremely important part of the diagnosis since as long as the man's pathological control and the woman's reaction remain unchanged, any alteration to the script of the children's behavior in the home may place them at risk. Evaluation of the effect of the treatment on the parents must be performed by experts in the specific field of domestic violence, while also examining the children's perspective of what happens at home. Based on my professional experience, the children's perspective is very accurate. I frequently encounter gaps between the parents' reports of improvement and the children's deeper perception disclosing that although the physical violence has ceased, the psychological control and emotional abuse of the women and of the children have increased, including incidents of direct abuse. **If the circumstances do not allow us to move on to the second stage, the nature of the work with the children will continue to be as proposed in Sections 6.1–6.3.** (The direction will continue to refer the children to an out-of-home perspective to learn solutions for the future and to connect, in the here and now, to places of intense normality on all levels mentioned above.)

Corresponding to the findings of the first stage of studies regarding the existence of mediating variables that may either weaken or heighten the negative influence of exposure to violence also on the ability to recover, in the second stage of the therapy, I propose an intervention that contains components of resilience theory as well as of psychological cognitive-behavioral components.

Self-control is a psychology concept intended to describe a wide range of human behaviors adopted out of a freedom of choice while forgoing more attractive behaviors for the sake of behaving more appropriately (Mahoney & Thoresen, 1974). Self-control includes many behaviors such as the ability to delay gratification, to withstand temptation, to cope with stress situations, to overcome pain and unpleasant situations, to control one's anger, and more (Ronen, 1994, 2021).

The ability to find an appropriate solution to problems related to self-control is referred to in the literature as learned resourcefulness. This is an acquired repertoire of behaviors and competencies, mainly cognitive which, with their help, a person can manage events such as emotions, cognitions, and pain that impair intact performance of goal-driven behaviors (Rosenbaum, 1983, 1990, 2000). In other words, learned resourcefulness is the tool that the child or adult will activate to achieve self-control (e.g., self-talk and self-instructions, use of the imagination, diversion, planning, and problem-solving).

In the context of domestic violence, central issues are difficulties in emotion regulation surrounding anger management; inability to cope effectively with frustration; and difficulty in conceptualizing feelings and a lack of tools to cope effectively with them, as well as misinterpreting the situation. In other words, they are an inherent part of the basic components of the problem. Therefore, a therapeutic approach that is centralized on working with these issues and that channels the intervention to the problematic areas in these contexts may help the children to heal and to recover. The self-control model, however, is originally directed (Ronen, 1994, 2021) toward the explanation that the problem depends on the individual—on the child or the adult. But as I explained in detail in Chapters 4 and 5, the distorted perception with which these children are growing up becomes ingrained in their being and they have learned to read the world through this distorting filter. Therefore, a statement or explanation that the change depends on them when they do not understand what they must do to make this change and when they do not understand the confusion relating to the normative components in their upbringing becomes very complicated and even impossible.

Based on the art therapy proposed in Chapter 5, and elaborated on in the current chapter, it will be possible to create a basis for understanding and coherently constructing the components of normativity. Following on from this, it will be possible to direct work that will provide children with tools to help them develop means of thinking and planning.

In fact, when we talk about self-control behavior, we are referring to a situation in which individuals manage their lives independently, take responsibility for their actions and plan them, act to improve their lives, and use effective strategies to cope with stress situations (Meichenbaum, 1985; Rosenbaum, 1983). Studies that examined interpersonal differences in the level of self-control among adults found that people with high self-control can cope more easily with stressful situations, undergo painful treatments, and recover after surgery and from serious illnesses. Children and adolescents with high self-control had higher achievements in school and socially (Rosenbaum & Ronen, 2012; Ronen, 2021). A lack of self-control is a predicting factor for the need for therapy and therapeutic frameworks in the future. People who do not believe in their ability to cope with stress were found to be at risk of developing a sense of helplessness, depression, and apathy. In addition, their circle of activity gradually diminished (Ronen et al., 2016).

Children who experience domestic violence are exposed to a confused, unclear world without boundaries from two directions: From their father who, on the one hand, loses control and, on the other hand, creates deliberate control in the intimate relationship context; and from their mother, who has difficulty protecting her personal space—her body. In this situation, the children have no choice but to take responsibility and create their own boundaries. Since, in many cases, children do not know how to manage their behavior appropriately, and certainly not in complex situations, children who are exposed to violence often develop guilt feelings, a sense of failure, and an ever-deepening sense of chaos in their world.

Considering all this, I have chosen two themes from the self-control intervention model and have adapted them for working with this child population. The first theme attempts to teach the children how to think according to an optimistic schema, directed toward coping, action, and identifying different behavioral options; and the second theme attempts to provide the children specifically with effective coping skills (such as anger management, stress, frustration, fear, temptation, and delaying gratification).

On the practical level, the challenging-optimistic thinking schema is imparted by developing the children's/adolescents' ability to identify a specific strength that may help them to cope with a certain type of difficulty and to lead them to general action. For example, courage versus fear; resourcefulness (the ability to create solutions) versus impasse or difficulty; hope versus despair; and happiness versus sadness. When working with **young children**, we could say, for example, "you told me that you are frightened to climb the ladder to slide down the slide. So, let's see: How can you get over that fear? What do you suggest?" Or, "the man in the picture is crying. What do you suggest he do to make himself feel happy?" Or, "you want to copy the lion in the picture but didn't succeed. Do you have an idea of how you could do it differently?" Ideas for working with **older children** are as follows: For example, if a child talks about classroom ostracism or difficulties in creating interpersonal relationships, we could expose him to stories based on social issues and ask him questions of the following type: "How did the children in the group understand the boy's behavior? What led them to think that the boy didn't want to be part of them? What could they have done to find out what the boy was thinking? What could the boy have done to make them understand the real reason for his behavior?" Or, "you told me today that you find it hard to fall asleep because you are thinking about sad things that happen at home. Which of the ideas that appeared in the story as ways to cope with sadness speak to you? In what way do you think you could adopt the idea yourself?" **With teenagers**, we could create work groups surrounding different subjects that arise and brainstorm using work cards that will present different cases from daily life. Films, drama, and the use of visual art can serve as an opening for discussion and for learning through examples of the use of humor, the imagination, and literature as a platform for ideas of how to behave in different situations.

The second theme—teaching the children effective coping around situations of stress, frustration, anger, etc.—will be taught on the practical level by imparting techniques of using the imagination, diversion, self-instruction, and self-talk and practicing them in emotional situations. Self-control will also be taught by imparting problem-solving tools and use of thinking and planning processes. Through practicing these tools, the children will experiment with developing behaviors that take gain and loss into consideration (actions to counter impulsive behaviors that they learned at home). In addition, the therapist will also set clear boundaries, give positive reinforcement, and, throughout the therapy, will be a role model demonstrating how to cope with unpleasant situations.

Thus, for example, when I worked with children exposed to domestic violence in a shelter for women victims of violence, I clarified to all the children that when I am working with one of the children, the other children must not enter. They must find themselves something else to do. At the same time, I suggested an alternative: Drawing outside and playing a game. Setting a boundary such as this helps them develop one of the central behaviors of self-control: The ability for self-restraint and for delaying gratification.

When one of the children bursts in or becomes so angry that he loses control within the therapy framework, I talk to him in a conversational and explanatory way, thus becoming a kind of role model of how to behave when faced with anger. For example, in one of the sessions, a girl flew into a rage over a subject on which we were working, which was fear. She began cutting up sponge balls that were in the room. My talking about how she was feeling, while suggesting that we draw the anger, dance the anger, or drum the anger while taking care of the objects that are important for our work, succeeded in calming her down. Once she was calm, she looked around, collected the cut-up balls, and said: "Look what they did to the balls!" I said:

> That is a shame. Those balls were useful for our work—and now we won't be able to use them. But never mind. We're in a learning process of how to cope with anger, so next time, the one who gets angry will practice the proper way to cope with anger and will know what to choose for getting angry.

The girl responded: "You know, I was the one who cut up the balls." Her response teaches us not only that my behavior was a new kind of role model for her (different from the explosive model) but also that the new model allowed her to take responsibility.

An example for strengthening self-control behavior could be as follows: When one of the children succeeded in looking at a coloring page, choosing which animal he would like to color in, and coloring in the drawing without scribbling over it, I compared this to his work in a previous session and drew his attention to the change. I showed him that, this time, he colored within the lines, whereas the previous time, he had scribbled all over the drawing. I also tried to examine with him whether he could think what had made him work differently this time. He replied: "This time I was concentrating." When I asked him if he could identify what helped him to concentrate this time, he answered: "I said to myself that, this time, I will prove to myself that I am capable, and every time I succeed in coloring in one part, I will give myself a round of applause." This type of work illustrates the result of practicing goal setting and intermediate targets, self-evaluation of behavior, use of self-strengthening, and activating specific tools of self-talk, problem-solving, and coping with failure.

The following case can serve as an example of training the development of modes of thinking and planning: In one session, as part of strengthening the sense of bodily boundaries, I showed one of the girls how I place the palm of my hand on a sheet of paper and draw around it, and she tried to copy me; however, she did not succeed, became irritated, and quickly gave up on the attempt. I suggested to her that, instead of giving up on the task that she had set herself, she could try to think what had caused her not to succeed. She placed the palm of her hand on the paper once again, and I showed her, using her sketch, that she had moved her hand while drawing. I suggested that she make several attempts, taking into consideration that she would not succeed immediately while suggesting she use techniques of self-talk ("now I need to do it like this").

The themes mentioned above (optimistic thinking schema and teaching the children effective coping behaviors) are integrated at the stage of identifying the type of experience through which the children understand their world and defining the appropriate intervention (Chapter 5, Section 5.8.1). Nevertheless, the identification focuses on imparting the different competencies, whereas the intervention itself focuses on using these competencies to confront those beliefs that are responsible for the child's cognitive gaps in understanding. Specifically, if the type of experience is "**living with loyalty of conflicts**," the beliefs that justify the perpetrator go hand in hand with empathy for the victim; thus, the therapy will be channeled toward confronting this splitting. Similarly, but with a difference, if the experience is "**living in fear and terror**," the choice of a violent, aggressive model in cases where they feel helpless signifies a powerless attitude toward the world. In that case, the therapy will be channeled toward confronting the perception that violence brings security. If the type of experience is "**adopting a violent model**," the perception is that violence is a legitimate and effective mode of behavior. In this case, the therapy will be channeled toward changing the perception of the use of violence as an advantage and to construct it as a disadvantage. The therapy must challenge the perception of abuse as a legitimate way to behave. In the context of the type of experience of "**living with the secret**," the confrontation will be with the perception of denial (there was no such thing) as an effective way of behaving and coping. In this context also, it is necessary to construct blurring and erasure as disadvantageous. If I deny what happened, I cannot develop tools to deal with the problem. The problem will continue to exist and will cause me serious harm.

References

Anderson, K. (2017). Children's protective strategies in the context of exposure to domestic violence. *Journal of Human Behavior in the Social Environment, 27*(8), 835–846. https://doi.org/10.1080/10911359.2017.1339654

Buckley, H. (2018). Editorial. *Australian Social Work, 71*(2), 131–134. https://doi.org/10.1080/0312407x.2018.1438029

Carmel, Y. (2010). *Escalation of interparental conflicts from the children's perspective* (Unpublished doctoral dissertation). University of Haifa, Israel (Hebrew).

Douglas, H., & Walsh, T. (2015). Mandatory reporting of child abuse and marginalized families. In B. Mathews & D. C. Bross (Eds.), *Mandatory reporting laws and the identification of severe child abuse and neglect* (pp. 491–512). Springer.

Eisner, E. (2008). What education can learn from the arts. *Learning Landscapes, 2*(1), 23–30. https://doi.org/10.36510/learnland.v2i1.271

Eisner, E. W. (2002). *The arts and the creation of mind.* Yale University Press.

Garrigan, B., Adlam, A. L. R., & Langdon, P. E. (2018). Moral decision-making and moral development: Toward an integrative framework. *Developmental Review, 49*, 80–100. https://doi.org/10.1016/j.dr.2018.06.001

Graham-Bermann, S. A., Cater, A. K., Miller-Graff, L. E., & Howell, K. H. (2017). Adults' explanations for intimate partner violence during childhood and associated effects. *Journal of Clinical Psychology, 73*(6), 652–668. https://doi.org/10.1002/jclp.22345

Howarth, E., Moore, T., Welton, N., Lewis, N., Stanley, N., MacMillan, H., Shaw, S., Hester, M., Bryden, P., & Feder, G. (2016). Improving Outcomes for children exposed to domestic violence (IMPROVE): An evidence synthesis. *Public Health Research, 4*(10). https://doi.org/10.3310/phr04100

Jenney, A., & Alaggia, R. (2012). Children's exposure to domestic violence: Integrating policy, research, and practice to address children's mental health. In R. Alaggia & C. Vine (Eds.), *Cruel but not unusual: Violence in Canadian families* (pp. 303–336). Wilfrid Laurier University Press.

Katz, E. (2022). *Coercive control in children's and mothers' lives*. Oxford University Press.

MacMillan, H. L., Wathen, C. N., & Varcoe, C. M. (2013). Intimate partner violence in the family: Considerations for children's safety. *Child Abuse and Neglect, 37*(12), 1186–1191. https://doi.org/10.1016/j.chiabu.2013.05.005

Mahoney, M. J., & Thoresen, C. E. (1974). *Self-control: Power to the person*. Wadsworth.

McTavish, J. R., MacGregor, C. D., Wathen, C. N., & MacMillan, H. L. (2016). Children's exposure to intimate violence: An overview. *International Review of Psychiatry, 28*(5), 505–518. https://doi.org/10.1080/ 09540261.2016.1205001

Meichenbaum, D. (1985). *Stress inoculation training*. Pergamon Press.

Miller, L. E. (2015). Perceived threat in childhood: A review of research and implications for children living in violent households. *Trauma, Violence, and Abuse, 16*(2), 153–168. https://doi.org/10.1177/1524838013517563

Ronen, T. (1994). *The way to self-control: A guidance for children's education*. Keshet (Hebrew).

Ronen, T. (2021). The role of coping skills for developing resilience among children and adolescents. In M. L. Kern & M. L. Wehmeyer (Eds.), *The Palgrave handbook of positive education* (pp. 345–368). Palgrave Macmillan.

Ronen, T., Hamama, L., Rosenbaum, M., & Mishely-Yarlap, A. (2016). Subjective well-being in adolescence: The role of self-control, social support, age, gender, and familial crisis. *Journal of Happiness Studies, 17*(1), 81–104. https://doi.org/10.1007/s10902-014-9585-5

Rosenbaum, M. (1983). Learned resourcefulness as a behavioral repertoire for the self regulation of internal events: Issues and speculation. In M. Rosenbaum, C. M. Franks, & Y. Jaffe (Eds.), *Perspectives on behavior therapy in the eighties* (pp. 54–73). Springer.

Rosenbaum, M. (1990). *Learned resourcefulness: On coping skills, self-control, and adaptive behavior*. Springer.

Rosenbaum, M. (2000). The self-regulation of experience: Openness and construction. In P. Dewe, T. Cox, & M. Leiter (Eds.), *Coping, health, and organizations* (pp. 51–67). Taylor & Francis.

Rosenbaum, M., & Ronen, T. (2012). Emotional well-being and self-control skills of children and adolescents: The Israeli perspective. In C. L. M. Keyes (Ed.), *Mental well-being: International contributions to the study of positive mental health* (pp. 209–229). Springer.

Shlonsky, A., Friend, C., & Lambert, L. (2007). From culture clash to new possibilities: A harm reduction approach to family violence and child protection services. *Brief Treatment and Crisis Intervention, 7*(4), 345–363. https://doi.org/10.1093/brief-treatment/mhm015

Vu, N. L., Jouriles, E. N., McDonald, R., & Rosenfield, D. (2016). Children's exposure to intimate partner violence: A meta-analysis of longitudinal associations with child adjustment problems. *Clinical Psychology Review, 46*, 25–33. https://doi.org/10.1016/j.cpr.2016.04.003

Chapter 7

Summary and implications for policy

The aim of this book is to expose the complexity of the phenomenon known as children exposed to domestic violence. This was done by presenting a comprehensive phenomenological study that attempted to inquire into: 1) The children's understanding of the interparental conflicts throughout all stages of the escalating confrontation; 2) the children's involvement in the various escalation stages; and 3) the way in which they experience their internal home environment (what they think, feel, and do). The rationale for this in-depth study was the lacuna in the scientific literature of in-depth understanding of the phenomenon. Over the years, researchers have pointed to this lacuna and the importance of studying this topic, specifically to fill this void, to create genuine understanding of this unique type of child abuse as well as to create a precise solution for these children (e.g., Carlson, 2000; D'Andrea & Graham-Bermann, 2017). Therefore, **an additional aim** of the book was to investigate the reasons for the vacuum that had been created in the research surrounding learning about the phenomenon. Researchers themselves have indicated the need for this learning but, for many years, have either distanced themselves from it or avoided dealing with the issue.

These two axes, the theoretical, critical review (presented in Chapters 1–3) and the empirical study (presented in Chapter 4), are the basis for proposing a context-based intervention program that has implications for treatment policy for children exposed to domestic violence and outlines a framework for working with their parents (Chapter 5 and 6). Recent literature has begun to address the need to connect research and practice to new policy in the field (Schreier & Hansen, 2022).

The literature review in Chapters 1 and 2 shows that the more these children's reactions to their violent daily reality were researched, the more the severe, multifaceted abuse experienced by these children was exposed (e.g., Kitzmann et al., 2003; Vu et al., 2016; Negriff, 2020). The revelation that witnessing violence (seeing, hearing, exposure to outcomes of violence, or finding themselves involved in interparental conflicts) constituted the same intensity of abuse as other forms of child abuse created a new status quo. It had become clear that this child population must be recognized as direct victims of domestic violence—rather than indirect victims, as was previously thought (e.g., Edleson et al., 2007; Katz, 2022). This was alongside recognition of the women who, until then, had been considered as the only direct victims.

As part of this important research development, there was growing understanding that concrete and therapeutic responses were needed to help children cope with the complex reality of their home environment. Empowering the mothers, together with the provision of home support and parenting counseling, all came under the creation of a support system. Psycho-educational groups for the children with close follow-up of their clinical reactions was another means of treating the problem (e.g., Howell et al., 2015; McDonald et al., 2011). The assumption was that the moment at which the woman (a direct victim of violence herself) would receive appropriate support and the necessary help, she would be able to break the circle of violence and release herself and her children from the complex situation of captivity in which they were living (e.g., Edleson, 2004; Hollin, 2016).

This assumption turned out to be incorrect, however. The scientific literature shows that very often, despite the help they had received, women had difficulty leaving the violent couple relationship (e.g., Jenney & Alaggia, 2012). At the same time, the chosen method for working with these children, psycho-educational therapy with emphasis on imparting strategies for how to act in the home reality, was not proven to be effective enough (e.g., Romano et al., 2021). In this context, clinicians and researchers raised the hypothesis that part of the problem was the double message being conveyed to the children. On the one hand, the clear message that violence is dangerous while emphasizing the adults' responsibility to stop it, but on the other hand, placing responsibility on the children to behave properly in the home space (through the action strategies that they acquired during the intervention e.g., McTavish et al., 2016).

A critical analysis of policy for treating the children, starting from this stage (Chapter 3), points to the existence of a "zig-zag" action pattern, moving back and forth between two directions. When one direction has been exhausted, they move to the other. When that one is exhausted, they attempt to redefine the first one in a similar and yet different way, and so on. Each direction's definition changes while its essence remains the same. Specifically, directions for work, as I have learned, are as follows: 1) Attempts to incorporate the field of exposure to violence under the heading of child protection, which mandates the obligation to report and to treat the children as high risk. An at-risk evaluation of children dictates that they be removed from the violent home environment. In practice, in cases where the mother is unable to do this and to leave her violent partner, the State will find a safe, alternative care framework for the child. 2) Attempts to shape treatment in the field of children exposed to violence within the framework of women's abuse. In this context, children can remain within the home framework while receiving treatment in the community, with proper guidance for the woman combined with constant supervision.

It must be noted that the first direction suggests relating to and treating the children as victims of the domestic captivity circumstances. In other words, often, when the woman, who is in captivity herself, is unable to remove the children from the domestic violence situation, intervention by the State is required. This strategy was criticized by the feminist research approach, claiming that it places responsibility on the woman, who may feel blamed by society and, even worse, may feel that she is being held responsible for the children's difficult situation. The other, contrasting, direction suggests relating to and treating the children as victims of the abusive man. In this context, the child abuse (whether direct or indirect) is perceived as an extension of the violence against the woman and assumes that the woman's risk considerations for herself will always be suitable for her children as well. Even though this approach resolves the issue of placing responsibility on the woman, it disregards the unique nature of the child abuse. In captivity circumstances where the woman needs to survive, she must take her captor's perspective into account, often placing her in a problematic position vis-à-vis the children.

In any case, this repeated back and forth between the two approaches over many years, which has not succeeded in creating genuine solutions for the children, either through legal means (Macdonald, 2017) or through intervention (Berg et al., 2020), has led to an impasse. In the context mentioned above, current studies indicate the gaps between the policy declared, over the years, and its practical implementation (e.g., Black et al., 2020). In my view, the gaps are even less understandable when considering the researchers' proposal to discontinue interventions for which proving their effectiveness was problematic and to adopt a new direction for working with children—evidence-based programs that were found to be suitable for working with trauma (Cameranesi & Piotrowski, 2020). If these programs have been evaluated by researchers as suitable for working with children, why have they not been adopted in practice but have remained as a theoretical suggestion? Another element of this confused state of affairs is the legal proceedings surrounding child arrangement orders in cases involving domestic violence. A bizarre situation has been revealed in this context: Despite clear empirical findings pointing to violent men's dangerous parenting, the courts have not taken this into consideration, neither on the default level of temporary suspension of visitation rights nor on the level of reducing the number of meetings and introducing supervision. These measures are necessary to evaluate the risk to the mother and the child, to evaluate parental functioning, and to ensure the child's physical and psychological safety and well-being (e.g., Perrin, 2017; Henry, 2017; Birchall & Choudhry, 2022).

To attempt to explain the gradually increasing gaps between recognition of the severity of the harm caused to the children and the solutions offered in practice, one must refer to the considerations that guided the policymakers in shaping directions for child intervention. One must refer also to criticism voiced by researchers in the context of intervention development for these children.

Specifically, when the situation of captivity sometimes means that their mother can neither protect the children nor remove them from the situation, emphasizing the children as victims would damage or erode the mother's victim status. This situation might even be a pretext for placing some of the responsibility on the mothers for the children's predicament. This ethical conflict and the fear of turning the victim into the guilty party by society as well, constituting secondary victimization, have become a central consideration that overshadows the children's victim status. Furthermore, this fear of blaming the victim has also created a practical obstacle for the children regarding the legal option, an option that advocates compulsory reporting and removal of the children from the violent situation.

Based on what has been said, intervention programs that would successfully overcome the problem of "conflict of interest" created by the captivity situation for mothers and their children could provide at least a partial solution. However, none of the existing programs succeeded in considering those parameters that place the children at risk in their violent home reality. That includes those interventions that are based on trauma theory. Specifically, the problematic components are as follows: Imparting action strategies suitable for the children, but that may put the women at risk, or vice versa; contradictory messages that the internal home reality is dangerous for the children while simultaneously leaving them there; and imparting knowledge about how to interpret the violent home reality—knowledge that may alter the children's behavioral script in the home reality and thus put them at risk or distance them emotionally from their parents.

The inability to weigh up the women's sensitive position as victims and the absence of appropriate solutions for the children has led to an insurmountable and perplexing situation. The policy-level "solution" that was found for this complexity was, and continues to be, to emphasize the children's difficult position while obstructing infiltration of work directions that were found and perceived by researchers and clinicians as unsuitable, on the one hand, and on the other hand, simultaneously obstructing the direction that proposes out-of-home placement for the children.

The issue of child arrangement orders in cases where the woman is trying to separate from her violent partner is another dimension that can complete the rationale for shaping child treatment policy. In this context, analysis of the criteria that have guided the law courts for years (based on study findings in the United States, Canada, the United Kingdom, other European countries, Australia, New Zealand, and Israel) when dealing with exposure to violence shows that priority is given to the relationship with the noncustodial parent—usually, the violent man. Specifically, the analysis reveals that despite the fact that in contexts of violence against women, reducing the interparental conflict to a minimum and protecting the child from a violent and abusive environment were found to be essential for children's recovery and healing, the subject that was given the highest priority was their relationship with the father and not child protection (e.g., Feresin, 2020; Galántai, 2019; Jackman-Ladani, 2020; Gezinski & Gonzalez-Pons, 2022; Macdonald, 2017; Mackenzie et al., 2020; Meier, 2020; Ministry of Justice, 2020; Thiara & Gill, 2012; Webb et al., 2021).

The question to be raised based on what has been written is: What does this course of action achieve? Who is served by the division between violence against women and child abuse? It seems that relating to the man as the abuser of the woman **while disregarding** the home captivity circumstances that he creates also for the children, in fact, makes an immediate distinction between the men in the couplehood context and the men in the parental context. This view, which makes it possible to relate to the man on two dimensions, is consistent with social processes that attempt to shape the perception of egalitarian and involved fatherhood in all the family domains. If that is the case, it can be claimed that drawing attention to child abuse may create a threat to the group of men, in general, returning them to what they consider to be a regression, i.e., being judged from a distanced and pathological perspective. The imprecise definitions of the phenomena relating to violence against women over the years and the blurring of the distinction between "domestic violence," "intimate violence," and "gender-based violence" have created the impression that there is a very large group of men who are violent toward women, and from here, it is a short step to accusing men as a whole and putting them on the defensive.

In summary, a situation in which a large group of men consider themselves under attack will motivate the blurring of violent men's responsibility for abuse of their children and the promotion of a line that stresses the importance of the parent–child relationship. From this point of view, the assumption that the relationship with the parent is the most important factor for the child's psychological well-being—more important than creating a safe environment for the child—serves this motivation.

If so, the social-ethical conceptualization of the woman as victim, alongside complex social processes that have led a large group of men to feel threatened, provides the context that appears to be responsible for the adamant policy of considering the children's treatment within the framework of their mother's abuse. Specifically, it can be said that **the theoretical-critical study presented in this book shows** that repeated rejection of recognizing the children as victims in themselves, as well as the absence, over the years, of a response by researchers to their own call to understand more deeply the nature of the harm caused by witnessing violence, are an outcome of a complex gender-based discourse between women and men. This discourse enabled diminishment and blurring of the severity of the child abuse while preserving the rights of women and the rights of men. Although there is a proposal for treating the children on the declared policy level, in practice, they are entrapped once again by the gaps described above, in addition to the domestic captivity. As shown by my theoretical study, there is, in fact, no solution—there is no suitable treatment and no way of changing their daily life reality.

Based on this clarification of the gap in the scientific literature and out of the wish to attempt to create a fitting solution for these children—both a treatment and a solution for their daily lives—Chapter 4 presents a comprehensive phenomenological, qualitative study. In this study, I performed an in-depth examination of the children's lives in an attempt to understand the way in which they perceive, are involved in, and experience the escalation of their parents' conflicts to all-out violence.

The findings of the study expose the essence of the abuse named "witnessing violence" (directly and indirectly). It involves constructing the perception of the violent internal home reality as normative resulting from assimilating violence as part of the trivia of day-to-day life. The parents achieve this by dictating scripts that blur the violence,[1] enabling the children to utilize pseudo-normative components within the violent reality. In this manner, the violent incidents appear to be exceptional events that are not part of the daily routine. This distorted perception is enfolded in an experience of intense vitality that serves as an antidote to their boring, suffocating everyday reality, and therein lies its power. The experience of violence is so dramatic and so intense that it is almost like an addictive drug for the children. Therefore, a parallel experience is needed, equally intense and powerful, to offer as an alternative. There is no doubt that these findings leave no room for "running between the raindrops" and demand that full responsibility be taken for the children's protection.

The script that the parents outline for the children, to restore the broken reality "after the violence" to the state that it was in "before," is predetermined and imitates previous behavior. In contrast, the script that the parents create for the children, to lead the violent incidents to a climax and then to bring them to an end, requires management of the situation in real time, using initiative and tools for resolution. In addition, this script requires flexibility and a course of action in situations of uncertainty. It involves creative thinking using multiple senses, requiring imagination and refined intelligence. This type of thinking is at the center of art in all its variations.

The parallelization between two types of thinking—internal home creativity, required of the children during the interparental conflicts, **and art—is the basis for the proposed intervention.** As explained in Chapters 5 and 6, due to the need to build an indirect therapy for the children to enable them to understand the essence of normativity without creating direct confrontation with their parents—which may well put them at risk—I propose an intervention that uses several components of art therapies. This intervention is intended to provide the children with an extremely positive experience, based on authentic elements of normativity, as a genuine alternative to the intensely violent experiences. Following on from this, future directions for working with children are suggested, which will have implications also for the type of work with the parents.

These work directions are detailed below:

1. Given a complex situation in which the children's best interest is not in keeping with the interest of the parents, a seemingly insoluble situation is created: 1) How can the mother as a non-abusive parent continue to preserve her victim status without being harmed by society when she is incapable of leaving the violent reality at home? 2) How can men as a gender-based group avoid being on the defensive, enabling the definition of a specific group of men as abusers? I use the relative term "seemingly" since, in my view, **new conceptualizations** relating to **women as surviving mothers** as well as **precise definitions** of **different types of violence phenomena** will facilitate a solution to the problem.

Specifically, relating to women as victims who have done everything to protect their children in the violent home reality, on the one hand, but who, on the other hand, are simultaneously suffering from post-trauma resulting from an ongoing life in captivity, will enable them to be treated from a non-judgmental stance. This position will demand that they be included and supported throughout their children's recovery and healing, clearly recognized as beneficial parents. This situation will also allow **child-focused** treatment, including, when necessary, the child's temporary out-of-home placement (when it is estimated that the child is at either physical and/or psychological risk). This is based on the recognition of the woman as a victim of trauma who needs time for her own healing. In other words, a change of approach from placing the responsibility on the woman to remove her children from the captivity situation to an approach that acknowledges her own victimhood in the captivity circumstances will enable the woman's essential inclusion in the children's healing process also in the temporary out-of-home space. It will also legitimize providing long-term treatment for the woman herself.

Regarding the men, precise definitions of content that come under the concepts of domestic violence,[2] intimate partner violence,[3] and gender-based violence[4] will enable a clear distinction between different areas of abuse. Moreover, precise definitions of content will enable better measurement and evaluation of the prevalence of the different phenomena. Therefore, these precise definitions will enable recognition that violent men who are characterized by pathological control are a **specific group** whose behavior can certainly not be projected onto the rest of the male population. In addition, these definitions will not allow violence that creates pathological control to be placed on the same continuum as non-controlling violent behaviors. If a situation is created in which the male population itself legitimizes acknowledgment of the existence of a group of men whose inherent problem is child abuse, it will be possible **to advance the issue of child protection surrounding child arrangement orders** (by taking a break from them, reducing their number, or introducing supervision).

The practical significance of promoting the issue of child protection in the law courts (as part of shaping supervised child arrangement orders) is to adopt a child-focused approach also in the context of interviews with the children for reports to the court. In other words, to understand the significance of the psychological and/or the physical risk to the child, s/he should be asked questions that will attempt to understand the internal home experience in-depth: What happens to him/her there? What is s/he frightened of? What does s/he think, feel, do during the escalating interparental conflicts? To what extent does s/he feel in danger and what, if anything gives him/her some sense of safety?

2. In a violent reality in the home, abusers (those who exert pathological control over the woman) as well as victims (those who develop posttraumatic reactions to the circumstances of captivity) require complex ongoing treatment. The significance of this situation is the absence of the ability to create a genuine change in the children's lives on the practical level. In my view, therefore, a change **in the working assumption** is needed. Instead of expecting the children to be healed because their parents undergo a change, the **focus of the work needs to be with the children while strictly ensuring appropriate conditions for therapy.**

Specifically, I am referring to the creation of the following conditions: 1) In cases where the woman has made attempts to leave the relationship, assisting her by shaping child arrangement orders that are appropriate to the circumstances of her captivity. This can be achieved either by reducing the number of visits and introducing supervision or, alternatively, suspending the visits for the purpose of evaluating the risk. Thus, it will be possible to reduce the interparental conflicts significantly as well as the woman's risk, thus creating a safer day-to-day space for the children, both emotionally and physically. 2) In cases where the parents continue living in the same environment, i.e., the woman continues to live in the violent relationship, the children's time spent at home can be significantly reduced by including them in community projects and meaningful and empowering social initiatives. These projects will genuinely create a safe everyday routine for the assimilation of normative components. Spending most hours of the day in a normative space outside the home will be part of the child protection program as an alternative to an out-of-home residential placement. 3) In cases of concrete suspicion of direct abuse, in addition to the abuse that constitutes direct or indirect witnessing violence (when the mother is not capable of leaving the couple relationship), the child will be placed outside of the home with the mother's full inclusion in parenting.

3. With the creation of the conditions described above, the child intervention program proposed in Chapters 5 and 6 can be implemented fully. While one of these conditions does not exist and the working assumption is the same as it has been thus far, the work with the children must be indirect, with no intention of making changes in the home. (This situation is also discussed in the relevant chapters.)

In conclusion, the theoretical-critical review reveals three central obstacles to outlining new directions for work in the context of the phenomenon known as "children exposed to violence:" 1) Rejecting the understanding of the essence of the field as well as rejecting the recognition of the domestic violence field as gender-based. 2) Distinguishing between violence against women and child abuse, a distinction expressed in a claim heard repeatedly in the courtroom regarding the need to separate violence in a couplehood context from the issue of deficient parenting. 3) The absence of insight regarding the need to recognize the children as direct victims of domestic violence as well as being victims distinct from the woman.

Overcoming these three basic obstacles, in **situations of suspected domestic violence** (the claim of the existence of such violence is frequently raised in high intensity conflict contexts), will enable **action in the legal context according to the following guiding criteria:**

1. Evaluation of the woman's risk by skilled professionals, specifically in the domestic violence field.
2. Evaluation of the child abuse by professionals whose specialization is abuse related specifically to exposure to violence. In this context, evaluation will be performed out of a deep understanding of the meaning of the complex and destructive experience of actual witnessing of violence. In other words (direct or indirect) witnessing of violence will be a basic criterion for evaluating emotional and psychological child abuse, not only in cases of suspected physical and/or sexual abuse.
3. Evaluation of the woman's position regarding leaving the violent relationship, her support systems (if any) and the help she requires from the various systems to leave the relationship. The likelihood of her leaving is small without the provision of practical responses and trauma-focused emotional support.
4. Following on from this, **child arrangement orders will be shaped to allow the children to unravel the captivity circumstances.** In other words, the child arrangements will be limited and supervised in a manner that will reduce exposure to the poisonous interparental conflict to a minimum. **Joint parental responsibility** in the framework of the custodial parent, with child arrangement orders of 30% with the other parent, **is inappropriate in cases of domestic violence.**

5. In cases where risk to the children is evaluated from the fact of witnessing violence and/or from suspected direct abuse and when the woman is unable to leave the couple relationship, an out-of-home solution will be recommended while leaving the woman in the picture as part of the child's healing.

In cases in which the violence began surrounding a dispute between the partners (i.e., the violence was not an inherent part of the relationship from the outset and does not include elements of a ring of captivity), the criteria for shaping a healthy environment for the child will be shaped according to a different context of understanding.

Notes

1. As explained at length in Chapter 4—the man, from the stance of the perpetrator who tries to conceal the existence of violence, and the woman, from the stance of the victim who, out of no choice, uses a defensive mechanism of survival that will justify her staying in the relationship.
2. Domestic violence—characterized in the scientific literature as men's extreme, multidimensional controlling behavior toward women, placing women in a state of captivity (Dobash & Dobash, 1979; Dobash et al., 1992; Dutton & Goodman, 2005; Kurz, 1989; Monckton-Smith, 2020; Stark, 2012).
3. Intimate partner violence—characterized in the scientific literature as behavior that uses physical strength in intimate relationships. In this context, studies found that although such behavior is more typical of men's violence toward women, the opposite phenomenon also exists. Still, in the former context, the violence will be more frequent and its outcomes more serious (Chan, 2011; Hardesty et al., 2015; Haselschwerdt et al., 2019; Johnson, 2008; Straus, 2008).
4. Gender-based violence—characterized in the scientific literature as men's (physical or sexual) abuse of women outside of a couple relationship (Council of Europe, 2011; Watts & Zimmerman, 2002; WHO, 2013; 2016; 2020).

References

Berg, K. A., Bender, A. E., Evans, K. E., Holmes, M. R., Davis, A. P., Scaggs, A. L., & King, J. A. (2020). Service needs of children exposed to domestic violence: Qualitative findings from a statewide survey of domestic violence agencies. *Children and Youth Services Review*, *18*, 105414. https://doi.org/10.1016/j.childyouth.2020.105414

Birchall, J., & Choudhry, S. (2022). "I was punished for telling the truth": How allegations of parental alienation are used to silence, sideline and disempower survivors of domestic abuse in family law proceedings. *Journal of Gender-Based Violence*, *1*(17). https://doi.org/10.1332/239868021X16287966471815

Black, T., Fallon, B., Nikolova, K., Tarshis, S., Baird, S., & Carradine, J. (2020). Exploring subtypes of children's exposure to intimate partner violence. *Children and Youth Services Review*, *118*, 105375. https://doi.org/10.1016/j.childyouth.2020.105375

Cameranesi, M., & Piotrowski, C. C. (2020). Critical review of theoretical frameworks elucidating the mechanisms accounting for the adverse developmental outcomes observed in children following exposure to intimate partner violence. *Aggression and Violent Behavior, 55*, Article 101455. https://doi.org/10.1016/j.avb.2020.101455

Carlson, B. E. (2000). Children exposed to intimate partner violence: Research findings and implications for intervention. *Trauma, Violence, and Abuse, 1*(4), 321–342. https://doi.org/10.1177/1524838000001004002

Chan, K. L. (2011). Gender differences in self-reports of intimate partner violence: A review. *Aggression and Violent Behavior, 16*(2), 167–175. https://doi.org/10.1016/j.avb.2011.02.008

Council of Europe. (2011). *Council of Europe convention against women and domestic violence.* https://www.ojp.gov/ncjrs/virtual-library/abstracts/council-europe-convention-preventing-and-combating-violence-against

D'Andrea, W., & Graham-Bermann, S. (2017). Social context and violence exposure as predictors of internalizing symptoms in mothers and children exposed to intimate partner violence. *Journal of Family Violence, 32*(2), 145–155. https://doi.org/10.1007/s10896-016-9869-0

Dobash, R. P., Dobash, R. E., Wilson, M., & Daly, M. (1992). The myth of sexual symmetry in marital violence. *Social Problems, 39*(1), 71–91. https://doi.org/10.1525/sp.1992.39.1.03x00641

Dobash, R., & Dobash, R. (1979). *Violence against wives.* Free Press.

Dutton, M. A., & Goodman, L. A. (2005). Coercion in intimate partner violence: Toward a new conceptualization. *Sex Roles: A Journal of Research, 52*(11–12), 743–756. https://doi.org/10.1007/s11199-005-4196-6

Edleson, J. (2004). Should childhood exposure to adult domestic violence be defined as child maltreatment under the law? In P. Jaffe, L. Baker, & A. Cunningham (Eds.), *Protecting children from domestic violence: Strategies for community intervention* (pp. 8–29). The Guilford Press.

Edleson, J. L., Ellerton, A. L., Seagren, E. A., Kirchberg, S. L., Schmidt, S. O., & Ambrose, A. T. (2007). Assessing child exposure to adult domestic violence. *Children and Youth Services Review, 29*(7), 961–971. https://doi.org/10.1016/j.childyouth.2006.12.009

Feresin, M. (2020). Parental alienation (syndrome) in child custody cases: Survivors' experiences and the logic of psychosocial and legal services in Italy. *Journal of Social Welfare and Family Law, 42*(1), 56–67. https://doi.org/10.1080/09649069.2019.1701924

Galántai, J., Ligeti, A. S., & Wirth, J. (2019). Children exposed to violence: Child custody and its effects in intimate partner violence related cases in Hungary. *Journal of Family Violence, 34*(5), 399–409. https://doi.org/10.1007/s10896-019-00066-y

Gezinski, L. B., & Gonzales-Pons, K. M. (2022). Legal barriers and re-victimization for survivors of intimate partner violence navigating courts in Utah, United States. *Women and Criminal Justice, 32*(2), 454–466. https://doi.org/10.1080/08974454.2021.1900991

Hardesty, J. L., Crossman, K. A., Haselschwerdt, M. L., Raffaelli, M., Ogolsky, B. G., & Johnson, M. P. (2015). Toward a standard approach to operationalizing coercive control and classifying violence types. *Journal of Marriage and Family, 77*(4), 833–843. https://doi.org/10.1111/jomf.12201

Haselschwerdt, M. L., Hlavaty, K., Carlson, C., Schneider, M., Maddox, L., & Skipper, M. (2019). Heterogeneity within domestic violence exposure: Young adults' retrospective experiences. *Journal of Interpersonal Violence, 34*(7), 1512–1538. https://doi.org/10.1177/0886260516651625

Henry, C. (2017). Expanding the legal framework for child protection: Recognition of and response to child exposure to domestic violence in California law. *Social Service Review, 91*(2), 203–232. https://doi.org/10.1086/692399

Hollin, C. R. (2016). *The psychology of interpersonal violence* (pp. 77–89). John Wiley & Sons.

Howell, K. H., Lilly, M. M., Burlaka, V., Grogan-Kaylor, A., & Graham-Bermann, S. (2015). Strengthening positive parenting through intervention: Evaluating the moms' empowerment program for women experiencing intimate partner violence. *Journal of Interpersonal Violence, 30*(2), 232–252. https://doi.org/10.1177/0886260514533155

Jackman-Ladani, O. (2020). *Custody and child support: Chaos and judicial activism in the family courts* (Unpublished master's thesis). Tel Aviv University (Hebrew).

Jenney, A., & Alaggia, R. (2012). Children's exposure to domestic violence: Integrating policy, research, and practice to address children's mental health. In R. Alaggia & C. Vine(Eds.), *Cruel but not unusual: Violence in Canadian families* (pp. 303–336). Wilfrid Laurier University Press.

Johnson, M. (2008). *A typology of domestic violence: Intimate terrorism, violent resistance, and situational couple violence*. Northeastern University Press.

Katz, E. (2022). *Coercive control in children's and mothers' lives*. Oxford University Press.

Kitzmann, K. M., Gaylord, N. K., Holt, A. R., & Kenny, E. D. (2003). Child whitnesses to domestic violence: A meta-analytic review. *Journal of Consulting and Clinical Psychology, 71*(2), 339–352. https://doi.org/10.1037/0022-006X.71.2.339

Kurz, D. (1989). Social science perspectives on wife abuse: Current debates and future directions. *Gender and Society, 3*(4), 489–505. https://doi.org/10.1177/089124389003004007

Macdonald, G. S. (2017). Hearing children's voices? Including children's perspectives on their experiences of domestic violence in welfare reports prepared for the English courts in private family law proceedings. *Child Abuse and Neglect, 65*, 1–13. https://doi.org/10.1016/j.chiabu.2016.12.013

Mackenzie, D., Herbert, R., & Robinson, L. (2020). 'It's not OK'. But 'it' never happened: Parental alienation accusations undermine children's safety in the New Zealand family court. *Journal of Social Welfare and Family Law, 42*(1), 106–117. https://doi.org/10.1080/09649069.2020.1701942

McDonald, R., Jouriles, E. N., & Minze, L. (2011). Intervention for young children exposed to intimate partner violence. In S. Graham-Bermann & A. A. Levendosky (Eds.), *How intimate partner violence affects children* (pp. 109–131). American Psychological Association.

McTavish, J. R., MacGregor, C. D., Wathen, C. N., & MacMillan, H. L. (2016). Children's exposure to intimate violence: An overview. *International Review of Psychiatry, 28*(5), 505–518. https://doi.org/10.1080/ 09540261.2016. 1205001

Meier, J. S. (2020). U.S. custody outcomes in cases involving parental alienation and abuse allegations: What do the data show? *Journal of Social Welfare and Family Law*, *42*(1), 92–105. https://doi.org/10.1080/09649069.2020.1701941

Ministry of Justice, UK. (2020). *Assessing risk of harm to children and parents in private law children cases* (Final Report). https://assets.publishing.service.gov.uk/government/uploads/system/uploads/attachment_data/file/895173/assessing-risk-harm-children-parents-pl-childrens-cases-report_.pdf

Monckton-Smith, J. (2020). *In control: Dangerous relationships and how they end in murder*. Bloomsbury.

Negriff, S. (2020). ACEs are not equal: Examining the relative impact of household dysfunction versus childhood maltreatment on mental health in adolescence. *Social Science and Medicine*, *245*, Article 112696. https://doi.org/10.1016/j.socscimed.2019.112696

Perrin, R. L. (2017). Overcoming biased views of gender and victimhood in custody evaluations when domestic violence is alleged. *American University Journal of Gender, Social Policy and & the Law*, *25*(2), 155–177. https://digitalcommons.wcl.american.edu/jgspl/vol25/iss2/2/?utm_source=digitalcommons.wcl.american.edu%2Fjgspl%2Fvol25%2Fiss2%2F2&utm_medium=PDF&utm_campaign=PDFCoverPages

Romano, E., Weegar, K., Gallitto, E., Zak, S., & Saini, M. (2021). Meta-analysis on interventions for children exposed to intimate partner violence. *Trauma, Violence, and Abuse*, *22*(4), 728–738. https://doi.org/10.1177/1524838019881737

Schreier, A., & Hansen, D. J. (2022). Family violence and public policy: Existing trends and emerging needs [editorial]. *Aggression and Violent Behavior*, *65*, 1–3. https://doi.org/10.1016/j.avb.2022.101724

Stark, E. (2012). Looking beyond domestic violence: Policing coercive control. *Journal of Police Crisis Negotiations*, *12*(2), 199–217. https://doi.org.https://doi.org/10.1080/15332586.2012.725016

Straus, M. A. (2008). Dominance and symmetry in partner violence by male and female university students in 32 nations. *Children and Youth Services Review*, *30*(3), 252–275. https://doi.org/10.1016/j.childyouth.2007.10.004

Thiara, R. K., & Gill, A. (2012). *Domestic violence, child contact, post-separation violence: Issues for South Asian and African-Caribbean women and children: A report of finding*. NSPCC.

Vu, N. L., Jouriles, E. N., McDonald, R., & Rosenfield, D. (2016). Children's exposure to intimate partner violence: A meta-analysis of longitudinal associations with child adjustment problems. *Clinical Psychology Review*, *46*, 25–33. https://doi.org/10.1016/j.cpr.2016.04.003

Watts, C., & Zimmerman, C. (2002). Violence against women: Global scope and magnitude. *The Lancet*, *359*(9313), 1232–1237. https://doi.org/10.1016/S0140-6736(02)08221-1

Webb, N., Moloney, L. J., Smyth, B. M., & Murphy, R. L. (2021). Allegations of child sexual abuse: An empirical analysis of published judgements from the family court of Australia 2012–2019. *The Australian Journal of Social Issues*, *56*(2), 1–22. https://doi.org/10.1002/ajs4.171

World Health Organization. (2013). *Global and regional estimates of violence against women: Prevalence and health effects of intimate partner violence and non-partner sexual violence.* https://apps.who.int/iris/bitstream/10665/85239/1/9789241564625 _eng.pdf

World Health Organization. (2016). *Global plan of action to strengthen the role of the health system within a national multisectoral response to address interpersonal violence, in particular against women and girls, and against children.* https://www.who.int/reproductivehealth/publications/violence/global-plan-of-action/en/

World Health Organization. (2020). *COVID-19 and violence against women: What the health sector/system can do.* https://www.who.int/reproductivehealth/publications/emergencies/COVID-19-VAW-full-text.pdf

Index

abuse 87–89, 94–95, 195–196, 210; children as distinct victims of domestic violence dynamics 153, 206–209; direct abuse 18, 20; mandatory reporting of 89; sexual abuse 152
abusive domestic reality 153; *see also* captivity
adolescents' experiences, interventions for children exposed to interparental violence 69–71
Adopting the Victim Model 184–185
Adopting the Violent Model 23–27, 117, 183–185, 203
age, impact on children exposed to interparental violence 17
aggression 51–52
allowing expression of escalation norms and preparing for active involvement 129–132
ambivalent state 185
anger: sides' management of escalation process 148; variables that impact escalation of conflict to a violent quarrel 144; *see also* escalation
arrangement orders 208–209
art: connection do violent reality 161–162; learning as discipline 196–197; as therapy 162
art education 164–165, 168–169, 194–195
art psychotherapy 162, 193; integrating 169–170
art psychotherapy groups 165–166
art studio groups 166
art therapy 162–164, 166–175, 193–195, 211–212; in groups 170–171
art therapy groups 165–166
artistic intelligence 169

assessing type of experience that characterizes the child's reality and drafting appropriate intervention 176–182
assimilation process 24
at-risk evaluation 207
attachment theory 20, 54
attitudes justifying violence 198

captivity 4–5, 93–97, 103, 114–115, 188, 195–196, 207–213; abuse domestic reality 153; coercive control 13, 18, 96; domestic violence dynamics 18, 27, 153; obsessive control 4; pathological control 4, 198, 212–213
causality 24
child abuse 195–196, 210; *see also* abuse
child arrangement orders 208–209; *see also* custody
child harm 94; *see also* abuse
child protection 90–91, 195–196, 213; through legislation 96; women's situation 102–103
child protection system 87–89
children, helping to end conflicts 132–133
children as distinct victims of domestic violence dynamics 18, 27, 153, 206–209
children exposed to interparental violence 2, 214; definition 11–12; drafting new policy 188–189; witnessing violence 192; *see also* exposure to interparental violence
children's coping strategies 18–19, 201–202; approaching for studies 120
children's development, negative impacts of interparental violence 12–16

children's perspective 5, 199
circumstances of the violence, perception of escalation of interparental conflicts 139–142
clinical consulting intervention 176; assessing type of experience that characterizes the child's reality and drafting appropriate intervention 176–182; diagnosing the types of experience and presenting ways to treat them 182–186
coercive control 13, 18, 96; see also captivity
cognitive maturity 72
cognitive-contextual theory 52
communication: evoking through images of art 164; internal home communication 124–125
communicative components, signs of conflict escalation to a violent quarrel 142
community activism 197
community projects/initiatives 195–196
contact arrangements 175; see also custody
control 26
coping strategies 201–202
creativity 161, 163; see also art therapy
cultural values 125–126, 134
custody 98–100; arrangement orders 208–209

data analysis, perception of daily reality among children exposed to their father's violence against their mother study 123
data collection, perception of daily reality among children exposed to their father's violence against their mother study 122–123
dating relationships 13
departing from violent reality 160
development stage of conflict, escalation 129–130
developmental psychopathological theory 54
diagnosing types of experience 182–186
direct abuse 18, 20; see also abuse
discrimination against men 100
distorted perception/filter 70, 153, 183, 192, 200, 211

domestic violence dynamics 18, 27, 153; see also captivity
domestic violence phenomenon 4–5, 31
double abuse 18; see also abuse, children as distinct victims of domestic violence dynamics
dynamic perspectives and attachment theory 54

early parenthood 13
ecological theory 55
ecological-transaction model of development 71–72
educational consultants, locating children exposed to interparental violence 186–188
elementary-school-age children, impact on children exposed to interparental violence 17
emotion regulation mechanisms 53, 73
emotional components, signs of conflict escalation to a violent quarrel 142
emotional occurrences 150
emotional protectiveness 74
emotional regulation 199; see also emotion regulation mechanisms
emotional relief 13
emotional security 20, 52–53
escalation 127–128, 134–135; allowing expression of escalation norms and preparing for active involvement 129–132; taking an active part in helping to end conflicts 132–133; of violence in intimate relationships 30–36; see also anger; perception of escalation of interparental conflicts
escalation dynamics 145–146
evidence-based intervention for treating children who have experience maltreatment 74–75; ecological-transaction model of development 71–72; trauma-focused cognitive-behavioral therapy (TF-CBT) 72–75
existential emptiness 166
existential reversal 166–167
expectations 135–136
experience of children exposed to interparental violence 23–27, 115–116, 159–161; perception of daily reality among children exposed to their father's violence against their mother

Index

116–124; *see also* perception of escalation of interparental conflicts
experience of nothingness 123–124, 134; internal home communication 123–124; internalized cultural values 125–126; parenting styles 126–127
experiencing violence 11
exposed to violence 11
exposure to abuse, direct abuse 18, 20
exposure to interparental violence 23, 114–115, 198; art therapy interventions 171–175; as form of abuse 87–89; history of treatment policy 92–103; implications of abuse for working in the school context 186–188; negative impacts on children's development 12–16
external normative reality 160
externalized behavioral problems 17

factors that mediate impact of interparental violence on development 16–19
failure to protect 89, 94
family, cultural values 125
family group conference (FGC) model 90–92, 95
family system approach, escalation of violence in intimate relationships 33
family system theory 12, 16, 31, 53
father–child relationships 127
fatherhood, as a movement 100–102
fathers' rights groups 101
feminist approach: to intercouple violence 31, 34–35; to understanding violence against women 102
FGC model *see* family group conference (FGC) model
first wave of evaluation (mid-1980s to the beginning of the 2000s); evaluating results 58–59; programs for children aged 0-3 and their mothers 55–56; programs for kindergarten- and school-age children and their mothers 56–58
forgotten victims 11
framing expectations 135
frequency of violence, impact on children exposed to interparental violence 18

gender, impact on children exposed to interparental violence 17

gender symmetry or asymmetry 31
gender-based violence 212, 215n4
goal of intervention 94
groups, art therapy 170–171, 194

harm reduction (HR) approach 90–91, 94
helping to end conflicts 132–133
heterogeneity, first wave of evaluation (mid-1980s to the beginning of the 2000s) 58–59
high-school-age children, impact on children exposed to interparental violence 17
history of treatment policy, for exposure to interparental violence 92–103
Home Visitation 55

images of art to evoke verbal communication 164
impact of interparental violence on children 23; direct abuse 20; factors that mediate impact on development 16–19; limitations of research 21–23; negative impacts on development 12–16; resiliency among children 19; theoretical formulation 16; theoretical reevaluation 19–20
Infant-Parent Psychotherapy Program 55
influence of interparental violence on children 12
initial stage of conflict, escalation 129
integrating: art psychotherapy 169–170; principles of art education 168–169
integrative view 33–34
intense fighting stage, escalation 130–132
intercouple relationships 33
intergenerational transmission theory 12, 16
internal home communication 124–125
internal home creativity 211
internalized behavioral problems 17
internalized cultural values 125–126
interparental violence 12, 23; children's experience of 23–27; impact on children 12–23; influence on children 12
intervention programs for men 93
interventions for children exposed to interparental violence 51, 54–55; adolescents' experiences 69–71; art therapy 166–175, 193–195; assessing

type of experience that characterizes the child's reality and drafting appropriate intervention 176–182; clinical consulting intervention 176–186; cognitive-contextual theory 52; dynamic perspectives and attachment theory 54; emotional security 52–53; family system theory 53; first wave of evaluation (mid-1980s to the beginning of the 2000s) 55–60; knowledge building 67–69; second wave of evaluations (beginning of 2000s to the present) 60–67; self-control 200–202; social learning theory 51–52; trauma theory 53–54
interventions for treating children who have experienced maltreatment: ecological-transaction model of development 71–72; trauma-focused cognitive-behavioral therapy (TF-CBT) 72–75
interventions with violent men 103–104
intimate partner violence 13, 31, 153, 212
intimate relationships, escalation of violence 30–36

Kids' Club Program 63–64
knowledge building, interventions for children exposed to interparental violence 67–69

language development 15
learning about the subjective experience of the mothers living in circumstances of domestic violence 90–91
limitations of research 21–23, 27–30
Living in Terror and Fear 23–27, 117, 203
Living with Conflicts of Loyalty 23–27, 117, 184
Living with Loyalty of conflicts 203
Living with the Secret 23–27, 117, 184, 186, 203

male clients, approaching 120
mandatory reporting of abuse 89
mediation 164
men 193, 210; discrimination against 100; escalation 138; *see also* violent men
modes of exposure 11
moralization 24
mother–child relationships 126–127; impact on children exposed to interparental violence 18

motherhood 94
mothers: interventions for victims 104; preserving position as victim 96
mother's behavior as motive for father's escalation: sides' management of escalation process 148–149; variables that impact escalation of conflict to a violent quarrel 144
motivation: to argue, sides' management of escalation process 147–148; to quarrel 143–144

negative impacts of interparental violence on children's development 12–16
neglectful behaviors 97
nihilist ideology 123
normative reality 160, 192

obsessive control 4; *see also* captivity
open studio groups 166
optimistic thinking 201
out-of-home sphere 194

parental education 12
parent–child relationships 26; *see also* mother–child relationships
parenting, cultural values 126
parenting styles 126–127
parents' motivation to quarrel 143–144; sides' management of escalation process 147–148
participants, perception of daily reality among children exposed to their father's violence against their mother 118–121
pathological control 4, 198, 212–213; *see also* captivity
perception of daily reality among children exposed to their father's violence against their mother 116–118; data analysis 123; data collection 122–123; findings 123–133; overview 133–136; research instruments 121–122; research questions 118; sample and participants 118–121; study method 118
perception of escalation of interparental conflicts 137, 150–154; circumstances of the violence 139–142; escalation dynamics 145–146; literature review 137–138; sides' management of escalation process 146–150; signs of conflict escalation to a violent quarrel

142–143; study methods 138–139; *see also* escalation
perpetrator--victim relationships 5
perspective of children 199; distorted perception/filter 70, 153, 183, 192, 200, 211
physical health, negative impacts on children's development 15
physical protectiveness 75
pre-school age children, impact on children exposed to interparental violence 17
Preschool Kids Club program 57
present ways to treat experiences of violence 182–186
preserving mother's position as victim 96
principles guiding treatment of exposure to violence 86–87
programs for children aged 0-3 and their mothers: first wave of evaluation (mid-1980s to the beginning of the 2000s) 55–56; second wave of evaluations (beginning of 2000s to the present) 60–61
programs for kindergarten- and school-age children and their mothers: first wave of evaluation (mid-1980s to the beginning of the 2000s) 56–58; second wave of evaluations (beginning of 2000s to the present) 61–62
Project Support 57, 62
pseudo-normative reality 136, 151, 168
psycho-educational lessons 196
psycho-educational therapy 207
psychopathology 72
psychotherapy 162

quarrels: signs of conflict escalation 142–143; variables that impact escalation 143–145

real parenting 126
reality: external normative reality 160; normative reality 192; pseudo-normative reality 136, 151, 168; *see also* violent reality
recollection 24
recruiting interviews for studies, perception of daily reality among children exposed to their father's violence against their mother study 119–121

relational posttraumatic stress 18
relationships: dating relationships 13; father-child relationships 127; mother-child relationships 126–127; parent--child relationships 26
removal of children to foster care 90
research, limitations of 21–23, 27–30
research instruments, perception of daily reality among children exposed to their father's violence against their mother study 121–122
research questions, perception of daily reality among children exposed to their father's violence against their mother 118
resilience theory 54
resiliency among children, exposed to interparental violence 19
risk factors for violent intimate relationships 13
risk management: family group conference (FGC) model 95; following separation 98

samples, perception of daily reality among children exposed to their father's violence against their mother 118–121
school, helping children exposed to interparental violence 186–188
School-Age Kids Club 57
schools, art 197–198
scripting expectations 135–136
second wave of evaluations (beginning of 2000s to the present); evaluating results 64–66; Kids' Club Program 63–64; programs for children aged 0-3 and their mothers 60–61; programs for kindergarten- and school-age children and their mothers 61–62; Project Support 62
self-control 199–202
self-esteem 19
self-restraint 201
separation 97–100
sexual abuse 152
shared custody 99
shelter-based studies 21
sides' management of escalation process 146–150
signs of conflict escalation to a violent quarrel 142–143
silent victims 11

skill-building stage 73
social learning theory 12, 16, 51–52
socioeconomic status, impact on children exposed to interparental violence 17
spatial arrangements: during developmental stages of conflict 132; tensions 136
The Storybook Club 56
stress 16
study methods: perception of daily reality among children exposed to their father's violence against their mother 118; perception of escalation of interparental conflicts 138–139
supervised visitation 99

teen dating violence 13
TF-CBT *see* trauma-focused cognitive-behavioral therapy
theoretical reevaluation, impact of interparental violence on children 19–20
theoretical sampling, perception of daily reality among children exposed to their father's violence against their mother study 119
thinking 164–165
togetherness 125
trauma theory 53–54
trauma-focused cognitive-behavioral therapy (TF-CBT) 72–75
treatment policy for exposure to interparental violence 103–104
treatments for: Adopting the Victim Model 185; Adopting the Violent Model 184–185; Living with the Secret 186
types of violence 18

unintended victims 11

variables that impact escalation of conflict to a violent quarrel 143–145
verbal aggression stage, escalation 132
verbal communication, images of art 164
victimized parents 94
violence 160; gender-based violence 212, 215n4; intimate partner violence 13, 31, 153, 212; against women 2–5, 12, 30–31, 33–35, 88–89, 93, 98–102, 114, 152, 175, 188, 214
violence prevention centers 28
violence stage, escalation 132–133
violent men: interventions with 103–104; separation 97
violent reality 213; connection to art 161–162; departing from 160
vitality 30, 127, 160, 163, 165, 167, 169, 171, 192–193

wholeness 159–160
witnesses of violence 11, 206
witnessing violence 211
women 193; escalation 138; role in child protection 102–103; *see also* mothers
women victims of violence 96; interventions with violent men 103–104; *see also* violence
work, art therapy 196–198